# Race, Racism and the Geography Curriculum

John Morgan and David Lambert

BLOOMSBURY ACADEMIC
LONDON • NEW YORK • OXFORD • NEW DELHI • SYDNEY

BLOOMSBURY ACADEMIC
Bloomsbury Publishing Plc
50 Bedford Square, London, WC1B 3DP, UK
1385 Broadway, New York, NY 10018, USA
29 Earlsfort Terrace, Dublin 2, Ireland

BLOOMSBURY, BLOOMSBURY ACADEMIC and the Diana logo are trademarks
of Bloomsbury Publishing Plc

First published in Great Britain 2023

Copyright © John Morgan and David Lambert, 2023

John Morgan and David Lambert have asserted their right under the Copyright, Designs
and Patents Act, 1988, to be identified as Author of this work.

For legal purposes the Acknowledgements on p. xv constitute an extension
of this copyright page.

All rights reserved. No part of this publication may be reproduced or transmitted
in any form or by any means, electronic or mechanical, including photocopying,
recording, or any information storage or retrieval system, without prior
permission in writing from the publishers.

Bloomsbury Publishing Plc does not have any control over, or responsibility for,
any third-party websites referred to or in this book. All internet addresses given in
this book were correct at the time of going to press. The author and publisher
regret any inconvenience caused if addresses have changed or sites have ceased to
exist, but can accept no responsibility for any such changes.

A catalogue record for this book is available from the British Library.

A catalog record for this book is available from the Library of Congress.

ISBN: HB: 978-1-3503-3665-0
PB: 978-1-3503-3664-3
ePDF: 978-1-3503-3666-7
eBook: 978-1-3503-3667-4

Typeset by Newgen KnowledgeWorks Pvt. Ltd., Chennai, India
Printed and bound in Great Britain

To find out more about our authors and books visit www.bloomsbury.com
and sign up for our newsletters.

*To the students we serve, and their teachers*

# Contents

The Authors — viii
Preface — ix
Foreword, *Julian Agyeman* — xii
Acknowledgements — xv

## Part one  Contexts

1. Introduction: Changing Geography, Changing Curriculum — 3
2. Changing Geography and the Rise of Multicultural Britain — 17

## Part two  Theoretical Perspectives

3. Changing Perspectives on 'Race' and Education — 33
4. Overcoming the Whiteness of Geography — 53

## Part three  Remaking Geography

5. Learning to Talk about Racism in School Geography — 95
6. Knowledge and the Geography Curriculum — 123
7. Changing the Geography Curriculum — 151
8. Conclusion — 171

**Coda: Positionality** — 177

Appendix 1 *Critical Realism, Powerful Knowledge and Future 3* — 179
Appendix 2 *Why Future 3?* — 183
References — 187
Index — 205

# The Authors

**John Morgan** is Professor of Geography and Environmental Education at the IOE, UCL's Faculty of Education and Society, University College London, UK, and Head of the School of Critical Studies of Education at the University of Auckland, New Zealand, having previously worked as a geography educator at the University of Bristol, UK (2000–12), and a senior researcher at Futurelab (2005–8). His interests are in geography education, curriculum studies and the political economy of schooling. He is the author of *Teaching Secondary Geography as if the Planet Matters* and *Culture and the Political Economy of Schooling: What's Left for Education*?

**David Lambert** is Emeritus Professor of Geography Education at the IOE, UCL's Faculty of Education and Society, University College London, UK. He was a secondary school teacher for twelve years, becoming deputy principal of a comprehensive school. He wrote award-winning school textbooks and became a teacher-educator from 1986, since when he has published widely on the curriculum, pedagogy and assessment of geography in education. He was appointed chief executive of the Geographical Association (2002–12), returning to the university sector as Professor of Geography Education in 2007. Recent books include *Learning to Teach Geography* 4th edition. In 2014, he coauthored with Michael Young *Knowledge and the Future School*.

## Foreword

**Julian Agyeman** is Professor of Urban and Environmental Policy and Planning and Fletcher Professor of Rhetoric and Debate at Tufts University, Massachusetts, USA. He is a former geography teacher in England and a cofounder of the Black Environment Network. He is the originator of the increasingly influential concept of *just sustainabilities*, which explores the intersecting goals of social justice and environmental sustainability.

# Preface

In choosing this book, readers will have a variety of possible motives. To find out more about race and racisms in education maybe, or to discover how geography has evolved as a discipline to become more inclusive and diverse. Or, to learn more about contemporary debates about how to change the geography curriculum in school. Whatever the primary motives, we, the authors, take it as given that readers will possess critically reflective dispositions. Such readers will be ready for challenge and, in some cases, to change what may be long held assumptions about the story of race in the UK and beyond, and how racisms work in society. In the world of teacher education and training, it is de rigueur that critical reflection be a key part of teacher professionalism. One of our purposes is to provide a conceptual knowledge base to enable informed and thoughtful critical reflection on the geography curriculum. We are addressing all concerned, from policymakers to the writers of textbooks and especially teachers – who are the curriculum makers. In so doing, we are of course sharing the fruits of our own critical reflections over several decades of engagement in geography education.

A point reiterated throughout this book is that issues of race and racism are both complicated and dynamic. The issues do not stand still. How race and racism are conceptualized has changed enormously during the period covered by this book, and they continue to change. We set out to trace these developments at three levels: in society, in the world of education and in the discipline of geography (in Chapters 1–4). Our goals in doing this are twofold and became the focus of the following chapters (Chapters 5–8): First, to account for the difficulties and challenges faced by geography teachers in schools in addressing racism – for although geography likes to project a progressive, aware and contemporary image, its track record is at best patchy. Second, to analyse and then make some bold proposals about ways forward, which require teachers' involvement in, and taking responsibility for, curriculum making in the increasing number of schools that aspire to anti-racist principles.

One of the challenges we all face is *how* to talk or write about race and racism. The language used in discussions of race and racism changes. Some turns of phrase deemed acceptable by one generation, or by one group, become unacceptable by the next. Some offensive words can be appropriated and used defiantly in order to show ownership and a form of power over the oppressor. We thus have a potential minefield which, ironically, can have the effect of stopping conversation altogether, for fear of using the 'wrong language' in a particular setting or context.

In other words, although the words we choose to use matters, let's agree to use language with some 'allowances'. Throughout the book we have tried to show how ideas such as colour, multicultural, intercultural, race, black and white have evolved and that nothing is 'settled' forever: occasionally, our choice of words may not suit all readers.

Our approach to writing has been guided by these principles:

- The need to avoid accepting without question simple binaries, such as black and white. This is because even though there is a collective strength to be found in groups, assigning people into pre-existing groups is hazardous and often limiting.
- Some speakers and writers therefore qualify Black as 'black and brown', or 'people of colour'. In the UK, the acronym BAME has become common place.[1] However, we attempt to avoid all these catch-all groups – including the worst of all 'non-white' (which suggests that normality is white, and anything else is not).
- Extending the point still further, there is also a need to recognize that racism can impact negatively on groups who may identify as white: at various times Irish, eastern Europeans and Jewish people have all been subject to forms of racism.
- Furthermore, we are aware of how issues of race and racism are intersectional with, for example, poverty, class, culture and gender. Inequities are complex, but in this book, we focus mainly (but not exclusively) on race.
- Finally, and unlike the controversial 2021 Commission for Race and Ethnic Disparities (CRED) Report, we do not downplay the structural and institutional processes that show how racism 'works': racism is not just a matter of irrational personal prejudice (though, of course, where this is evident it needs to be called out and stopped).

In remaining resistant to rigid categorizations and 'solutions', we share the CRED's (2021) ambitions expressed in their conclusion: 'Rather than just highlighting minority disparities and demanding the government takes action, we have tried to understand why they exist in the first place' (p. 233). In this book, we show that the study of geography can make a significant contribution to this and help guide teachers of geography in schools on how to think about the subject curriculum.

One of the greatest challenges in talking and writing about race, which the limitations of language seem to exacerbate, is that try as we might the binaries often remain or are reinforced. Talk and action can then become divisive. But when it comes to the curriculum (the question of who studies what), division, even if it 'unintentional' or unconscious, surely should be avoided. A curriculum serving the interests of white privilege, and which distorts and/or is silent on black histories and

---

[1] Black, Asian and Minority Ethnic (BAME) was roundly rejected by the *Commission on Race and Ethnic Disparities Report* (2021): Recommendation 24 was to 'stop using aggregated and unhelpful terms such as "BAME". To better focus on understanding disparities and outcomes for specific ethnic groups' (14).

geographies, is unacceptable and requires change. Our position argues for a *racially literate* curriculum which provides all students with powerful knowledge. Our book is therefore addressed to *all* teachers of geography (and therefore indirectly to *all* students in school). Our concept of a racially literate geography curriculum not only avoids simplistic and endless binaries but also avoids policies and solutions that reinforce division.

We therefore agree with the view that,

> A well sequenced, knowledge rich curriculum, based around subject disciplines, can help students to acquire a sense of place and a framework for understanding cultural diversity. The national curriculum seeks to reflect this multi-layered story and is the product of years of dialogue and research. (CRED, 2021: p. 92)

However, we do not agree with the assertion that such a curriculum will be straightforward to assemble and 'roll out' across the nation's schools. This is naïve and misunderstands the active role that teachers must play in curriculum making, locally in thousands of unique classroom settings. Our intention in writing this book is to bring to the fore some of the essential 'dialogue and research' in geography education that will assist teachers grasp the importance and the potential impact of their work. Our hope that this will help what Kinder and Pike (2021) refer to as 'our subject community' open up and grasp the scale of the work ahead in its 'examinations of racism and neo-colonialism through the lens of the geography curriculum' (p. 9).

# Foreword

## *Julian Agyeman*

David, John and I have been discussing *Race, Racism and the Geography Curriculum* for a couple of years. Over that time, I believe the book has morphed into a timely, critical and clarion call for the centring of issues of race and racisms in geographical education, rather than their being an add-on. It warns of a 'partial and incomplete' geographical education if these issues are not prominent in curriculum planning and practice: 'A curriculum serving the interests of white privilege, and which distorts and/or is silent on Black histories and geographies, is unacceptable and it needs to change.' It calls, ultimately and incisively, for a racially literate geographical education, delivered to an increasingly diverse and different student body by geography teachers, the majority of whom are white.

However, what struck me in our Boston-London-Auckland Zoom meetings was how there were often two parts to our discussions. The first was substantive, about the challenging issues the book raises in relation to wider British society, the world of education and in the discipline of geography, a 'subject which likes to project a progressive, aware and contemporary image'. In effect, we were discussing *how* we can move forward, towards an anti-racist, de-colonial geography curriculum.

The second was intensely personal to David and John: Why should two older white guys be writing this book? My response was 'why *shouldn't* they?' Why shouldn't they wrestle with their own (and geographers') White fragilities and White supremacy more broadly toward the goal of an anti-racist, de-colonial geography curriculum? Why shouldn't they, with over eighty years combined geography teaching and training teachers, offer their thoughts about, and experiences of, race and racisms in 'a predominantly white subject'? If this were the only book on this topic, I would be worried. But it isn't, and it will spark discussion, debate and more books.

Ultimately, I see this book as a signal of David and John's bravery and frustration. Bravery in the sense that despite knowing that they would be criticized because of their White male positionalities, they continued because they truly believe in the goals they set out on: frustration in the sense that the entanglement of White supremacy, empire, colonization, race/racisms and immigration are (still) deeply imbued in the geographical imagination and education.

When they asked me to write a Foreword for the book, I accepted immediately because I saw myself in its narrative in two fundamental ways: as a Black British kid of English and Ghanaian heritage growing up in East Yorkshire in the 1960s and 1970s and as a geography teacher in the early 1980s.

Most of my schooling was during the 1960s and 1970s *integrationist* phase of education, before the *multicultural*, or later the *anti-racist* phases. We were educated in a matter of fact, colour/race blind way. Being one of only three kids of colour at my school, one of whom was my brother, we also experienced the *'there's no problem here'* mentality. The 'problem', presumably, to purveyors of this sentiment, was caused by there being 'too many' kids of colour in some schools.

I was totally immersed in nature at this time. On reflection today, perhaps it was in part to escape the direct racism, and microaggressions, I was experiencing, that I embraced the natural environment. Whether it was birdwatching at Spurn Point in the Humber Estuary, seeing the carpets of Bluebells at Wauldby Green in the Yorkshire Wolds or seeing my first magical Merlin on the North York Moors, I was filled with wonder. Family walks, school field trips, or camping with friends all deepened my love affair with nature and landscape. It was no surprise to anyone that I should go to university to study geography and botany.

The geography side of my joint honours degree was pretty much all physical geography, biogeography and soil science. And I loved it. I did have to take a Regional Geography class to fulfil requirements, and I chose Africa. It was a very traditional, 'factual', uncritical class, but I didn't know this at the time. I simply thought 'this is how you learn about Africa'. There was no discussion of racism, little critical comment on colonialism and lots of data on agricultural and other forms of production. All the professors during my undergraduate days were white men, and there were very few women lecturers. There were no Black faculty.

On graduation, I decided to become a geography teacher. In 1982, I began interviewing. On my second interview at a school (name withheld) in Forest Gate, London Borough of Newham, I came up against the most vicious racism I have ever experienced, even to this day. In my one-on-one interview with the head of Geography, I was asked if I'd dress up in African clothes when teaching about Africa. But it was in the head teacher's office that things got really ugly. As the head, his deputy and I sat down to chat in his office, a note was slipped under the door. It read, 'Nigger go home, your master is waiting'.

The deputy, albeit shocked, tried to argue that the note was from some random kid at the school. But the reality was, and she knew I knew, that the door under which the note had been slipped was in a 'staff only' corridor. I didn't get the job (would I have taken it if it had been offered?); the head teacher shook my hand and said, 'I really wish I could have hired my first black teacher.' I don't know about the student statistics in 1982, but I'd say well over half were African Caribbean, maybe even two-thirds. What kind of geographic education, what kind of education *overall*, did the students get in such a hate-filled environment?

After being rejected by a London school, my geography teaching career started in September 1982 at a school in Carlisle. As an aside, looking on the top shelves of the school's geography storeroom, I got a glimpse of geography textbooks derived from what David and John describe as the 'effects of North European and British imperialistic "adventures" '. I came across some dusty old textbooks from the past with titles like '*At Home in Distant Lands*' and '*Homes around the World*'. The former book's front cover showed a uniformed English schoolboy standing proud while all around him, kneeling and in a way idolizing him, there were an assortment of 'others', essentially bit players in the boy's (and England's) rise to supremacy. The latter book was a 'developmental' study of homes around the world from the least sophisticated (a 'Blackfellow's Wurley' in Aboriginal Australia) to the most sophisticated (a semidetached suburban home in England).

Top-shelf imperialistic adventures aside, I became immersed in a very forward-looking geography department with three passionate (white) colleagues. I led field trips to the Lake District, joined the Geographical Association and became involved in the emerging radical humanist, anti-racist and anti-sexist geography journal, *Contemporary Issues in Geography and Education* (CIGE), founded by the wonderful Dawn Gill. This opened a whole new world of possibilities for me, offering different lenses, ideas, methodologies and understandings. But more than this, it bought me into contact with other, like-minded people such as Ian Cook, Frances Slater, Peter Jackson, Hilary Strudwick, John Huckle, David Pepper and others. This eventually led to my working in a London Urban Studies Centre, then as an Environmental Education Adviser in two London boroughs, while studying for a master's in Conservation Policy and ultimately a PhD in Urban Studies, with David Lambert as my advisor.

Today, forty years on from my first geography teaching job, I'm a professor of urban planning in Boston, Massachusetts, teaching master's students on a professionally accredited degree. In many ways, I've come full circle. But instead of *Race, Racism and the Geography Curriculum*, my ongoing project is *Race, Racisms and the Urban Planning Curriculum* in a nation where the *primary objective* of urban planning was racial segregation. Whether it is the high school or master's curriculum, geography or urban planning, the project is the same but in different race/racisms contexts and locations: *how* to talk or write about race and racisms; *how* to foreground Black histories and geographies and *how* to develop and deliver an anti-racist de-colonial curriculum that engenders racial literacy.

David and John offer us a roadmap. Let's use it.

# Acknowledgements

We take this opportunity to thank several anonymous reviewers of the book. No fewer than seven individuals have been involved in providing feedback to us over a two-year period, from the initial book proposal to the whole final draft manuscript.

In addition, great thanks go to Julian Agyeman who has provided critical friendship throughout this project. As he shows in his Foreword, he has a lived experience of much of the story we tell of UK racism, and not least through the lens of a geography/environmental educator. He also brings the unique attribute of an insider-outsider, as he now lives and works in the United States. His counsel and encouragement through zoom meetings and emails has been invaluable.

A thoroughly outside perspective was also brought to bear by Kelly León who generously read the whole draft manuscript from start to finish, providing us with observations and insights that influenced the final drafting of our book. Kelly is a high school geography teacher from Southern California with many years' experience of teaching young people of colour, frequently those in precarious economic and social circumstances. Furthermore, as a doctoral candidate, she is grappling with the design and implementation of Ethnic Studies in schools, a 'new' subject with its origins in the identification of and resistance to the sources of structural oppression experienced by ethnic groups in society. It has been immensely valuable to benefit from her forthright comments – and her encouragement to complete this book.

In Auckland, Bo Zhou did a thorough and essential job of helping prepare the rather extensive list of references. We have therefore been the beneficiaries of much assistance, discussion and advice. But it goes almost without saying that all remaining deficiencies, errors or indiscretions are our own responsibility.

Taking our book from its original conception to publication has in some ways been a rocky road. Writing any book takes some kind of 'belief'– not least in the notion that one has something worth saying. But to publish a book like this, which addresses at least three fields of scholarship, really does take courage, and so to Alison Baker and all at Bloomsbury we offer our profound gratitude for taking us on. As a publisher, we could not wish for better. We just hope we have met her and Bloomsbury's exacting standards.

And for all those who told us that we could not write this book on account of our white privilege, we are glad to have had at least the chance to prove them wrong. For we all need to find ways to talk about race. Silence, we think, is a form of approbation of the status quo.

# Part one

## Contexts

# 1

# Introduction: Changing Geography, Changing Curriculum

It would be difficult to imagine anyone reading this book disagreeing with Rutherford's statement that 'racism is not simply wrong because it is based on scientifically specious ideas. Racism is wrong because it is an affront to human dignity' (Rutherford, 2020: 185). The author, a geneticist, makes much of the 'genetic isopoint' – the moment about 3,400 years ago when everyone alive on Earth were the ancestors of everyone alive today. The implications of this are clear: we are all related, and as Rutherford explains, any concept of racial purity is pure fantasy. Every white supremacist shares African, Indian and Middle Eastern ancestry, and more besides these.

And yet, racists repeatedly attempt to use science to justify racial hierarchies. Rutherford shows that this is not science but pseudoscience, much of which emerged during the period of empire building by European powers. The very idea of 'race' is socially constructed, and, therefore, invented during the era of global exploration and exploitation to excuse plunder, enslavement and genocide. White supremacy too is a social construct of course. It is ugly when overt but often remains 'hidden' in taken-for-granted structures and embedded in some of society's institutions to this day. White on black racism needs revealing, understanding and addressing, and one of the purposes of this book is to help all those involved in geography education, particularly teachers in schools, to do so. In writing this, we are mindful that racism *also* works insidiously in a multitude of ways and in many settings and is not related only to skin colour. There are many racisms. Furthermore, the way racism is understood and talked about changes, not only over time but also through space: British racism – how it has evolved through struggle and changing societal attitudes and policy norms – is not the same as racism manifest in other European countries, or nations further afield such as the United States.

The idea of race is therefore really tricky. Biologically, race is fake: 'racial differences' are literally phenotypic – that is, no more than skin deep and having zero explanatory power when it comes to academic intellectual, musical or sporting performance. For this reason, it is tempting to follow the logic of a colour-blind approach in our personal and professional lives. This is mistaken, and we come back to it later, because although race may have no biological justification, racism certainly exists. It is real.

Racism is real because it is *experienced*, frequently through thousands of microaggressions reserved only for individuals of certain groups. It can also be *observed* through the way institutions (including schools) operate – that is the way they look and present themselves to the world. And social scientists, including many geographers, in their *analyses* of the way economic, social and cultural processes work, have done much to reveal how the racialization of these processes has determined unjust outcomes – in migration, housing, employment patterns, environmental quality and so on.

Thus, race and racisms are all pervasive. By this we mean that they operate at all levels in society from the personal, everyday level of experience, to the way society is organized and structured and on to the very deepest levels of assumptions and beliefs. This book cannot and does not pretend to cover the field. Although we draw widely from race scholarship education, cultural studies and geography in the UK and the United States, we are geography educators and the question we address through this book is how issues of race and racism can be engaged with productively through the teaching of geography in schools in Britain. Even this aim needs some additional qualification, for the book is not a teaching manual with precise advice and guidance on how to 'operationalize' anti-racist techniques. Our focus is on the geography curriculum.

The curriculum is perhaps the most precious idea in education and although many institutions and interests have a role in shaping it – from government, though awarding bodies and the Office for Standards in Education, Children's Services and Skills (Ofsted) to textbook writers and agencies such as the Geographical Association – it is in the end in the hands of teachers. This book is addressed to all those with an interest in the curriculum but most of all to teachers. The book tells an unfolding story of race in Britain and how society at large, and also the discipline itself, has accommodated, assimilated and adjusted. It is a story of struggle, shocking injustice and setbacks, sometimes missed opportunities and occasionally false moves: but generally, and we realize this may be controversial, one of progress. The book is written in the firm belief that if we can raise the collective sense of 'racial literacy' in our personal and professional lives, then the geography curriculum actually enacted in schools can become increasingly anti-racist. Improved, more racially literate school geography may then contribute further to young people's understanding of fundamental divisions and injustices in the worlds that they may experience directly or are yet to encounter.

Geography is a subject that has the potential to help shed light on the way in which race and racism works in society. This point, of course, is relevant to *all* geography teachers and to *all* students who find themselves studying geography at school. We acknowledge that in many schools the majority of students are white, as are most of their geography teachers. We also acknowledge that these people have not directly experienced the microaggressions, the hurt and the frustrations of systemic racism that works against them. However, to assume that you need direct experience of phenomena (of racism or simply ethnic diversity) before you can study or even think about them undermines the whole process and purpose of education. As a school subject, geography contributes to the whole school curriculum which is designed to take young people beyond their direct experience. Educators understand that their role is to induct people into more abstract thought, how to make safe generalizations and appreciate the strength of theoretical perspectives and ideas in order to deepen students' knowledge and understanding of how the world works. As we both have an interest in notions of 'powerful disciplinary knowledge' in the school curriculum, we reject the notion that direct experience of the world is the only basis for legitimate knowledge acquisition and development (even though we accept that personal testimony and knowledge through acquaintance are both valid and an asset in the classroom). We are also doubtful that the aim of teaching geography is to adopt moral positions, although these can of course be explored. Thus, an essential component of this book is our exploration of geographical research and development and its implications for geography educators and schoolteachers. This is not definitive of course but serves as a way in to the proper consideration by school geography teachers of how the discipline itself not only has changed but also has contributed to insights and a better understanding of how racism works.

The intention of this book, then, is to show secondary school teachers (especially geography teachers), that issues of race and racism are of central concern to their work as curriculum makers. This is not meant as an add-on, or simply to signal virtue, but because geographical understanding is partial and incomplete without it. Our aim is to write a rigorous, comprehensive and usable book to enhance our collective racial literacy in the field of geography education. We believe that enhanced literacy of this nature, which we hope will inform conversation and dialogue, is a prerequisite for the improvement of the quality of the geography curriculum experienced in schools in years ahead.

In the past, it seemed that deeper, structural issues of race and racism in geography education could be wished away or ignored by way of necessary, though in themselves insufficient, measures such as countering racist imagery in textbooks. But not this time, we think. An achievement of the Black Lives Matter (BLM) movement, which saw an international surge of interest after the murder of George Floyd in May 2020, has been to show to diverse audiences across the world that the issue of race thinking is not just a matter of personal conscience or prejudice. Through our careful, sustained focus on the curriculum, seen as an expression of society's conversation with its next generation, we seek not to adopt one ideological position and grind any particular axe. We are not seeking to create just another description of society's divisions and hierarchies but also a platform for deeper understanding. In Paul Gilroy's words, 'For me, a critique of racism and *race-thinking* provides a route into clearer, deeper understanding of humankind and its contested nature' (emphasis added; 2019). We have tried, therefore, to produce a resource that will enable geography teachers to develop and deepen their professional confidence in understanding and teaching issues of race and racism – maintaining a deep respect for shared humanity and shared space.

## The Book in Overview

It is impossible to understand contemporary British society without paying attention to issues of race and racism. However, it is quite possible to teach geography in schools without paying such attention. As we show in Chapters 2 and 3, one of the main challenges facing educators in the period after 1945 has been largely conceptualised as how to 'manage' the presence of children in schools arising from successive waves of migration to Britain. Any discussion of this in geography teaching has been patchy to say the least. Chapters 2 and 3 set out to explain the backdrop to this, while Chapter 5 zooms in on the actual history of this on-off conversation about race in school geography.

As we shall show, much has been made of how schools, including geography teaching, served to train British workers to support imperialism which has promoted racism and reflects geography to this day as a predominantly white subject. One of the most telling quotes comes from a woman interviewed by Beverly Bryan et al. in *The Heart of the Race*, a history of black women's lives in Britain:

> I didn't do Geography after the Third Form, but when I realised that the countries the teacher was talking about in that far-off, abstract way, were actually countries which Black people came from, Africa, the Caribbean etc. I realised that teachers didn't always speak the truth. It was so inaccurate, so biased, such a negative way of showing how we were meant to live. (Bryan, Dadzie and Scafe, 1985: 65)

In the years immediately following migration, it was assumed that immigrants would *assimilate* – that is, come to accept their place in British society and that cultures would somehow merge. In such circumstances, there was little apparent need to change the natures of teaching and learning. This was followed, in the 1960s and 1970s, by the policy of *integration* and gave rise to multicultural education. *Multicultural education* pointed to the importance of recognising the existence of a plurality of cultures and finding ways to make sure these were represented in the school curriculum and classroom. However, in the 1980s, this was challenged by more radical forms of *anti-racist education* which stressed on the importance of power and economic structure in creating racism. In a famous formulation – that is, Racism = Prejudice + Power – anti-racist education attempted to acknowledge the roots of racism.

Another approach altogether, which might still be prevalent in many settings, was to declare that there is *no problem here* and thus avoid discussion of the issues.

We are tempted to suggest that in school geography, perhaps unconsciously in an unexamined way, this has been the default position over many years. These are, after all, very difficult matters to discuss and as we shall show, frequently subject to change in how the issues and their politics are understood. It is perhaps easier to retreat to the comfort of received custom and practice of what counts as legitimate, progressive enquiry-based geography. Even in our own writings, we are aware that issues of race and racism sometimes only had a walk-on part (Biddulph, Lambert and Balderstone, 2021; Lambert and Morgan, 2010; Morgan and Lambert, 2005), although we tried occasionally to suggest these were matters of central concern (Morgan and Lambert, 2001, 2003) to the teaching of geography in schools.

Chapter 4 is the longest chapter and arguably the cornerstone of this book. It is here that we examine the story of how geography as a discipline, which emerged in the UK during the twentieth century (the learned Institute of British Geographers [IBG], now merged with the Royal Geographical Society [RGS] since 1995, was not established until 1934), has evolved its attitude to race and racism since its early imperialistic days (see Kearns, 2020, 2021). The story is complicated but it is true that the subject was slow to register the effects of North European and British imperialistic 'adventures' (and the legacy of white supremacy) so that the link between empire, decolonization and immigration to Britain from different parts of the Commonwealth was not really researched nor communicated. From the 1960s, 'new' social and economic geographies concerned with the mapping of space and looking for scientific spatial processes became more important. Although this seeded an interest in segregation and measurement of indices of difference, race was treated mainly as a variable, based upon 'given' social classifications.

However, from the 1980s, the subject took a more critical turn that assessed the role of the state in promoting and sustaining racial division. There were early studies of South African apartheid and the emergence of 'welfare geographies' which asked who got what, where, when and occasionally why. Geographers began to explore the relationship between society and space and how these were mutually constituted. Broadly, approaches varied between political economy, which focused on the way that race was used to structure a socially and economically divided society, and a cultural approach, which stressed the construction of identity.

As noted in the previous section, there has been a different trajectory between UK-based and US-based approaches to the study of racialized identities including whiteness, and this is reflected in the emergence and rapid growth of 'Black geographies' in the United States – studies more closely associated with cultural studies and sociological processes in the UK. In addition, geography's own involvement with the Western project of 'development' has been subject to reflexive challenges and adjustments, reflected in ideas of 'post-development geographies', 'postcolonial geographies', and, most recently, 'decolonizing geography'. We attempt to overview these developments and suggest that from them we can discern several very powerful concepts, ideas which might be highly productive to recontextualize in school geography settings. At the very least, we argue, such ideas contribute directly to the racial literacy of geography teachers: they may not tell us what to teach exactly, but they do provide strong indications of how to think geographically about content areas such as migration, development and so on.

In Chapter 5, we explore how geography teachers responded to these developments in teaching about race and racism. The highpoint of this engagement was the so-called GYSL[1] affair, prompted by the decision of the Schools Council *not* to publish a report it had commissioned from Dawn Gill (1982), a geography teacher at Quintin Kynaston School in Westminster, on how syllabuses and examinations could meet the needs of all pupils in a multicultural society. Gill concluded that important though it was for more black children to achieve better grades, this was not really the point. She argued that it was structural racism, not formal educational qualifications, that was the main determinant of life chances for black students in the UK. As we report in Chapter 5, the reluctance to publish Gill's findings caused a minor storm, even leading to correspondence in the pages of the *Guardian* newspaper. Despite the Geographical Association's (GAs) response, in the form of a report (Walford, 1985), we portray this whole affair as a missed opportunity. But it also may point to a lack of engagement between school geography and the wider discipline – a matter we hope to address in this book.

The final section of the book focuses on the curriculum, or more precisely how to think about the curriculum. As with race and racism in the UK, and the ways in which education, geography as a discipline and as a school subject have responded to issues of race thinking, there is a story to tell. Curriculum is a deceptively straightforward idea: it concerns the question of *what to teach*. However, the question is far from straightforward to answer. Thus, in Chapter 6, we examine carefully issues around knowledge and the geography curriculum. Even if we can easily say what we mean by geographical knowledge (and this is surprisingly difficult), we immediately confront a slew of concerns over who actually controls the curriculum and how, at all levels, from the national curriculum down to the level of individual classrooms in local schools, curriculum content is decided. Curriculum making is not simply a technical matter as described in detailed 'toolkits' (for a recent example see Gardner, 2021) and manuals. It is rather a matter of moral judgement as to how material can be studied in order to impart to students a better, fuller and more adequate understanding of how the world works. (Or else why send children and young people to school?) We believe that the study of geography can contribute to this task, and in Chapter 6, we develop our position in relation to what has now become known as powerful disciplinary knowledge. There is both a shine and a shadow to knowledge conceptualized as 'powerful', and we discuss this crucial matter head on.

In Chapter 7, we then attempt to apply our discussion about knowledge matters to curriculum making in geography. We are careful to show that the task of planning, making and enacting the subject curriculum is also a complex process which we analyse at three levels: the macro, meso and micro levels. Our argument – for what we call a Future 3 curriculum scenario – is that a sustainable anti-racist curriculum

---

[1] The Geography for the Young School Leaver Project (GYSL) was one of three Schools Council geography curriculum development projects of the 1970s.

in geography (or any other subject for that matter) is elusive. But quick fixes are also an illusion, and we conclude that a defensible and productive curriculum is almost certainly one that is in a constant state of becoming. This dynamic, contingent and responsive curriculum is – has to be – in the hands of teachers who need to balance their knowledge of the students (including existing experiential and cultural 'funds of knowledge' of the students) with their understanding of what the subject has to offer.

We hope this book, taken as a whole, serves as source book for teachers' curriculum thinking and practical curriculum making. In particular, we hope that teachers' work becomes more racially literate and finally addresses the unavoidable truth that geography in school is still perceived as a white subject – in which white normativity shapes the data selected for study and the explanations offered.

## Improving Geography Teachers' Racial Literacy

The Runnymede Trust's report *Race and Racism in English Secondary Schools* (Joseph-Salisbury, 2020) argues strongly for greater *racial literacy* among teachers, candidly observing that even now 'the National Curriculum does not mandate for engagement with colonial legacies – or the racist underpinnings – of contemporary Britain' (2). The Runnymede Trust's recommendation is for teachers more fully to grasp how race and racisms work in society. For without this, the way teachers interpret and enact the curriculum will be limited or even faulty. After all, 'colonial legacies' can be taught more as a triumphalist moment of white supremacy and not necessarily in a way that adds understanding to how racial injustice was the root of exploitation and genocide. An important message of this book is that it really matters whose definitions we take on and the ways in which we interrogate the content of what is taught. It is important, we argue, for both teachers and students to grasp such a relational approach to how we make sense of the world through the study of geography.

So, *what is racial literacy?* There are at least two ways to look at this. For example, it is a sociological term to describe strategies that may be employed by parents and teachers to help young black people understand and counter the racism they encounter in their daily lives. This is important of course. However, used this way, it unintentionally treats racism as an inevitable component of society which black people just have to 'deal with'. We take a broader approach based on the concept of 'race literacy' originated by Lani Guinier (2006) and which has been developed by social studies educators in the United States (e.g. King, Vickery and Caffrey, 2018). In essence, this is a critique of the liberal assumption that racism resides in the faulty prejudice of individuals – the sort of thinking that often results in a 'colour-blind' approach to race. When operating in this way, people try to convince themselves that they do not 'see' race. They claim instead to choose equity and that they just see people, all people, as equals. But this is problematic. Not only does it wash over and ignore an important element of any person's being and identity, but it also tends to equate issues of race and racism with historical enslavement, for example, and therefore conveniently residing in the past – or happening somewhere else.

Though in some ways a clumsy term, 'racial literacy' at least asks us to consider what knowledge, understanding and skills are required by teachers in contemporary classrooms. As we have made clear, our definition of racial literacy begins with an understanding that race is a socially constructed idea: that race is not a biological fact. It is a concept designed *to create* a hierarchy and, through cultural, social, economic and political manipulation, the means to govern, control or oppress people on the basis of the colour of their skin or origin. As we shall go onto argue below, the acceptance of this position is no longer exceptional, or even controversial. After all, it is now rare to find a politician, captain of industry or even the chief commissioner of police deny the insidious effects of 'institutional racism' in society. Although there are still doubtless some individuals in positions of responsibility with 'tin ears' or some form of sociocultural myopia that prevents them from really seeing this in *their* everyday lives, the question now is not whether or where racism is a problem but what to do about it. In the precise context of this book, this means what and how to teach in school geography. Our argument is that racial literacy involves a body of knowledge and the ability to understand how race and racism works in shaping society – and that for geography teachers, this has implications for their curriculum making. We take it as read that the goal of curriculum making in geography is to furnish young people with better explanations in our task to help them make sense of the world.

Our working definition of racial literacy suggests that there are five areas that any geography teacher needs:

1. an understanding of the history and geography of Britain as a diverse society – that has, in identifiable ways, perpetuated race thinking;
2. a conceptual and theoretical understanding of race and racisms and how these have been mobilised and used in educational contexts;
3. an analysis and understanding of how race and racisms have been linked in the past to geography as a subject discipline;
4. a consideration of the ways in which geography educators and geography teachers have attempted to teach about racisms and an ability to assess the successes and failures of these efforts; and
5. an ability to plan and teach a curriculum that addresses issues of race and racisms (this will reflect a synthesis of the knowledge and understanding of areas from points 1 to 4 above).

These areas of interest form the agenda for this book. We necessarily attempt to cover a lot of ground in a relatively short book and try to knit together three intellectual domains: race and racism, geography, and curriculum studies. Some of this ground will be new to some readers. For example, the essential historical contextualization (addressing points 1 and 2 above) may only have a sketchy presence in contemporary debates (e.g. 'Windrush'), and we attempt to help join the dots to create a meaningful narrative of change. For others, the developments we describe in geography as a discipline, both in the United States and the UK, may be news and might require some staying power on behalf of the reader. Possibly more readers may be familiar with the developments we discuss in relation to the curriculum and the narrative to support our argument for 'Future 3' curriculum scenarios (see Appendix 2) – the product of critical thought and development by both of us over a considerable period: this is not merely grasped from the air.

However, we trust that this ambitious investment of 'think space' will be rewarded by what could emerge in the form of revised teaching approaches or even the selection of entirely new content. Thinking theoretically, which is necessary in developing geography as powerful disciplinary knowledge, and then developing ways to teach and communicate in ways that move from the concrete to the abstract, or vice versa, is hard intellectual work. This is a point we have been consistent about in our writings – for example, exploring teaching as knowledge work in our book from over a decade ago (Lambert and Morgan, 2010).

## Turning the Page

The BLM movement, which originated in the United States in 2013,[2] really took off following the horrific, video-recorded murder of George Floyd in Minneapolis by a white police officer Derek Chauvin, in May 2020. This event symbolized the continuing, extreme forms of trauma violence and oppression experienced by black people in the United States. 'Enough is enough' seemed to be the clarion call from the notably diverse groups of largely peaceful protesters in cities throughout the United States and the world. The brilliance of the movement was epitomised by its ability to isolate, resist and dismiss the weak and dishonest counterargument put up in defence of the status quo: that '*all* lives matter' – an empty slogan that seeks to use the cover of colour blindness. The BLM message travelled widely to other countries and contexts which have different but equally shocking stories of racism, including the UK.

With the widespread acceptance and support for BLM (including premiership footballers, following the example of US National Football League star Colin Kapaernick, 'taking the knee' through 2020–21 and into the 2022 season) it seems that British society is ready to face some home truths about race and racism. As a sign of the times, this was symbolised when protesters in Bristol toppled the statue of Edward Colston (a prominent 'dignitary' of the city whose wealth was gained through enslavement). BLM sentiments were not uncontested, however, as we saw when the BBC announced that the singing of Rule Britannia and Land of Hope and

---

[2] https://blacklivesmatter.com/about/ (accessed 30 September 2022).

Glory would be dropped from the annual 'Last Night of the Proms'. Following howls of protest, including from the Prime Minister himself, arrangements were hastily made to reinstate these anthems.

Nevertheless, the GA's journals published articles on race and geography for the first time in twenty years, and questions are now being asked about the school curriculum. For example, would it be possible to teach the British industrial revolution as something other than a happy accident based solely on the presence of 'abundant coal' and exceptional British 'ingenuity'? What is usually overlooked is that industrialization was fuelled by the enormous profits that accrued from enslavement and the slave trade. Rather than excuse this inconvenient truth with stirring stories of William Wilberforce and abolition (which resulted in compensation for UK slave owners but not the freed people), it may be more helpful and responsible to engage candidly with the geography and the history of racism which has underlain British capitalism to this day. In doing so, young people may better understand British society and the world in which they live.

This is of course 'political' but is not in any sense anti-British. It is an appeal for educators in a mature democratic state to aspire to teach material that seeks the broader truths that reflect a diverse – and plural – society. The populist media may wish to appeal to and promote an unhealthy sense of national exceptionalism (e.g. that stirred up by Rule Britannia media storm). However, national exceptionalism (not to be confused with patriotism) is based upon the very idea of white supremacy that made enslavement possible in the first place and enabled the enduring myth of colonialism as a 'civilizing' mission. The 'harmless tradition' of pomp and circumstance is part of the continuing delusion that 'we' were on the right side of history because Britain was among the first nations to abolish the slave trade in 1807 (even though the use of slave labour in British colonies remained legal until 1833). Fair enough, and credit where credit is due. But prettifying the horrors of the middle passage of the triangle of trade with 'abolitionist myth' is for many people nothing less than a polite continuation of white British supremacy.[3]

The abolitionist myth arises from the history of enslavement which is

> viewed backwards, through the history of its abolition ... not a complex story involving slave resistance and economic causation ... but as a story of heroic moral efforts of a mainly white and mainly British abolitionist movement. (Smith et al. 2011: 28 cited in Bunce and Field, 2017: 15)

As the great Black activist Darcus Howe remarked, 'My life has been largely spent in trying to help force an often reluctant and purblind England to be true to the benign "Motherland" of my parent's vision' (Bunce and Field, 2017: 3). Decades earlier he had written ironically about his and the (British) Black Power Movement's civilising mission – the British had travelled the globe to civilise Africa, India and the Caribbean, and now it was time 'to return the favour' (ibid). This precisely expresses

---

[3] 'Rising British capitalism had a magic money machine, an endless chain with three links: sugar cultivation; manufacturing industry; and the slave trade. And the slave trade was the essential link' (Fryer, 1984/2018: 16).

the failures Howe identified in Britain, to acknowledge a more complicated and less self-righteous understanding of what was destroyed through the colonial period, including a sense of humility. As Gary Younge writes in the Foreword to the 2018 edition of Peter Fryer's brilliant history of Black people in Britain, *Staying Power*, we now know 'that whatever multicultural bonhomie we enjoy now is a product not of Britain's innate genius and sense of fair play, but of bitterly fought struggles in which the political and media class have often resisted progress' (Younge, 2018: xii). For the book 'provides us with the necessary tools to unravel the morass of self-congratulation, myth, melancholic nostalgia and hollow, narrowly tailored remorse that tends to underpin scheduled moments of racial commemoration' (xi).

Although black, Asian and minority ethnic (BAME) voices have been articulating these kinds of critical perspectives for many decades, it has been as if the majority population has been hard of hearing, or at least very selective in what it chooses to hear. There have, after all, been other gross and urgent inequalities to take on board, understand and address, and perhaps race has been drowned out (or, we have told ourselves this particular aspect of disadvantage has already been dealt with, and is historical). Issues of inequality are *intersectional* – creating overlapping and interdependent systems of discrimination and disadvantage. We certainly recognise this, but in this book, we prioritize racism as a deeply ingrained issue which, after a long period of quiet, is overdue serious attention.

Having withdrawn reluctantly from its 'imperial destiny', and also failing to secure a future as part of the European Union of nations, the UK must now fully come to terms with its pluralism – rather than risk any retreat to a whitewashed fiction of 'global Britain'. In order to do this, the nation needs to acknowledge and then address not only the historical roots of racism in the UK but also the myriad ways in which racism operates in contemporary society. There are implications of this 'big picture' project for education, including for the teaching of geography. The main concern of our book is to excavate and open up this big picture and hopefully provide a resource for this ongoing project.

## Deliberating and Talking about Race Thinking

Our claim to be able to write this book is based on our experience of teaching geography in schools and training geography teachers. But we are also two white men who typically are said to 'move through the world blissfully unaware of their own race until its dominance is called into question' (Eddo-Lodge, 2018: xvi). As she explains, 'To be white is to be human; to be white is universal. I only know this because I am not' (xvii). We fully acknowledge that we cannot, by definition, claim to have the direct *experience* of British racism. Nevertheless, we are alert to the risk Eddo-Lodge identifies, that 'people like us' can all too easily *normalize* not only our privilege but our ways of even seeing the world. The danger is that we fail to acknowledge the accumulation of microaggressions and aggravations faced by BAME people out shopping, applying for a school place or a job, getting a mortgage and so on.

However, we do not think that you can *only* talk about race and racism if you are BAME. Indeed, like US author Robin DiAngelo in *White Fragility: Why It's so Hard for White People to Talk about Racism* (2018), we argue the reverse – that white people *must* talk about race and racism. However, to have a meaningful conversation about race and racism requires white people to listen carefully to BAME voices. It is incumbent on us to hear what Eddo-Lodge (and others) are saying. She (and others) have caught our attention. We can acknowledge the challenging idea of white privilege implied in her statement quoted in the previous paragraph. We must then seek to understand it (and its cousin white fragility) as an essential part of acquiring racial literacy. But in doing so, we do not deny additional complexities and hazards, including the danger of seeing categories such as white and black as essentially monolithic. There are, for example, white people who are also oppressed and who feel no sense of 'supremacy' – such as, eastern Europeans in parts of the UK in the first decades of the twenty-first century, and of course Jewish people (and again eastern Europeans) who suffered at the hands of state-sanctioned, scientific racism associated with Nazi Germany in the mid-twentieth century.

The question is what to do now. We hope that geography teachers in school, equipped with enhanced racial literacy, have a part to play in helping 'turn the page'. Of course, geography as a subject has moved on from the overt racist thinking that underscored environmental determinism and geographical study from what Halford Mackinder called 'the British standpoint'. But if the messages given more urgent exposure from BLM are to be acted on, then a number of very searching, practical questions follow for geography teachers:

- What do we teach children and young people about the economic geography of the UK?
- What do we teach about development and the so-called developing world?
- What do we teach about global food and or water security?
- How do we address, in geography, the meaning and impacts of the climate emergency?
- What do we teach about human populations and migrations?
- What do we teach, if anything, about the structures that govern nations and the boundaries between them and attempts to create international and global governance structures?
- Does physical geography also have scope to change?

Geography is a dynamic discipline that helps us address these questions (it is not an exhaustive list). Geographical scholarship has revealed how racist regimes have used space to organise society along racist lines, how social and economic processes operating in the housing market are racialized, how certain places are coded along racial lines, how some environments are perceived as white and how the negative externalities of economic activity, or the consequences of so-called natural disasters, are often borne unevenly by racialized populations. The challenge for geography teachers is to be part of a widespread move to recontextualize new and revealing geographical ideas into the school curriculum.

This book does not deal directly with everyday racism, for example, in the form of microaggressions vividly described by Luke de Noronha in his blog post (2022) for Decolonising Geography Educators Group. We accept that everyday superficially innocuous 'acts of racism' occur, and frequently in school. He asks rhetorically, 'What does it feel like to be stared at, whispered about, or treated as if invisible?' to make the point that 'racist resentments do not come from nowhere'. We agree and argue that to make the link between unacceptable everyday racism and the structures that support this requires enhanced racial literacy.

As Layla Saad (2020) points out, 'Systems do not change unless the people who uphold them change, and each person is responsible for upholding the system.' The part of the 'system' we examine here is the *geography curriculum* in schools. This system is quite well identified by the three-part curriculum making model (Biddulph et al. 2021: 35–7). This captures the interplay between *teachers/ teaching*, the *subject* matter and the *students*. Each element contributes to the enacted curriculum. The focus in this book is on teachers and teaching and how they can interpret and use the subject matter of geography in a way that is just and fair. We argue that this requires a continuing and deepening understanding of how racism works, how space and place are implicated in this and how place and space might be remade otherwise.

Of course, the third element of curriculum making – the students – is where many (including the influential GeoCapabilities project)[4] think curriculum making should start (see also Hammond, 2021). To conclude this introduction, we should acknowledge the significance of this question: *Who* are the people we teach? Many black children will understand instantly the recollections of Jimmy Akingbola reported by Hanna Flint in the *i newspaper*[5] (6 October 2020):

> At secondary school in Canning Town, east London, during the 1990s, he was taught 'a little bit on slavery', while the majority of the curriculum, as it is still today, was delivered from a white perspective.

If many children *know* that the curriculum is partial, failing to provide full access to knowledge and information, then it is obviously quite alienating. Classrooms are increasingly diverse, and the curriculum, through its content selections, must reflect this. It is just as important that in schools and classrooms, which remain predominantly white, children and young people are also provided with the means to grasp and think about how racism has shaped the economy, society and environments.

---

[4] https://www.geocapabilities.org/ (accessed 4 October 2022).
[5] https://inews.co.uk/culture/television/sorry-i-didnt-know-jimmy-akingbola-black-history-month-677691 (accessed 14 September 2022).

## Questions for Discussion and Reflection

- What is racial literacy in geography education?
- Why have geography teachers found it hard to talk about race and racism?

# 2
# Changing Geography and the Rise of Multicultural Britain

This chapter provides some of the essential background required to develop racial literacy by providing an account of migration and the development of race and racism in Britain. The chapter also sets out the problem that we seek to engage with in this book, which is, how school geography has made sense of (and continues to grapple with) the reality that it is taught to an increasingly diverse population, yet has been shaped by (and continues to be shaped by) a 'white imaginary'. Stating the problem in this way means that we have to take seriously arguments about what we mean by the 'British nation'. Since the Second World War (1939–45), the idea of the nation has been popularly represented by the welfare state, Imperial consciousness, and the Monarchy. This imagined country was based on a solid geography represented by places, events and landscapes. However, the period since then has been characterized by attempts to come to terms with the dismantling of this 'imaginary'. This is what makes race and racism such a challenge for geography teachers in schools.

## Migration to Britain

There is a long history of immigration to Britain. A key historical source remains Peter Fryer's (1984/2018) *Staying Power*. Its first line reads: 'There were African people in Britain before there were English people' (1). That point is rhetorical. Global lives were lived in the past, only in different ways. There have been black people in the British Isles since the Romans occupied it, guarding Hadrian's Wall. Perhaps the most telling period of 'global Britain' was that of mercantile dominance leading to the extraordinarily profitable 'Age of Empire', which involved the occupation and exploitation of territories across the world and the subjugation of people. It was financed to a large extent by the slave trade which was also a key component of the industrial revolution.

Our account focuses on the period after the Second World War and attempts to resolve the problem of labour shortages in key sectors of the economy. This was part of a wider story of migration. As Peter Gattrell (2019) shows in *The Unsettling of Europe*, it was the extraordinary growth of the European economy in the thirty years after the Second World War that saw the European states seek new sources of labour.

For its part, Britain had operated its Empire with a dual system. On the one hand, it had developed systems of exploitation including the sugar and tea plantations of the Caribbean, the Indian subcontinent and parts of East and Southern Africa. On the other hand, it had established 'white' Dominions overseas, such as Australia, Canada and New Zealand. Faced with labour shortages after the war, the UK devised complex ways to meet the demand for workers. At home, there were preferred sources of labour, not least from Poland and the Ukraine, Italy, and, after that, Ireland (this of course complicates the idea that racism is just about skin colour. There is racism other than colour-based racism, something that needs to be factored into any discussion about teaching race). The overall policy aim was to 'Keep Britain White' (Paul, 1997). At the same time, despite intense labour shortages at home, Britain continued to export citizens to its settler colonies. To solve the labour shortfall, workers were imported from the former colonies. The 1948 British Nationality Act made clear that the peoples of the Commonwealth were subjects of the British Crown and had the right to live and work in Britain.

After the Second World War, as the British working classes achieved occupational mobility and social status, they vacated low-paid, low-status jobs. These were filled by migrants. An initial source of migrant labour was the Caribbean. The West Indies' were facing economic pressures, with unemployment and underemployment, low wages and lack of opportunity. The immediate choice for those seeking a better life was the United States, but as the door closed on this in the early 1950s, Britain became the preferred choice. So-called West Indians were British subjects, had been brought up with British values (the 'mother country') and had a legal right of entry. Thus, began migration from the islands to Britain, though it is important to acknowledge the relatively small numbers involved. Initially, settlement was concentrated in large cities. Within London, two-fifths of the West Indian population settled in two areas: in the west, stretching from Paddington, through North Kensington and Notting Hill to Shepherd's Bush and Hammersmith; and the south, in Brixton, Stockwell and south Lambeth. Despite the fears of some commentators, there were no 'ghettos'. But the newcomers found themselves in the parts of the cities that were not being redeveloped, and faced problems of housing, employment and schooling.

It is important to note the significance of these developments for a nation that had hitherto imagined itself white. One of the insights of cultural geography is that space is freighted with meaning. Nations live via their imaginations, and the presence of 'dark strangers in our midst' was symbolic. It came at a time when the wartime unity of the nation was fracturing during a period of intense social change. This narrative of 'newcomers' to an 'old country' shaped the political response to immigration.

## Politics and the 'Control' of Immigration

The economic background for migration is worth stating again. Britain faced the prospect of labour shortages. A Royal Commission on the British population reported in 1949. It forecast a shortage of labour in certain sectors of industry where the conditions of work were unattractive. It estimated that some 140,000 young people might have to migrate to Britain annually to meet the shortfall. The Commission concluded that 'large-scale immigration' was both undesirable and impracticable. However, in the 1950s, it became a reality. Faced with shortages of labour, employers launched campaigns to attract workers from the West Indies, India and Pakistan.

From the start, immigration was constructed as a political issue. On the day that the *Empire Windrush* arrived in Britain (22 June 1948), eleven Labour MPs wrote a letter to the Prime Minister Clement Attlee expressing their worries about what 'coloured' migration might do to a 'white' nation:

> The British people fortunately enjoy a profound unity without uniformity in their way of life and are blest by the absence of a colour racial problem. An influx of coloured people domiciled here is likely to impair the harmony, strength and cohesion of our public and social life and to cause discord and unhappiness among all concerned. (cited in Webster, 1998: 25)

Political leaders in Britain were concerned with the potential for 'racial prejudice', the discrimination migrants might face finding accommodation and employment and the dangers of immigrants being forced into 'ghettos'. They were also conscious that colonial immigrants were British subjects and were more likely to settle permanently rather than return 'home'. This meant that their response was hesitant and ambiguous, and little positive was done to assist settlement, integration and acceptance. This sensitivity to the social and political 'costs' of migration meant that Britain moved to a position of introducing legal measures to limit migrant numbers sooner than other Western European countries.

However, the 'campaign for control', which was led by the Conservative MP Cyril Osborne, met with resistance from the Conservative governments of the 1950s for a range of reasons:

- Cabinet ministers were motivated by the principle of free movement of Commonwealth citizens.
- Levels of migration were low and limited to a few urban areas: outside of these areas, there was little pressure for control.
- There were acute labour shortages.

The Notting Hill and Nottingham 'race riots' of 1958 were a turning point in immigration policy. Tensions between 'locals' and 'immigrants' broke into open violence in 1958 with attacks by white youths (so-called Teddy Boys) on immigrants. The response was widespread condemnation of violence by politicians, church leaders and the media, who assumed that the riots were a response by the 'host' population to the visibility (and perceived lack of 'assimilation') of black people. They led Osborne to step up his 'campaign for control' and created a climate in which the limitation of numbers was taken more seriously.

Although race did not feature as an issue in the 1959 General Election, by the summer of 1960, it was clear that a significant rise in the number of West Indian migrants was taking place, prompted by a wish to 'beat the ban' which was beginning to look inevitable. In 1962, the Commonwealth Immigration Act was passed, introducing quotas to limit the number of migrants.

By 1962, the presence of migrant labour from the Caribbean and Indian subcontinent had become the focus of political debate in Britain. Many employers eagerly sought this source of labour power, but a small group of politicians and activists conducted a hostile campaign against their presence. The lack of increased investment by the state in housing, education and welfare created the conditions for prejudice and hostility among those sections of the working class which the migrants joined. The 1962 Commonwealth Immigration Act effectively meant that British politics were racialized at the highest level (Miles and Phizacklea, 1984).

The 1950s was the decade of Conservative political control; Labour dominated the 1960s. Labour politicians grappled with the tension between the socialist principle of fairness and the more sectional interest of defending workers' rights and jobs. Some Labour MPs needed to respond to constituents' concerns about immigration, especially in parts of London. In 1964, the newly elected Labour government renewed the Commonwealth Immigration Act, effectively accepting the argument that numbers should be restricted (this was a U-turn – Labour had opposed the 1962 Act). But Labour also acknowledged that new policies were needed to deal with the fact that a new generation of migrants' children was here to stay. Britain was now a multiracial society, one whose economy required the presence of Commonwealth immigrants. Its 1965 White Paper (Home Office, 1965) states the challenge of integration:

> At the same time, it must be recognized that the presence in this country of nearly one million immigrants from the Commonwealth with different social and cultural backgrounds raises a number of problems and creates various tensions in those areas where they have concentrated. If we are to avoid the evil of racial strife and if harmonious relations between the races who now form our community are to develop, these problems and tensions must be resolved and removed. (10)

This is doubled edged. It is an example of the political construction of race as a problem, along with the acceptance of 'race' as a common sense and therefore 'natural' way of thinking about social relations. At the same time, it was a statement of the liberal desire for people to live harmoniously. The Race Relations Act of

1965 established what became known as the 'race relations industry'. Bodies such as the Community Relations Council, the Race Relations Board, the Institute for Race Relations and the Runnymede Trust were established, all concerned to promote racial harmony and integration.

Overall, in the 1960s, both major parties sought to maintain a bipartisan consensus towards immigration policy. Both insisted on the need for strict control of the number of immigrants. This consensus was shattered in 1968 when the Conservative MP for Wolverhampton, Enoch Powell, made an incendiary speech – often referred to as his 'Rivers of blood' speech – in which he warned of racial tension turning to violence at some point in the future.[1] Powell's intervention continues to resonate in discussions about race and immigration.

## Thinking Black

The 1970s and 1980s saw the emergence of a distinct 'racial formation' centred on 'Blackness'. Note here the shift from 'black' to describe settlement from the New Commonwealth and Pakistan to 'Black' to denote a distinctive political identity. As a positive label of racial pride, Black was imported from the United States during the new social movements of the 1960s and 1970s but was shaped by the British geographical context. As Chambers (2016) describes it:

> Within two or three decades, Caribbean migrants had, literally and metaphorically, given birth to Black Britain … In the 1950s … there was no such entity as Black Britain. Nor did such a thing exist in the 1960s. Yet the 1970s saw the astonishing emergence of not only a distinct Black-British identity, but within a few years, the emergence of incredible artistic and cultural practices. (8)

Many of the first generation of people from the Caribbean found themselves in a social landscape that was not geared up to meeting their needs – and indeed many imagined returning 'home'. The new generation of children developed their own cultural responses, and were 'at best ambivalent about their Britishness' (6). Within two generations, a community shifted from being West Indian to Afro-Caribbean to Black-British. In the 1970s, a generation of children who had been brought up in highly religious Christian households began to take up the symbols of the Africanist religion of Ras Tafari, which originated in Ethiopia and resonated with ideas of exile, return and the Promised Land. Rastafarianism 'provided a compelling and indeed, mesmerising template for those Black youth for whom Britishness was an ill-fitting garment' (p. xiii) It appealed to blackness, had a mythical African homeland,

---

[1] Such remarks cost Powell his career in the Heath government, but they also unleashed a surge of racist – and, indeed, segregationist – sentiment among the general public. This helped stimulate the popular patriotism which swept the Conservatives to power in 1970. It was so successful in this respect that, in Bulpitt's (1986: 32) opinion, if Powell had not existed 'it may have been necessary to invent him'.

spoke a language of sufferation and downpression and communicated via powerful reggae music.

Whereas the 1950s and 1960s might be characterized as decades in which the West Indian communities were concerned with the question of 'home', by the 1970s, the focus had turned to the 'street', as second-generation African Caribbean youth sought to establish their right to occupy public space (Proctor, 2003). Thus, the struggles that took place over public space and in the 'street' were crucial to the making of Black Britain. For example, the dress of the Rastafarians presented a challenge to mainstream (i.e. white) society.

A key site of tension was the annual Notting Hill carnival (first held in 1959). As relations between black youth and the police deteriorated, the carnival became a site of struggle. Marred by violence in 1976, the police sought to prevent it taking place in 1977 and 1978. The Black community resisted (celebrated in Linton Kwesi Johnson's poem 'Forces of Victory'). Tensions continued: the 'riots' of 1980 in the St Paul's area of Bristol, followed by Brixton in 1981 (which followed the infamous 'SUS laws', which allowed the police to stop and search on 'suspicion') were important moments in the making of Black Britain. The events at Brixton should be seen in a wider context, which included the New Cross Fire of January 1980 in which thirteen young black people had been killed. The police discounted a racial motive, which was challenged by Black-community activists. That this event did not reach the national television news revealed the invisibility of black people in the national media.[2]

The political turmoil and economic collapse of the 1970s had an impact on a black population largely concentrated in the inner areas of large cities that bore the brunt of cuts in welfare, education and social support. A new sensibility of resistance emerged in these areas. At a moment when British politics was moving to the right (Thatcher came to power in 1979), and as British capitalism struggled to overcome its long-term crisis, Black struggle challenged the assumptions of better 'race relations' and instead asserted the need for Black power.[3] In the meantime, while the Conservative government and the popular press blamed trouble-making minorities and criminal behaviour, the official report into the riots, led by Lord Scarman, concluded that they were the result of a complex range of economic and social factors. While the report received criticism for its liberal assumptions, to a largely complacent public who assumed that black people lived a contented life in Britain, the riots and the Scarman

---

[2] As Diane Abbott, daughter of 'Windrush' immigrants and Britain's first Black female MP, has remarked, 'If the same things happened today, the slogan would be Black Lives Matter. What we felt was that for the state, black lives didn't matter, and that was what was electrifying about the response to the New Cross fire' (Bunce and Linton, 2020: 100).

[3] As Chris Mullard (1985), a black teacher who went on to become Professor at the Institute of Education, put that, as white voluntary bodies scrambled to get in, black people got out of the official race relations network. Black activists were disillusioned with government policies, disturbed by the growing bureaucratization of the community relations commission, and frustrated by society's tolerance of white racism.

Report brought some understanding of the reality of race and racism in British cities (Benyon and Solomos, 1987).

Even as 'inner city' became a euphemism for areas of black settlement, we should note that the streets also appealed to others, especially white youth who shared the sense of alienation and lack of entitlement (Hebdige, 1983). It was reflected in cultural movements such as Rock against Racism, which challenged the visible rise of the neofascist National Front from the mid-1970s (Goodyer, 2009). This coalition between Black and white youth raises an important point. Political blackness became more about the willingness to 'Think Black'. The term 'Black' acquired a political meaning which incorporated the interests of a range of ethnic groups.

The moment of this Black political formation lasted from the late 1960s to the mid-1980s, and to this day, it continues to shape debates about race and racism in Britain (see Waters, 2020). However, from the mid-1980s, global and local political and cultural trends converged to pull apart this particular articulation of blackness and radicalism. There were a number of elements to this, including the apparent failure of 'Black power' as a revolutionary movement, the rise of radical Islam as well as a growing dissatisfaction with blackness as a political identity in itself, linked to the renaissance of Black cultural expression which challenged the hegemonic, masculine, heteronormative and often Afro-centric conceptions of blackness. In short, it was no longer so easy to assume common experiences of racism as the basis for 'Black' identity.

## The Political Construction of 'Asian'[4] Britain

So far, our focus has been largely on migration from the Caribbean. This risks downplaying the role of migration from South Asia, but it also reflects the way in which, for significant amounts of time, race relations in Britain tended to be refracted through the prism of the relationship between black (i.e. African Caribbean) youth and the police.[5] By comparison, Asians were frequently portrayed as a 'model minority', passive, hardworking and law abiding (McGhee, 2005: 41–2).

The pattern of migration and settlement in Britain of people from South Asia exhibits similarities as well as important differences from that of migration from the Caribbean. Following the partition of India and Pakistan in 1947 and encouraged by

---

[4]The complexities of nomenclature continue to raise questions. Here we follow Avtar Brah (1996) in her general account of the making of Asian identity in Britain. As this section will highlight, though, there are different sources of Asian migration.

[5]For example, McGhee makes the point that the Scarman Report noted the context of unemployment and lack of opportunities and explained that this was exacerbated by the loose family structure within Afro-Caribbean communities. The report noted that Asian youth were likely to suffer the same problems and were more likely to be the victims of racial violence, but that Asian youth had not been involved in confrontations with the police. This was attributed to the closer family structures and patterns of childrearing of Asian communities.

the labour shortages of the late 1940s and the early 1950s, South Asian immigrants came to be concentrated in the inner areas of older industrial towns and cities, living in close proximity to white working-class communities. The migration streams were predominantly male, as earnings were sent home (repatriated) to families back home, and the peak years of migration were in the early 1960s. However, the 1962 Commonwealth Immigration Act limited migration to skilled workers, but it also led to an increase in numbers, as wives and families joined their husbands, in an attempt to beat the ban.

Asian people in Britain faced racism and discrimination (Wilson's (1978) *Finding a Voice* offers a portrait of the time). There were collective concerns about the potential undermining of Asian lifestyles, and these were brought to a head occasionally by particular issues, such as schools insisting that girls wear skirts, or the wearing of turbans by Sikh men in the workplace. Thus, as with the Caribbean community, Asian people were constructed as a problem. So, for example, as families expanded and women began to take up employment, significant industrial disputes took place as Asians began to challenge their subordinate position in the labour market.

The picture was complicated by the arrival of East African Asians, Indian workers who had been indentured to build roads and railways in Britain's East African colonies. Illegal indenture lasted until 1922, but many Indians came to occupy a middle-class position in between the white colonial elite and the African workers. They were mainly of urban rather than rural backgrounds, and Gujarati speaking (rather than mainly Punjabi South Asian migrants). In the 1960s, when Kenya, Tanzania and Uganda gained their independence, East African Asians were offered the choice of UK citizenship. Furthermore, in 1972, Uganda's President Idi Amin suddenly expelled all Asians from the country. In the refugee crisis that followed, East African Asians were dispersed to Britain, Canada and South Asia. Upon arrival in Britain, Ugandan Asians faced discrimination and the UK government policy of zoning their residential choices. This meant that many felt isolated, lonely and faced with the reality of downward social mobility and incorporation into the British working class.

All this took place in the context of the 1970s and deepening of Britain's economic recession. In 1978, Prime Minister to be Margaret Thatcher made an (in)famous speech in which she warned that British people felt 'swamped' by the arrival of people from different cultures. The 1981 British Nationality Act was seen to represent an attack on migration and was wrapped up with a campaign of state surveillance, 'virginity tests' and raids on factories in search of illegal immigrants and 'overstayers'.

To Asian youth, however, it was clear that they were here to stay, and the late 1970s saw a surge in political activism among young Asian people who adopted a highly visible, militant stance against racism. In April 1979, a large police operation saw many Asian young people arrested in Southall, London, prompting a march to Ealing Town Hall during which Blair Peach, a white teacher, died. In July 1981, following the riots in Brixton and Toxteth, there were further disturbances in Southall (Ali, 2020).

## Multicultural Drift and the Highpoint of State Multiculturalism

The 1990s saw a gradual shift in the cultural mood of many parts of life in Britain. The 1980s neoliberal rollback in services was experienced as a painful economic restructuring that made way for new economic spaces and opportunities. Whereas the 1970s and 1980s were marked by a kind of white defensiveness and siege mentality matched by an increasingly assertive Black consciousness, in the 1990s, there was more sense of becoming 'Black British' and the state actively pursued pluralism and multiculturalism (Arday, 2019). The hardened race-based identities of the 1980s began to be replaced by hybrid, playful youthful identities (this is explored further in Chapters 3 and 4). Nowhere was this more evident than in relation to new British Asian identities. In the 1990s, positive representation of Asian culture in the media included characters in *Eastenders* and comedy programmes such as *Goodness Gracious Me*, which consciously critiqued and ridiculed earlier stereotypical and racist representations. Successful films such as *Bhaji on the Beach* and *Bend it like Beckham* seemed to be in line with the culturally inclusive social policies of New Labour, which won a landslide election in 1997.

This 'multicultural drift' was reflected in the Parekh Report (2000) on *The Future of Multi-ethnic Britain*. It captured what had been termed the 'irresistible rise of multiracial Britain' (Phillips and Phillips, 1998). It coincided with a project of state multiculturalism (no longer assimilation, nor integration) that sought to address and challenge racism. This multiculturalism defined diversity as a positive good that could foster a more open, expansive notion of nationhood and citizenship. New Labour promoted the idea that Britain was a 'young country' at ease with itself.

The optimism was short-lived, lasting from approximately 1997 with the setting up of the Commission on the Future of Multi-Ethnic Britain to the publication of (and reaction to) the Parekh Report in 2000 (Carrington, 2008). The Commission was given a remit to 'analyse the current state of multi-ethnic Britain, and to propose ways of countering racial discrimination and disadvantage and making Britain a confident and vibrant multi-cultural society at ease with its rich diversity' (Parekh, 2000 p. xvii). The Report identified a series of social and cultural changes which had 'eroded the patterns of gender, class and regional and generational differences that stabilized Britain in the past as an imagined community' (23). These changes – such as moves towards devolution, accelerating globalization, membership of the European Union (EU) and the end of Empire – had:

> shaken the unified conception of Britishness hitherto taken for granted and have injected a sense of fluidity and uncertainty into what was formerly experienced by many as a settled culture. (23)

*The Future of Multi-ethnic Britain* offered an account of how Britain could respond to these trends and of the multiple stories that could be told about Britain. It seemed to offer a range of possible identities that were in tune with more fluid or mobile ideas of belonging. Thus, Britain, the report suggested, was at a turning point requiring a rethinking of the national story so as to recognize the development of a multiethnic and diverse society.

The Parekh Report offered a 'serious and thoughtful opportunity to link discussions of race with those of nation' (Carrington, 2010). However, its analysis and a modest series of proposals were buried in the press coverage of the report, which focused on one issue: that the dominant or mainstream representation of Britishness had racial connotations (McGuigan, 2010).

Subsequent events sealed the fate of the report. In the summer of 2001, there were disturbances in several northern towns and cities such as Oldham, Burnley and Bradford, with Asian youth fighting with white youth and the police. Dubbed the 'Asian Riots' by sections of media, British Society appeared fragmented and rife with divisions – a broken society. In his report into the riots, Sir Ted Cantle concluded that people in the same towns and cities were, in effect, living 'parallel lives' and that there was a need for explicit policies that would promote community cohesion (Cantle, 2008). Trevor Phillips (2005), the CEO of the Commission for Racial Equality, warned that Britain was 'sleepwalking to segregation'.

The idea of social cohesion, linked to other terms such as 'inclusion' and 'exclusion' in the context of wider society and its institutions, certainly added to the analysis in the Parekh Report. In addition, another conversation was taking place in the wake of the 1999 Macpherson Report into the Stephen Lawrence murder in Eltham, southeast London in April 1993. This report confirmed what anti-racist educators had been arguing since the 1980s: that racism was not simply a matter of personal prejudice but existed at institutional levels. Today, this argument, identifying institutional racism, is widely accepted and, at least until recently, has been officially acknowledged. The report called for anti-racist education in schools, though, in a portend of what was to come, the Education Secretary at the time, David Blunkett called institutional racism an 'empty slogan'. Instead, he argued for the importance of British values and British culture, associated with the new integrationist agenda after the 2001 Bradford disturbances.

By the early 2000s, the political ground had shifted once more. The *multicultural drift* that the Parekh Report considered inevitable and inexorable appeared to be halted. There has been a renewed set of arguments about the balance of benefits and costs of immigration, and which overtly challenge the assumption that multiculturalism and cultural diversity are necessarily positive features of society. The outrage caused by the destruction of New York's Twin Towers on 9 September 2001, and the attacks on London's transport networks on 7 July 2005, dramatically altered the political landscape. There are efforts to reassert and promote 'British values' as a way to shore up a fragile, fractured and traumatized national body politic – and the development of a 'new integrationism' (Kundnani, 2007).

## Halting the Drift

For most of the period described in this chapter, major political parties campaigned on the basis that immigration to the United Kingdom should be restricted. The goal was zero migration, and within that governments placed a focus on 'integration', symbolized by a 1983 General Election poster which depicted a black man with the tagline, 'Labour says he's black; we say he's British'. As we saw, by 2000, there was an acknowledgement of state multiculturalism. This all seems a long time ago. After 1997, the consensus over migration policy broke down. Declining birth rates, an ageing population and shortages of skilled and unskilled workers led the New Labour governments (1997–2010) to reassess the economic benefits of immigration. In 1997, the number of immigrants was 362,100. In 2004 the figure was 582,100. The net inflow of migrants almost quadrupled from 46,800 in 1997 to 222,600 in 2004. After 2004, the widening of the EU to include fourteen new nation-states, with the right to free movement to seek work, cemented these policies. The shift was from zero migration to 'managed migration'. The UK was one of only three existing member states of the EU to open its labour markets immediately with no limits. This decision was remarkably uncontested and had bipartisan support. Given that most major economies in the EU imposed restrictions on free movement and the British economy was booming, very large numbers of east European migrants arrived in the UK, particularly between 2004 and 2007.

Throughout the 2000s, New Labour pursued policies that favoured migration to Britain in order to service the expanding financial services and the low-wage service economy. Managed migration entailed the liberalisation of the economic migration system, restrictions on asylum seekers, increased surveillance of unauthorized migrants and measures to ensure the integration of newcomers, including citizenship tests to ensure adherence to 'British values'. The 2002 White Paper *Secure Borders, Safe Haven* signalled the end of the old consensus on race and immigration and focused the arguments on belonging and identity. It led to the introduction of a citizenship test, the assumption being that differences should be reduced or set aside to ensure that migrant communities would integrate or assimilate into the dominant (British) culture.

This 'new integrationism' signalled the end of multiculturalism as a policy goal and emphasized the importance of a national story based on 'core British values'. Allegiance to these values would be the basis for assessing the merits of different categories of migration as well as requirement for the settlement of immigrants. The role of schools in this process was to help the children of newly arrived immigrant to integrate into British society.

The end of the consensus on limiting immigration had important implications. It ensured that race and immigration were high on the political agenda. Multiculturalism and cultural diversity were no longer viewed as an unalloyed good, and this argument has gained prominence in the past two decades. There is a growing literature in this vein, which represents an important strand of British social conservatism. In 2004,

David Goodhart, then editor of the political magazine *Prospect*, caused controversy when he argued that rising levels of diversity undermine the collective forms of solidarity at the heart of the welfare state. The willingness collectively to support institutions such as state education, or the NHS and social security, he suggests, rely heavily on an imagined community made up of 'the likes of us' (Collins, 2004). Thus (the argument runs), mass immigration threatens this by making the collective nation 'too diverse'. In this sense, non-white immigration presents a threat, as 'indigenous' communities ask why their taxes should be spent on different kinds of people – outsiders. The solution, according to this argument, is to emphasize the importance of a *progressive nationalism* based on accepted British values that 'newcomers' should be compelled to learn. Goodhart argued that immigration had been sold to the 'indigenous' (i.e. white-British) population without a clear explanation of how it benefits them. Indeed, he suggested that it is 'ordinary' Britons who have borne the costs of immigration (Goodhart, 2004).

There are a number of problems with this account. One is the tendency to imagine the nation as made up of a largely homogenous settled people: people who were already there, so to speak, with unspoken dominance as the 'host' population. The second problem follows this directly, in that it stresses on the reality of successive waves of migration to Britain. Immigrants, therefore, become the problem, the source of internal class, regional, ethnic and linguistic and cultural cleavages (many of which, of course, are present within the 'already there' population). Finally, Goodhart conflates questions of Britishness, or perhaps Englishness, with questions of state belonging and citizenship, assuming that sameness is the key to solidarity. As Gilroy (2005) noted, Goodhart's arguments may be read as an 'adaptation and updating of well-worn themes drawn from the Powell lexicon. Immigration is always an invasion'. (41)

Despite these flaws, Goodhart's arguments have received extensive and positive coverage within the liberal media, and in his subsequent book *The British Dream* (Goodhart, 2014), he noted how the political climate had shifted and his earlier arguments no longer appear extreme. Indeed, over the past decade or so it has become a standard argument that politicians have betrayed the working classes through encouraging immigration. Thus, Nick Timothy (2020) felt able to state (with limited referencing): 'We know from almost every poll published that most people think immigration is too high and ought to be reduced. Research shows that this view is shared across every age group and every part of the country including liberal London' (137). He goes on to assert that although migration may have little impact on the overall size of the economy, it does have local effect upon particular sections of the labour force and in particular localities, where it increases competition for scarce resources and adds pressure on infrastructure and services (the alternative case – that immigration is beneficial for the economy is set out by Phillippe Legrain (2020). The argument that any economic benefits from migration accrue to the wealthy while the costs are borne by the 'have nots' became an oft-repeated refrain in the years leading up to and following the Brexit referendum in 2016. Commentators, such as Goodhart, and academics, such as Eric Kaufman (2018) and Matthew Goodwin

(Eatwell and Goodwin, 2018), draw attention to a divide between the 'liberal elites' and the 'left behinds'. In the context of Brexit, they suggest that votes for anti-immigration policies reflect the sense that the white working class, itself an historical and political construction (Shilliam, 2018), feels increasingly marginalized and left out of mainstream political debate.

## To the Present and Black Lives Matter

The previous section describes how the faltering progress in Britain towards a more open, inclusive and equal society has been interrupted, culminating in the Brexit vote. This is not how the story ends. As the editors of *Soundings* wrote in 2020, 'We are living through a moment of multiple disruptions ... the racialized dispossessed and their allies are destabilizing the forces of white nationalism that have been in the ascendant in recent years' (Davison, Grayson and Forkert, 2020: 4). This reflects the fact that race is a continuing strand within the cultural politics of British society.

The Brexit vote has generated a counter-movement visible in a variety of developments. Examples of this include the scandal of the Windrush inquiry in which long-standing residents who came to Britain in the 1950s had their citizenship rights revoked, highlighting the arbitrary nature of national belonging; the political response to the Grenfall fire which revealed the scant regard to the lives of working-class and Black and Minority Ethnic (BME) tenants and the failure of the state to look after its most vulnerable and marginalized citizens; widespread awareness of the well-documented impact of Covid-19 and its disproportionate impact on BME groups; the knowledge and experience of policies of policing revealed through the murder of George Floyd and the subsequent mobilizations of Black Lives Matter; and the statements made by the England footballer Marcus Rashford, the taking the knee at football matches and the racist response to England's penalty shootout defeat in the European Championship final in 2021. These are indicative of the role that race is playing in the present moment and that race and racism is the frame with which young people make sense of events. This is reflected in books written by young Black Britons such as Afua Hirsch's (2018) *Brit(ish)*, Akala's (2018) *Natives*, and Reni Eddo-Lodge's (2018) *Why I'm no Longer Talking to White People about Race*; based on an earlier (2014) blog, Eddo-Lodge explained:

> Not all white people, just the vast majority who refuse to accept the legitimacy of structural racism ... It's like they can no longer hear us. (p. ix)

This is the context in which horrific images of a white police officer murdering George Floyd were received by a nation locked down with their mobile devices. This was about white supremacy, white privilege, white fragility and a failure to acknowledge how the wealth of developed societies had been built on histories of slavery, dispossession and genocide. It led crowds of protestors in Bristol to topple the statue of Edward Colston, a wealthy trader who earned profits from slavery and who was celebrated by the city, and the National Trust to publish a report acknowledging how many of its properties were built with the proceeds of slavery. When professional football resumed (albeit to limited crowds), players 'bent the knee' to recognize that Black Lives Matter. Corporations made statements to acknowledge the movement and educational organizations such as the Geographical Association issued statements that recognized the need to teach geography for a diverse and multiracial society.

## Conclusion

The narrative offered in this chapter confirms Sivanandan's (1983) comment that racism does not stay still. We have provided an abbreviated account of the changing meanings of race and racism in Britain since 1945 (the end of the Second World War). There is nothing inevitable or natural about these changes: they are political constructions of race and racism. This is the context in which school geography provides successive generations of young people an answer to the question, 'To which space do I belong?' As individual geography teachers, we can choose to be more or less aware of these issues, more or less prepared to raise them in classrooms, but until around 1980, the polite thing to do was to ignore them, in line with the commonly held view that mention of race and racism exacerbated problems or incited racial animosity (Small, 1994: 165). Such a position is no longer tenable.

## Questions for Discussion and Reflection

1. Postwar migration has changed the economic, social and cultural geography of Britain. How is this reflected in geography teaching?
2. The 2000 Parekh Report offered a positive vision of the future of multiethnic Britain. What happened next?

# Part two

## Theoretical Perspectives

# 3
# Changing Perspectives on 'Race' and Education

## Introduction

The previous chapter explored the changing politics of race and racism in Britain. It showed how, in response to postwar immigration, there were intense arguments about belonging, culture and the nation. Education – and schooling in particular – is a key site in which these arguments have been interpreted and worked through. In this chapter, we examine the ways in which schools and teachers have responded to the development of a multiracial society. Teachers operate at the sharp end of social and cultural change. However, they are, to a large extent, unprepared by their training to make sense of these changes. This chapter introduces debates about 'race' and education. Before we start, it will be useful to remark upon the approach we take.

Our approach is chronological. We broadly follow the narrative provided in Chapter 2. Indeed, it ought to be possible to map the different approaches to thinking about race and education to the developments described in that chapter. We are aware that one of the dangers of that approach is that it risks suggesting that there has been an ordered procession of theoretical perspectives as old (less useful) ideas are replaced by new ones that are more valid. Reality is not so neat and tidy. There is considerable overlap. This means that ideas associated with, for example, Critical Race Theory (which developed in the United States in the 1970s) are often linked to older ideas associated with anti-racist education. Second, reading this chapter, you might get the impression that schools and staffrooms are hotbeds of race thinking. In our experience, this is not the case. Indeed, as we suggest at various points in this book, for geography teachers, there is little trace of these arguments and debates in the literature. Finally, it is not our plan in this chapter to advocate one approach over another. Our goal here is to provide a map of the perspectives that have informed (and continue to inform) debates about race and education.

## Learning to Speak to Each Other

The 1944 Education Act provides a convenient starting point for our discussion. It was part of the establishment of the welfare state, an attempt to ameliorate the effects of the trade cycle and to ensure a degree of equality of opportunity. The school leaving age was raised, in 1948, to fifteen years. As postwar austerity eased, new schools were built. There were cultural changes too: an expanding economy meant that young people could leave school and take up jobs. They had money in their pockets, and the 1950s gave rise to the birth of the teenager and the consumer society. In *The Uses of Literacy*, Richard Hoggart (1958) documented the changes to traditional ways of life, and schooling was an important part of this modernization. In a 1958 essay, 'Speaking to Each Other', Hoggart invited readers to consider a typical scene from the new society. It is significant that this typical scene was of a classroom:

> It shows the classroom of a bright new secondary modern school on a public housing estate outside a busy provincial city. Almost all of the large class of thirteen-year-olds look healthy and are decently clothed; their young teacher wears what is by now almost a uniform – sports jacket and charcoal-grey flannels. A sense of vocation still gives something of a glow of idealism in his face, though it is confused with signs of strain. He is taking a poetry lesson and finding it at times surprisingly rewarding, at times extremely disillusioning. He knows most of his pupils go to the pictures at least once a week and watch television for two or three hours a night. They tell him about the programmes in a friendly way; they know he hasn't a TV set. He is an ex-scholarship boy, by choice committed to educating people whom he knows as deeply as one only knows those one was born among – and whom he yet feels he does not know. (121)

Hoggart saw in this scene a modest yet widespread prosperity, a new kind of working class, a society that was shaped by the mass media and an increasingly mobile society. But the scene he is describing is one of a largely white society. Into this picture – of a Britain, 'which has not yet learned to speak seriously to its new self' – must be inserted the 'newcomers' – the children of immigrants from the Caribbean and India and Pakistan.

A sense of this 'other Britain' can be glimpsed in Stuart Hall's (1967) essay, 'The Young Englanders', which was clearly influenced by Hoggart's method of the close analysis of culture. Hall noted how immigrants' encounters with the white British took place as a rule in particular parts of Britain and with particular kinds of people. In short, in the so-called 'twilight' areas of large industrial cities. These were places of intense competition for limited resources and ones that had still to benefit from the coming of affluence. The encounter with otherness on both sides was often mistrustful and led to the adoption of defensive inward-looking attitudes. Hall's young Englanders lived 'between two worlds'. Hall ended his essay with the observation that the young immigrants he had met were 'falling back on their own reserves'. They were rediscovering their own racial and national identities and stereotyping their white counterparts. While in some ways this was positive, in other ways it represented 'lost ground in the struggle for integration'.

The schools that the children of migrants attended were likely to be low status and lacking in resources. Secondary modern schools were sold as an alternative route to qualifications and well-paid jobs. In reality, these assumed and reinforced the idea of an academic-manual divide (20 per cent or so of the cohort going to grammar schools having been selected via the 11+ examination). They were drab buildings, staffed by teachers who were minimally prepared and less well paid. Pupils were frequently bored and uninterested. There were important cultural changes at work, but schools and teachers operated with a largely deficit view of the media cultures that pupils were increasingly engaged with. Schools were conservative places. To many of those living in an established and relatively homogenous culture, the presence of newcomers was literally shocking.

To head teachers and teachers, immigrant children presented a new challenge – they posed questions about education's capacity for responding to cultural and linguistic differences. The response of schools and teachers was 'panicky in tone' and 'assimilationist in content' (Jones, 2016: 68). Local authorities sought to limit the presence of immigrant pupils through policies of dispersal and bussing, and the limitation of the number of such pupils in schools. This was mirrored in national policy, which sought to ensure that no more than 30 per cent of any one school's intake would be immigrant children. The goal was rapid assimilation. As the authors of *The Heart of the Race* put it:

> It is no surprise that we were viewed as oddities, given the colonialist diet was still being fed. Our hair, habits, language and customs was seen as the manifestations of savagery, confirmation of our uncivilised past. Even to young children, and at a time when televisions were not a common feature of every working-class home, we represented the foreign hordes which had been tamed and disciplined in the flag and Empire. Indeed, it was the attitude of the teachers which did the most lasting damage. They were to interpret black children's disorientation and bewilderment as a sign of stupidity. The concept of us as simpleminded, happy folk, lacking in sophistication or sensitivity, became readily accepted definitions. Theories about us, put forward by Jensen in America and endorsed by Eysenck here in the late 1960s, gave such views a spurious credibility by popularizing the idea of race and intelligence are linked in some inherent way. (Bryan, Dadzie and Scafe, 1985: 34)

The reference to now discredited theories reminds us that teacher education courses are one of the ways by which teachers develop racialized ideas about the students they teach. Summarizing the response to the presence of black students in the school system, Hazel Carby (1982) argued that these were

> framed in terms of the problems to the system that the students pose. Since the 60s, educational theory has located these problems in the black child, his or her educational failure being explained through the application of common-sense racist assumptions. (183)

These assumptions included, for example, the idea that black students' linguistic structures were inadequate and inhibited learning (in contrast to ebonics in the United States, which regards American Black English as a language in its own right rather than a dialect of standard English). Furthermore, having thus situated failure in the individual black student, educational theories traced the causes of these problems to a 'cycle of pathology' in black communities. For example, it was suggested that forms of discipline tended to be authoritarian and repressive, and a deviation from what was considered to be 'normal', and thus desirable. The immigrant child was therefore at a disadvantage and more likely to be in need of remedial treatment. This was to be overcome through enlightened educational training of teachers so that they could recognize the specific needs of the immigrant child.

## From Assimilation to Integration

As we saw in Chapter 2, by the mid-1960s, official 'race relations' policy had come to recognize the limitations and failures of assimilation and moved towards ideas of integration and cultural pluralism. The period from 1962 to 1970 saw a distinct shift in the terms of the debate around immigration (Solomos, 1988). Prior to the 1962 Commonwealth Immigration Act, the concern had been about controlling the number of immigrants. Afterwards, the focus of official policy was the question of 'how to deal with the position of those black communities already settled in Britain'. The fear was that future generations of black people could grow up in conditions of social isolation and economic inequality which would impact relations between racial groups.

In response to growing concern about the educational position of black children in schools, the Local Government Act of 1966 made resources available for schools with significant numbers of black pupils. The Plowden Report (HMSO, 1967) criticized assimilation and instead spoke of cultural enrichment. A series of official reports singled out education as an area where action was necessary to meet the special needs of black children (and to overcome the opposition of white parents to the presence of black children in schools). Increasingly, state education was seen as a means to change attitudes towards race within the host society. Rather than simply seeing the 'problem' of black children, it was implied that society as a whole needed a greater understanding of race.

The state multiculturalism that emerged in the late 1960s and developed through the 1970s had two elements. The first was the requirement for more resources and emphasis on the 'special needs' of black children. The second was that if racism was challenged through education, then equality of opportunity would flourish. The objective was to produce more understanding of racial issues through the reform of the education system. It is striking that as early as 1978, a Home Office report stressed on the importance specifically of *curriculum* issues:

> For the curriculum to have meaning and relevance now in our schools, its content, emphasis and the values and assumptions contained must reflect the wide range of cultures, histories and lifestyles in our multi-racial society. The more informed teachers become about a wider range of cultures and communities and the more possibilities for all pupils to see their values reflected in the concerns of schools, the less likely is the alienation from schools and indigenous society experienced by some minority group pupils. (The Home Office, 1978: 6)

This model involved an incorporation of the assimilationist arguments within a more sophisticated concept of 'complex disability'. The rhetoric was that by

- learning about their 'roots' ethnic, children will improve their educational achievement;
- learning about their culture, its traditions and so on, ethnic children will have enhanced opportunities; and
- learning about other cultures will reduce all children's prejudice and discrimination towards those from different cultural and ethnic backgrounds.

This was a mix of what has been termed 'benevolent' multiculturalism with an approach targeting improved 'cultural understanding' (Bullivant, 1981).

To assume that the move towards integration was an act of political benevolence from a state that was in the process of modernizing and creating an inclusive, multiracial society downplays the fact that such moves were a response to campaigns, since the early 1960s, by black communities to improve the education offered to their children (Scafe, 1989). There was no easy path to integration, and Enoch Powell's infamous 'rivers of blood' speech ensured that any discussion of race and schooling was politicized. Between 1969 and 1971 parents' groups campaigned against policies of segregation and, as the existence and persistence of racism in schools became clearer, the black community rejected 'official' explanations for its children's educational failure. In 1971, Bernard Coard, a black educationalist, published *How the West Indian child Is Made Educationally Subnormal in the British School System*, which sold 10,000 copies. Drawing upon his own experience and on the social psychological research that was influential in the time, Coard suggested that black children tended to suffer from an insecure sense of identity. His conclusion was stark:

> Through the belittling, ignoring or denying of a person's identity, one can destroy perhaps the most important aspect of a person's personality – his sense of identity, of who he is. Without this, he will get nowhere. (31)

Coard's work drew attention to the effect that educational policy was having on black school children. As we have seen, an early response to the 'problem' of black children in schools was dispersal, or 'bussing' children to other areas (Richardson, 2005) and black children being allocated to schools for the 'educationally subnormal' on the pretext of providing 'special education' for them. Familiar (racialized) ideas about 'low IQ', 'broken English' and 'hyperactive behaviour' were used to justify these outcomes. In response, groups of black parents set up Saturday or Supplementary Schools to provide students with an understanding of their history and culture, recruiting volunteers to teach Black history alongside Maths and English.[1]

An important part of the approach to teaching and learning in Supplementary Schools was the use of autobiography as a means of encouraging black children to write about their experiences and to develop their own voice. This drew upon the tradition of progressive education which had been officially sponsored after the Second World War. In the hands of black teachers who were themselves developing a radical analysis of the racist society they found themselves in, it sparked a renaissance of Black writing. The effects were cathartic, and, for some at least, incendiary. For example, Chris Mullard (1973), commenting on the process of writing his book *Black Britain* noted that, 'In writing *Black Britain* I found not solace, comfort, or tolerance, but tension, a disturbing desire to break, smash and riot, to bellow: "Whitey! One day you'll have to pay!"' Mullard was talking about eruption of Black consciousness, and it was political dynamite: for example, English teacher Chris Searle was suspended from John Cass School in London for publishing an anthology of his students writing *Stepney Words*.

As well as Supplementary Schools, there were moves to challenge and modify the formal curriculum of state schools, leading to the development of 'Black Studies' in the 1970s and 1980s. For example, at Tulse Hill School in South London, sixth-form students were taught about black immigration to Britain and the history and cultures of the Caribbean, Africa, Asia and South America. At William Penn School (again in South London), teachers developed a two-year course aimed mainly at children of 'West Indian' origin. It adopted a historical approach progressing from the beginning of modern colonialism in the 16th century, to slavery in the plantations, the postcolonial developments in ex-colonies and analysis of the economic and social circumstances of immigrants in Britain. The preamble to the syllabus was uncompromising in its statement of purpose:

> A means of compensating for inadequacies of understanding, lack of identity, of poor self-image, sheer ignorance, the holding of myths and prejudices. (Pollack, 1972: 10)

The idea of Black Studies in schools, which may have parallels with Ethnic Studies in California (Lambert and León, 2022), was not universally accepted. The assumption that black children are in certain crucial respects culturally deprived fits in with 'deficit models' of education – in contrast to Ethnic Studies which stresses the cultural assets of students. Moreover, the Black Studies curriculum fix seemed to imply that racism could be countered by a rewrite of the history books. Bryan et al. (1985), warned that Black Studies risked being used to offer a second-class curriculum to black children:

---

[1] In his acclaimed *Small Axe* series made in 2020, Steve McQueen uses his own educational experiences of school in the 1970s to explore this issue: in the episode 'Education' https://www.imdb.com/title/tt10551106/ (accessed 30 September 2022).

> Taught alongside the geography lesson, which depicted the developing third world as being totally dependent upon Western generosity, and alongside the history lesson which concentrated on glorious white conquest, the value of Black studies alone was always debatable. (34)

Indeed, some critics worried that Black Studies could be used to 'ghettoize' black students while the white children got on with studying for high-status examinations. Thus, Dhondy, Beese and Hassan (1982) argued that Black Studies was designed specifically to pacify or even neutralize the potential of black students.[2] In an influential book, *The Education of the Black Child: The Myth of Multiracial Education*, Maureen Stone (1981) argued against the forms of multicultural education that focused on the affective dimension of students' experiences, rejecting the idea that black students suffered from low self-esteem. What was required, she suggested, was teaching 'associated with the mastery of skills and knowledge and the development of abilities' (254).

Despite these difficulties, the developments described in this section – alternative provision, black students' voice and curriculum change – amounted to the emergence of an approach to anti-racist education that was explicitly political and which challenged the 'liberal' assumptions of multicultural education. To reiterate, while we might assume that the shift towards multiculturalism represented an advance on assimilationist thinking, critics at the time argued that multicultural education was effectively a means of 'keeping the lid on' the pressures emanating from Black community groups and students themselves for more relevant curriculum and pedagogy.

## The Promise and Limits of Multicultural Education

In 1977, a Department of Education and Science Green Paper, *Education in Schools*, stated that

> ours is now a multiracial and multicultural country and one in which traditional social patterns are breaking down ... the comprehensive school reflects the need to educate our people for a different sort of society ... the education appropriate to our Imperial past cannot meet the requirements of modern Britain. (4)

This was a striking attempt to conjure up the idea of 'national interest' while acknowledging the existence of diversity. However, the Green Paper casts this as an historical rather than a structural issue. Similarly, the 'breaking down' of traditional

---

[2] These arguments about the value of Black Studies in many ways anticipate the arguments about standpoint curricula and powerful knowledge that have emerged more recently in the light of social realist arguments. See Chapter 6 for a fuller discussion.

social patterns was presented as a natural and evolutionary process, rather than one based around antagonism, conflict and contradictions. Schools were assumed somehow to reflect society: the classroom as a microcosm of society and at the same time a catalyst for social change.

Despite its calls for unity, the Green Paper was published at a moment when Britain was facing economic and social crisis. As such, it represented the moment of the break between two distinct ways of organizing the capitalist economy and society. The first has been termed 'social democracy'. It was marked by the 1944 Education Act, which established the idea of education for all and eventually led to the growth of comprehensive schooling. It was forged in a period of educational expansion, with the raising of the school leaving age to fifteen years in 1947 and sixteen in 1972, the incorporation of previously excluded working-class children and the assumption of a broadly common curriculum. However, by the early 1970s this, settlement was breaking down in the face of economic stagnation and cultural change. The promises of education for social mobility were revealed as just that – promises – and an increasingly restless youth culture was challenging the authority and discipline of the school. Politicians publicly questioned teachers' attitudes and moved to limit the profession's autonomy (Centre for Contemporary Cultural Studies, 1981).

One of the interesting things about the breakdown of the post–Second World War settlement, designed to heal society through the expansion of education and the inclusion of working-class children, was, by the 1970s, refracted through race. This was especially important, since the establishment of comprehensive schools often involved the merging of schools with very different racial and social mixes. The 1977 Green paper correctly judged that new approaches to schooling were needed. The social democratic postwar 'agreement' was crumbling, coinciding with the period in which 'Blackness' – the political formation described in Chapter 2 – came to prominence.

Of course, the postwar settlement did not dissolve overnight. Ways of thinking and acting that were habitual and embedded in common sense had to be challenged. The process involved creating moral panics and folk devils. The situation Hall had warned of in his 'The Young Englanders' article came to pass. A new sensibility of resistance had been developing in the inner cities throughout the 1970s, marked by tense relations between police and black youth. The economic downturns of the 1970s prompted cuts in welfare spending, education and social support. A section of the population, already radicalized in terms of Black consciousness, was exposed to the accelerating pace of the economic recession. At a time of youth unemployment, the state moved to discipline black youth, an overt example of the state racializing economic and social change. Conservatives considered that the urban disturbances in Bristol, London and Liverpool in 1980 and 1981 bolstered their case for a law-and-order society (Brake and Hale, 1992; Haider, 2018).

Education was an important part of this. Multicultural education, with its focus on cultural pluralism and diversity – caricatured as being focused on 'saris, samosas, and steel bands' – was ill-equipped to deal with the realities of life in 'multiracist Britain' (ALTARF, 1984). In opposition, a more radical form of anti-racist education was proposed. This was represented by the now-famous dictum that Racism = Prejudice + Power. The focus was on understanding the historical and economic forces that had led to immigration and the ways in which racism emerged from these relationships. As Salman Rushdie (1982) wrote, racism is not a side issue in contemporary Britain:

> And now there's a new catchword: 'multiculturalism'. In our schools, it means little more than teaching our kids a few bongo rhythms and how to tie a sari. In the police training programme, it means telling cadets that black people are so 'culturally different' that they can't help but make trouble. Multiculturalism is the latest token gesture towards Britain's blacks. It ought to be exposed – like 'integration' and 'racial harmony' – for the sham it is. (n.p.)

In the 1980s, anti-racist education insisted on the need to locate the problem directly with white racism, seeing racism as a structural rather than a matter of individual prejudice. Racism had to be understood as an integral feature of the educational system, with its roots in Britain's colonial history (Institute of Race Relations, 1983). The anti-racist remedy was the 'politicization' of race – and to acknowledge the role of the formal curriculum in the propagation of racism. Anti-racist proposals included:

- sharp scrutiny of the hidden curriculum;
- critical focus on processes of assessment and the allocation of resources;
- policies to employ more black teachers, especially into management positions; and
- requirements to record, track and deal with racist incidents.

In summary, while multiculturalism sought to maintain social stability and diffuse racial conflict, 1980s anti-racism sought racial equality and justice. Furthermore, it could be said that while multiculturalism represented the intentions of well-meaning white liberals, anti-racism eschewed concerns for harmony and integration, since it stemmed from a completely different primary source: black people themselves.

As this was happening, the New Right was gaining ascendancy. It focused on themes of culture and nation. In doing so, it sought to challenge 'the enemy within' such as striking miners, and even to ridicule anti-racist mathematics teachers who also (it was claimed) sought to undermine Britain's greatness. The Swann Report, *Education for All*, had been commissioned by a Labour Secretary of State for Education, but by the time it reported in 1985 the political landscape had changed. It was the last major report of the social-democratic era in education. The economic crisis had led to political and social division, and the Swann Report's liberal assumptions about diversity and cultural pluralism were subject to critique from all sides: from the radical left (which argued instead for anti-racist education) and the Conservative right, which called for a return to standards and tradition.

In Chapter 6, we will examine how arguments around multicultural and anti-racist education were received in the world of geography education. For now, we can simply note that the political formation of 'thinking Black', which underpinned anti-racist education, lasted from the late 1960s to the mid-1980s. After that, it lost ground. A key element of this was the establishment of a National Curriculum in 1988. There was much debate at that time about the extent to which the National Curriculum promoted a nationalistic and 'racist' worldview, a debate that was revived in 2020 in relation to Black Lives Matter. Under the national curriculum, Sivanandan (1990) argued, pupils:

> are not even be taught to relate healthily to the different experiences and cultures of the fellow students around them through education other cultures and in the racism of their own – which renders those of other cultures inferior. Instead, they are, if the new right continues to have its say, to be afforded a 'colour-blind', conflict-free education in a world replete with colour and conflict. (151–2).

## 'New Ethnicities'

By the mid-1980s the notion of 'Black' as a political category began to fragment. There was talk of 'New Times'. The economy appeared to be shifting, from one based around the heavy manufacturing industries and old, declining industrial regions to one based around services, and high technology. As the economy changed, people changed. Old ways of living organized around the factory and community were breaking down, and in their place were more fluid and open arrangements. People's identities, it was suggested, were fracturing and in flux. New forms of identity and belonging were emerging, and the crucial thing to note for progressive politics was that these were not fixed.

Ideas about 'race' and 'ethnicity' were not exempt. The presence of British-born black people meant that simple notions of 'hosts' accommodating 'newcomers' were less and less relevant. In addition, fresh critiques of the nation and the nation-state emerged, at least in part promoted by the quickening process of globalization. In this context, theorists, influenced by the rise of postmodernism and poststructuralism, developed concepts such as 'diaspora', 'new ethnicities' and 'hybridity', which were underpinned by a non-essentialist view of identity (McGuigan, 1996). This was popularly reflected in the idea that identity is less a matter of where you are from and more about where you are going – from 'roots' to 'routes'. As Avtar Brah (one of the most influential theorists of the term 'diaspora') later argued:

> It was a more positive way of conceptualizing communities, and a way to deracialize them. (Brah, 2020: 35)

The concept of 'new ethnicities' was coined in a 1988 lecture by the cultural theorist Stuart Hall. In that lecture, Hall did not want to give up on the possibility of some kind of Black identity but argued that racial identity is a fiction – a necessary fiction in order to make both politics and identity possible. As he once said, 'Identity is like a bus ticket. We use it to get from one place to another, but that is it' (Hall, 1989). Hall expanded this to insist on the importance of seeing Black cultural production in the context of global networks, showing how new identities are produced through a productive tension between global and local influences. All this gave rise to the notion that people can have multiple identities and culture.[3]

The implications of arguments about *fluid and non-essential identities* for any practice of teaching and learning about race are significant. They challenge the tendency, found in the anti-racist education of the 1980s, to construct a binary division between 'black' and 'white'. Faced with a model of changing and complex identities, anti-racist teaching cannot be simply a matter of providing 'positive images' in the classroom, or even providing accurate factual accounts of how 'we' underdeveloped 'them'. This is because racism goes deeper than that. Racism is located in identity, which is both a sociological and psychological construction.

Amid all this talk of openness, fluidity and multiple identities, and in a general mood of deconstruction, it was inevitable that attention would be drawn to the apparently natural and singular category of 'whiteness'. One of the ironies of the anti-racist argument was the tendency to leave whiteness unexamined. From the 1990s, this started to change. Thus, in media studies the early work of Richard Dyer (1988, 1997) drew attention to the invisibility of whiteness in studies of popular culture. In the United States, Ruth Frankenberg's (1993) in-depth interviews with white subjects revealed the ways in which their lives and the meanings they attached to places and location were shaped by race. Also in the United States, Peggy McIntosh (1989) popularized the notion of the 'invisible knapsack' that white people unknowingly carry around with them, carrying various forms of unearned assets, which focused attention on white privilege. Other studies have drawn attention to social construction of whiteness and how different groups were assimilated into the white majority (Allen, 1994; Roediger, 1991). In 1994, Howard Winant called the 1990s the 'incipient crisis of whiteness'. He attributed this to the fact that in some places white people were becoming minority groups, and in a time of intense competition some white people were critical of programs of affirmative action and financial aid. Together, such studies revealed that whiteness was not always equated with power, highlighting the diversity within the category of white. Analysing whiteness meant asking questions such as:

- How do people become white?
- How is whiteness socially constructed?
- What material and cultural resources are made available in how Anglo-ethnicity is compulsively and publicly performed? (Mac an Ghaill, 1999)

Critical whiteness studies were an important correction to the notion that white itself was a non-ethnic identity. They raised important questions about the process of becoming white and who was more or less regarded as properly white.

For example, in her study of Irish women in Britain, Bronwen Walter (2001) acknowledges that to be Irish in Britain is to occupy a complex reality. It is to be

---

[3]Hall's intellectual project is complex: spanning over six decades, it was a sprawling engagement with the questions of race, ethnicity, Englishness, nation and cultural change. At this point, Hall was interested in exploring the possibilities for more open, networked and fluid senses of identity to emerge in the spaces created by the breakdown of the postwar settlement.

both an insider and an outsider. Thus, as a white woman, Walter occupies a privileged position. However, there are subtle clues that give away one's Irishness, which mean that she is not quite white. These racialized boundaries are, inevitably, complicated by gender, class and region. Walter says she was able to grow up in England without even knowing she was Irish. It was only when she started to trace her family history that the extent of her family's geographical and social mobility was revealed. The concept that helped make sense of this for Walter was diaspora, and the idea of the nation-state (in this case, Britain) as a diaspora space: 'Englishness is continually reconstituted via a multitude of border crossings in and through other diasporic formations' (Brah, 1996: 209). As Walter explains:

> My father's mother was a Welsh-speaker from mid-Wales and even my 'English' grandparents came from Cumberland, Hampshire and Dorset, regions with differing relationship to the 'Deep England' of the 'Home Counties'. A crucial facet of the concept of diaspora space is its deconstruction of the monolithic 'sameness' of the 'centre', by revealing the hybridities which already constitute it. (28)

After a decade in which the New Right had dominated discussions of race, culture and nation, concepts such as the 'new ethnicities', 'diaspora', 'hybridity' were challenging and exciting; they appeared to offer new maps of meaning with which to make sense of social and cultural transformations. In retrospect, however, the focus on youthful, playful multicultural identities set up a new divide between older, traditional and exclusive identities. There was an all too simple binary between 'good new' hybridity in which people had fluid identities that were worn lightly and 'bad old' ethnicity in which people clung to older and less inclusive identities. Invariably, the latter were those members of the white working class. The work of Phil Cohen at the Centre for New Ethnicities at the University of East London and Roger Hewitt (2005) was important in drawing attention to the challenges of teaching against racism in schools where (some) white students resisted the messages of multiculturalism. Allowing space for students to voice their perspectives can lead to problems for teachers, who may decide that it is safer to avoid discussion of race altogether rather than make space for young people to explore their identities.

What it means in schools and classrooms to focus on whiteness is unclear, but it has become even more important in relation to the arguments around Black Lives Matter with its insistence that white people recognize and take responsibility for their privilege and to question the pervasiveness of whiteness as neutral or normal. For instance, what would it mean for teachers to teach with the aim to abolish whiteness? Should they seek to develop in students an oppositional whiteness that contests dominant forms of whiteness? There are few clear answers to these questions. In one of the earliest calls for the study of whiteness as part of a critical multicultural education, Kincheloe and Steinberg (1997) stated as their aims:

- understanding the positionality of whiteness,
- identifying and abandoning the practice of white racism, and
- developing a critical and progressive white identity.

Elsewhere, they expand on this, suggesting that their goal is 'creating a positive, proud, attractive, anti-racist white identity that is empowered to travel in and out of various racial/ethnic circles with confidence and empathy' (Kincheloe et al., 1998: 20).

## The Road to Critical Race Theory

Teachers often experience a mismatch between the pace and direction of social and cultural change and how this is (or is not) reflected in schools and classrooms. While concepts such as diaspora, hybridity and identities signalled significant shifts in the temper of multiracial Britain in the 1990s and early 2000s, these shifts were not always apparent in schools. We can see something of this in the developing work of David Gillborn, who is widely regarded as *the* leading figure in the field of race and education in Britain.

There is an interesting moment in his 1995 book *Racism and Anti-Racism in Real Schools*. In a section titled 'No One Asked about Us: White Students and Antiracism', Gillborn cites work by geographer Alistair Bonnett and others about the importance of deconstructing notions of whiteness. Gillborn acknowledges the discursive power of white as a category and how problematizing the category could counter the tendency in education to cast the white student's role as potential antagonist and racist, rather than fellow and anti-racist. As we saw in the previous section, this was an argument that had gathered force in the 1990s as anti-racism faltered. Gillborn states that it has always been clear that widespread progress to challenge racism depends on the involvement of white people:

> Indeed, as antiracist analyses and pedagogies become more sophisticated, it is increasingly obvious that white students occupy a pivotal role: any genuine attempt to challenge racism in education must engage with their perspectives and experiences. (1995: 168)

Thus, Gillborn acknowledges the criticism that in the world of anti-racism, there is all too often an oversimplistic assumption that 'black = victim and white = oppressor'. But he also suggests that in their push back, the New Right sought to build the consensus around a limited version of English identity that must be challenged through education. The move from anti-racism as a political struggle towards a position that acknowledges how race is linked with culture and nation raises difficult questions and issues for educators to deal with. Indeed, Mac an Ghaill (1999) concluded his survey of contemporary racisms and ethnicities with the comment that young people display a wide range of responses to life in a multicultural and multiracist society, and these responses do not 'translate easily into a political programme or policy approach' (151).

Indeed, educational policymaking in this period had its own momentum, which was not always helpful in supporting schools attempts to address diversity. The context for this was the drive towards standards and ensuring that schools met targets for the required number of GCSE A–C grades and could demonstrate value-added. This was linked to increased intensification of teachers' work and the rise of managerialism. It all amounted to nothing less than a rapid change in the culture of schooling. As always, there were winners and losers, and in *Rationing Education*, Gillborn and Youdell (2000) describe in detail how the 'A–C economy' serves to maintain and exacerbate historical patterns of inequality:

> The British school system is increasingly selective, disciplinary and discriminatory ... Equality of opportunity is denied many pupils, especially Black young people and their peers from working-class backgrounds. The obsession with measurable and elite 'standards', the publication of school 'league tables', heightened surveillance of schools, and increased competition for resources are all part of the problem, not the solution. (1)

It is possible to detect here a growing frustration with official policy, so much so that, a few years later, Gillborn (2005) starkly asserted that 'education policy is an act of white supremacy', a view he developed in *Racism and Education: Coincidence or Conspiracy?* (2008) – billed as the first book-length study of race and education in the UK to incorporate insights from Critical Race Theory (CRT), a radical intellectual development that originated in the academic domain of legal studies in the United States.

How can we explain this? The 1999 MacPherson report into the murder of the teenager Stephen Lawrence was widely regarded as an indication that racism was being taken seriously by educational policymakers. The 2000 Race Relations (Amendment) Act was an attempt to respond to MacPherson. It extended the 1996 Act to require public authorities (local authorities, schools, colleges, universities etc.) to prevent acts of racial discrimination before they occur. The Act was widely welcomed, but by the early 2000s, this commitment was being questioned. An Ofsted report in 2001 looking into thirty-nine local authorities with higher than average proportions of ethnic minority pupils concluded that schools were failing these pupils because they did not know how to raise attainment (Plomin, 2001). In 2002, Gillborn himself presented an inaugural lecture at the then University of London Institute of Education (now UCL Institute of Education) that set out the findings from his research that education was institutionally racist. He showed that African Caribbean boys in particular were frequently judged by teachers to be less able. Thus, although they started school at five years of age with high test scores, by the time they left at sixteen years they had the lowest attainment. Gillborn warned that policies for separate vocational and academic tracks at fourteen years, and so-called gifted and talented schemes would work to reinforce these trends (Smithers, 2002). All in all, the unwillingness of the new Labour government to return to its earlier commitments to state multiculturalism, the Bradford disturbances of 2001 and tensions between African Caribbean and Asian youth which in 2005 spilled into violence in the Lozells areas of Birmingham, all fuelled concerns about the role schools might play in reproducing segregation (Curtis, 2004). There was growing sense that, despite the claims of policymakers, racism in education – institutional racism – was a significant issue.

The various positions in the debate were rehearsed in relation to Stephen Strand's research at Warwick University (Curtis, 2008) – at the time of another subtle shift in nomenclature, whereby the catchall category of Black and Minority Ethnic (BME) entered the discourse. This suggested that teachers are likely to make decisions about what level of examination students are to sit for in a way that results in a disproportionate number of children from BME groups ascribed to the lower tier exams. This pattern is attributed to a process of institutional racism. If we accept the fact that ability or intelligence is distributed irrespective of race or ethnicity, then this outcome can only be explained in terms of what happens in the institution. As Strand suggests, the most likely explanation is that it is teachers who make these judgements according to how they perceive their pupils, and, since the majority of teachers are white, they are systematically making decisions based on a negative perception of the ability of BME students (Curtis, 2008). In response, Gus John, an inveterate campaigner on questions of race and education, raised the question of whether anything had been learned about racism in education over the past thirty years. However, not all agreed: in an early articulation of the 'post-race' argument (more in the next section) that has gained ground in debates about race and education, Tony Sewell (2008) argued that

> the idea that teachers are directly or indirectly holding back black pupils is questionable. More likely it is to do with the inability or unwillingness of these students to break away from an anti-education peer group that loves the street more than the classroom.

This statement appears to pathologize black youth. The take up of CRT in British educational studies can be understood as a response to the tendency to downplay discussions of race in educational policy and practice since the 1990s. Education policy had, according to this view, effectively become colour-blind (see Warmington, 2020) and CRT appealed as a response to the deep frustration felt by activist scholars to reverse long-standing educational inequality.

Thus, CRT argues that race is no longer just a variable to be plugged in or added on to any analysis of educational policy or practice. It argues that education is in itself a racial project. That race must be seen to be a dynamic that saturates the entire schooling process. Over the past decade, CRT has become *the* dominant theoretical position in discussions of race and education, having significant impacts on British academia and educational research (Warmington, 2014: 140). CRT has increasingly come to inform discussions of race and racism in schools. Its influence is found in a number of publications associated with the Runnymede Trust (which maintains a prominent role in connecting academic research with schools and teachers). Viv Lander's (2014) work on teacher education suggests that the Standards for Qualified Teacher Status (QTS) promote an unacknowledged whiteness, drawing on a long history of work that has pointed to how teachers are generally unprepared to deal with issues of race and racism.

However, just as in the United States, British versions of CRT have attracted criticism. The most serious of these have come from the inveterate researcher of race and education, Mike Cole (2009; 2017). His neo-Marxist analysis focuses on what he sees as a major problem – the separation of race and class. According to Cole, CRT prioritizes race over class, and that attempts to stress the intersectionality of race, gender and class (e.g. Bhopal and Preston, 2012) have not been successful. Cole concludes that CRT lacks a vision of the future, or a solution to racism. Warmington's (2020) recent review of the reception and impact of CRT in Britain, argues that there is a stand-off between CRT and those 'Marxist sociologists' who, it is argued, relegate race to an epiphenomena of class. This debate is heated, and complex (Walton, 2019). The important thing to note here is that CRT has inserted a particular kind of political Blackness into educational research and activism. Others, such as Hayes (2013) and Pluckrose and Lindsay (2020), have argued that CRT adopts a value-position that amounts to saying that to be white is to be 'inherently racist' (121).

At times there tends to be a collapsing of distinctions between anti-racism and CRT. The political temperature has been steadily rising, and this can lead to a sense of urgency. Thus, Sadia Habib (2018) asserts that a major challenge is how to ensure that Critical Whiteness Studies is incorporated into the pedagogical policies and practices of educational and social policy, and that teachers *must* come to understand and challenge white supremacy and white privilege. However, at the very least, these ideas require open discussion and argumentation. A good starting point for such a discussion is Kalwant Bhopal's (2018) *White Privilege: The Myth of a Post-Racial Society*. In exploring how race operates as a disadvantage in modern-day society, Bhopal argues that individuals from BME backgrounds, by virtue of their racial identity, are positioned as outsiders in a society that values whiteness and white privilege. Bhopal attributes this to neoliberal policymaking which suggests that education is neutral, and post-racial, while all the time privileging whiteness and white privilege.

Bhopal's characterization of neoliberalism as a project that benefits white people brings to mind Harvey's (2005) alternative assertion that neoliberalism itself should be understood as a *class* project. This is the conclusion also reached by other serious scholars of neoliberalism (e.g. Dumenil and Levy, 2011) and suggests how geographical perspectives can help develop a rich understanding of the complexities of the cultural political economy of race and racism in education.

## 'Post-Race'

CRT has focused attention on the role of racism in education. Its insistence on prioritizing race is in stark contrast to recent shifts towards 'colour-blind' policymaking in education. There are a number of elements to this, and it is important to further open up the beguiling notion of 'post-race' thinking. For one thing, there is the claim heard that we are now moving towards a post-racial society. In the United States, this idea is linked to the culture of black celebrities and especially the Presidential victory of Barack Obama in 2008 (Cashmore, 2012). As one commentator put it, how can you claim a society is racist in the face of the fact of the election of a black president. That comment did not anticipate the white supremacist backlash in the United States, resulting in the Trump presidency (2016–20). Nonetheless, in the United States, there is still at least some debate about the declining significance of race, as class becomes the main determinant of life chances.

The idea of a post-racial society takes its cue from the fact that capitalism has been (at least partially) successful in incorporating black populations into the circuits of the consumer society (Meghji, 2019; Pitcher, 2016), and in the UK at least, been promoted by a strand of 'Black conservative social commentary' (Warmington, 2014). The clearest statement to date of this post-race agenda is found in the Commission on Race and Ethnic Disparities (The Sewell Report, 2021) which stated:

> We do not believe that the UK is yet a post-racial society which has completed the long journey to equality of opportunity. And we know, too many of us from personal experience, that prejudice and discrimination can still cast a shadow over lives. Outright racism still exists in the UK, whether it surfaces as graffiti on someone's business, violence in the street, or prejudice in the labour market … [But] the country has come a long way in 50 years and the success of much of the ethnic minority population in education and, to a lesser extent, the economy, should be regarded as a model for other White-majority countries. (1)

According to this account, British society is increasingly colour-blind and a model of success (despite the continuing existence of 'outright racism'). There are four elements to this somewhat beguiling racism without racists. First, there is the appeal to 'abstract liberalism', most commonly expressed in educational terms through the idea of equal opportunity or meritocracy. There is no reason why educational success should not be available to all, according to Sewell. Indeed, the fact that certain ethnic groups achieve high levels of attainment proves that the system is working! Second, there is the idea of 'naturalization' or the idea that where differences exist, these are the inevitable result of cultural distinctions (e.g. segregation as a natural choice). Third, is the idea of 'cultural racism' – the idea that certain groups do not help *themselves* because of their cultural choices about how to live. And finally, the act of 'minimization' – the argument that claims of racism are overblown or overstated, and that, over time, there is less racism as it dies away.

All these elements are used to construct the argument – or perhaps mythologise – that advanced societies are moving towards the state of post-race. This idea has gained significant traction in Britain over the past fifteen years. David Goodhart (as we saw in Chapter 2) identifies the paradox that although we live in a time when historically there is much less racism, the changes of being called out for being a racist are higher than ever. As Munira Mirza (2010) puts it:

> Race is no longer the significant disadvantage it is often portrayed to be. In a range of areas – educational attainment, career progression, rates of criminality, social mobility – class and socio-economic background are more important. Indeed,

a number of ethnic groups in Britain, particularly Indians and Chinese, perform better than average in many areas. Today a higher proportion of people from ethnic minorities enter university than white people and these second and third generation Britons make ambitious career choices. (n.p.)

The 2011 riots in several English cities provides another example of this post-race framing, as efforts were made to show that these were not like the 'race riots' of the 1980s. Racism was yet again described as a regrettable but long-gone aspect of British life. In education, the development of a post-race agenda developing in Britain is perhaps represented by the outspoken headteacher of Michaela School – Katharine Birbalsingh – who is quoted advising parents to ignore young people's claims of racism:

> If [a] child says [a]teacher is being racist, back the teacher. Whatever the child says, back the teacher … if you don't you are letting the child down and allowing them to play you for a fool. (cited in Joseph-Salisbury, 2020: 3)

One of the unfortunate effects of statements such as these is to set up a simple divide between those who see race and racism 'everywhere' in schools and those who refuse to see it at all. They have the effect of 'reifying' categories such as 'black' and 'white', refusing to understand the social and historical processes that lead to their construction. It is important to remember that terms such as 'Black' or 'Asian', as well as 'white working class' are social categories. Their precise meaning, as well as how they are enlisted in debates, are capable of change, and they do change.

## Race and Class

These last comments remind us of the importance of exploring the intersection of race and class. Both CRT and post-race perspectives tend to place discussions of class in the background.

Coming back to the account we provided in the previous chapter, we were at pains to stress how race and racism in Britain are linked to the requirements of capital for labour. At one level, racism might be seen as a way of dividing the working classes. This is one small instance of the argument that capitalism and race cannot be separated when we come to analyse them. The classic statement of this position is found in Cedric Robinson's (1983) text, *Black Marxism*. It has been taken up and developed at length by Gargi Bhattacharyya (2018), and a clear account is found in the collectively authored *Empire's Endgame* (Bhattacharyya et al., 2021), which draws upon the work of Hall, Gilroy and Cultural Studies. The analysis recognizes how

> shifts in economic relations fundamentally shape political, ideological and cultural formations, and that crises of capital accumulation and profitability organize the more immediate terrain of political struggle. (3)

The authors stress how Britain is not a happy place. The years following the 2008 global financial crisis have been marked by austerity, the bitter division of Brexit and the ascendancy of Conservative administrations prepared to define the question of who belongs and who doesn't through the creation of a hostile environment for immigrants. Austerity has brought with it increased hardship and frustration, and the future for young people (with deregulated labour markets, zero-hours contract, the gig economy and precarity and low pay) looks bleak. In response, the state has sought a form of 'organized abandonment' (the term is Harvey's): the post financial crash common sense is that those most in need face scrutiny, neglect and criminalisation, so that any notion of the state as a redistributive actor has been abandoned. Young people are urged to give up hopes of landing a good job, lower their sights and prepare themselves for an age of diminished expectations. At one level there is a sense of what Paul Gilroy (2004) has called nostalgia for the past, but many young people have grown up in situations where they have never known this relative benevolence and are more open to embracing radical agendas. The trigger of Black Lives Matters and moves to decolonize the curriculum are examples of this.

Race is a term frequently used to divide the working class. Khan and Shaheen (2017) explain how, in the context of Brexit, it has become common to posit a widening gap between the white working class and black and ethnic minorities, with the assumption that anti-racism exacerbates the feeling of being left behind. It is important to recognize the common experiences of people. As McKenzie (2019) argues, the narratives that are frequently used of the 'left behind white working class' and the 'hard working but unappreciated ethnic minority working class' are inaccurate (see Embery, 2021). They focus on what divides rather than recognizing what unites both, which is the structural 'inequality and disenfranchisement entrenched in the experience of working-class life' (237).

## Conclusion

This chapter has developed an account of the changing politics of race and schooling. It started with the warm glow of post-war educational expansion and has ended with a call that we need to understand the complexities of 'racial capitalism'. We realize that what we have presented in this chapter is challenging for teachers who, after all, rarely come into teaching explicitly to teach about racism.

However, it is more and more difficult for teachers to avoid having a view on race; it is there in the wider society, it finds its way into schools, and students themselves speak from and to positions of race. The account we have offered here is a general one (and we hope many readers will follow up the references and argue with and against what we have written), and subject specialists will need to make connections to the developments and debates in their own subjects. Here, we write as geography educators. As we will suggest in the chapters that follow, geography has a complex relationship to issues of race. Our own interest in race stems from the critiques that took place in our discipline from the 1980s. We are interested in how the subject was dominated by the idea that space was a container of things that could be described, classified and enumerated. Where explanation was attempted, it was often in terms of 'neutral' spatial explanations. This well suited a gentlemanly and technocratic approach to teaching the subject – when geography was a largely white subject, taught by white teachers. The 1970s and 1980s provided a shock to that understanding. We started this chapter with a comment about how teachers are at the sharp end of social and cultural change but that their training rarely prepares them for this. We hope the account provided here can contribute to addressing this gap.

## Questions for Discussion and Reflection

1. How useful is the concept of 'new ethnicities' in challenging the black-white binary that tends to underpin anti-racism?
2. If 'whiteness' is an ethnic identity – and a powerful one at that – what should educators try to do with it? Abolish it? Reform it? Or what?

# 4

# Overcoming the Whiteness of Geography

## Introduction

An important theme in this book is the making and remaking of geography, reminding us that geography as an academic discipline has been shaped by successive generations of people working with abstract ideas, applying them and reworking those ideas or theories within changing geographical and historical contexts. This is what it means to say that geography as a discipline is a social construction. Recent critiques have focused on how geography has been constructed in ways that assume whiteness and that the discipline has been, from its inception, a 'racial project'. Thus, James Esson and Angela Last (2019) assert that

> geography as a field of study, a social institution, and a workplace, is underpinned by a 'racial project' that (has) sought to privilege an ideology of Eurocentric-white superiority. (Peake and Kabayasdhi, 2002) (230).

Natalie Oswin (2020) states the case even more strongly:

> The marginalization, sidelining, erasure and dismissal of 'othered' people and epistemologies persist within the discipline of geography today ... I discuss this fact as a source of harm for many individuals, a result of centuries of white supremacist heteropatriarchal grounding and a failure of the collective critical geographical imagination. (9)

Alistair Bonnett (1997), looking back on the subject's association with imperialism, has argued that

> it is difficult to underestimate the impact the ideologies and practices of empire have had upon the imagination of British geographers. Nowhere is this impact more evident than in their approach to race. Racial differences were seen by British Empire builders as one of the greatest challenges to colonial expansion.

> Geographers interested in issues of race saw their task as the elucidation of the hierarchy of the world's races and the provision of informed speculation on the implications of White settlement and colonial government. (193)

In short, the geographical tradition (Livingstone, 1992) has excluded black lives and experiences and has undertaken its work from a 'white' standpoint. As David Delaney (2002) remarked, Geography 'is nearly as white an enterprise as Country and Western music, professional golf, or the Supreme Court of the United States' (12).

We cannot quarrel with these assessments. Instead, we want to offer a 'map' of some of the ways in which geography as an academic discipline *has* engaged with the themes of race and racism. Our map reflects our own experiences as geography teachers and teacher educators. We both trained as geographers and worked as geography teachers as the subject was making its transition from spatial-quantitative perspectives through the geography of welfare and social concern into the society and space debates of the 1980s. Invariably, these intellectual shifts shaped our understanding of how geography is taught in schools. Throughout all our time as geography educators, the academic field has been marked by debates and arguments about race and racism.

Our discussion starts from the assumption that geographical knowledge is a social product that responds to both internal development within the discipline and external events that shape the content of study. Knowledge creation never stands still, and geography, like other disciplines, has seen continuous struggles over how to 'see' and understand the world. There is no single 'geography'. Geography teachers require an understanding of the various struggles and revolutions that have taken place in the discipline – and what ideas have had an influence, including those to do with race and racism.

In what follows, we discuss six sets of arguments and debates that inform our thinking about race, racism and the geography curriculum. These are

- arguments in British geography that respond to the challenges of race and racism in the UK space;
- Black geographies that originated in the United States;
- debates about 'development', the so-called Third World;
- postcolonial geographies that respond to the crisis of representation;
- historical geographies of modernity that result in attempts to decolonize geography; and
- political ecology and critical physical geography.

Readers will be able to follow these arguments through the chapter. There is an enormous literature, and our intention is to provide an accessible 'way in'. We intersperse our discussion with 'Boxes' that discuss key texts that have been influential in this evolving story. We make no claim to be definitive, and we repeat the position we have made elsewhere in the book: that race and racism are dynamic. They change both through time and in space. They do not stand still, and neither should we expect our understanding of how racism works in society to be static or given.

## British Critical and Cultural Geography

This section explores how geography as a discipline in the UK came to engage with questions of race and racism. University geography departments were established at the beginning of the twentieth century. Their purpose was to educate qualified geography teachers for the expanding secondary school sector after the Education Act of 1902. Regional geography was the main paradigm, heavily descriptive but with an emergent academic 'spirit and purpose' (Wooldridge and East, 1955). From the late nineteenth century to the 1930s, human geography was dominated by environmental determinism, which documented how the natural environment influenced, controlled or conditioned human societies, leading to an account of 'civilization'. Geographers such as Ellsworth Huntington, Ellen Churchill Semple, James Fairgreive and Halford Mackinder were important figures (both Fairgrieve and Mackinder were influential in the development of school geography). The reaction to this approach was environmental possiblism, which reversed the direction of the arrow of causation between man and nature.

## Applying Geography

The first half of the twentieth century produced 'an extremely conservative subdiscipline' (Cox, 2014: 21), one with an odd disinterest in modern, urban society. This is what made the spatial-quantitative revolution (in the 1960s in the UK) in geography so important. Science seemed to be the best bet to advance progress in geography. The context for this was the emergence, in the 1950s, of a welfare society in which academics were called upon to assist with and solve the problems of an expanding developmental state. This reinforced the importance of objectivity and rigour.

In the process, British geography was reinvented as an applied subject that supported the goals of welfare capitalism. The goals of full employment, modernizing economy and society and minimizing regional and social inequalities were, in part, achieved through the construction of the modern built environment (e.g. council estates, shopping centres, industrial parks and motorways – not to mention New Towns [1946] and National Parks [1949]). The human and natural sciences were mobilized to this end, and geography played its part, especially given its links to 'Town and Country Planning'.

At the same time, geography tended to exclude the interests of ordinary people, a minority of whom – in the context of postwar immigration – were black. David Harvey (1974a) caricatured the self-image of geographers:

> Tune into any discussion among geographers and as likely as not the discussion unfolds from the standpoint of the benevolent bureaucrat, a person who knows better than other people and who will therefore make better decisions for others than they will be able to make for themselves. (22)

A striking illustration of the geographer as a 'benevolent bureaucrat' is the book *Resources for Britain's Future*, a collection of articles that appeared in the *Geographical Magazine* at the start of the 1970s (Chisholm, 1971). The contributors were all men, all white and all confident and assured in their expertise. To take its place in this state project, the subject needed to exert its shift from a largely descriptive discipline to an objective, scientific discipline. The problems that they dealt with were concerned with the management of space and environments – for example, traffic flows, the maintenance of the green belt and ensuring that tourist sites were not overrun by an increasingly car-driving population.

It is not far-fetched to state that the imagined population of Britain in *Resources for Britain's Future* was overwhelmingly white. There is no recognition of one of the most pressing issues facing the UK state – the resolution of labour shortages through immigration and the question of how these new arrivals would settle and integrate. Over the next decade, however, social geographers *did* seek to contribute to understanding this issue, by devising measures and mapping the concentrations of different groups over geographical space. This work operated within a broadly empiricist and positivist framework, making use of concepts such as assimilation, segregation and integration (see Robinson, 1987, for an overview of this work). In accepting the common-sense term of 'race relations theory', academic geography tended to reflect the assumption that racism was a problem only where black people lived and that over time integration would occur naturally (Lawrence, 1982).

Slowly, British human geography came to terms with how to study and analyse a changing society. This required an acknowledgement that the space and politics were linked, and that it could not be assumed that the state operated as a neutral 'referee', balancing the interests of capital, labour and community (Clark and Dear, 1984). A decade later, when the *Geographical Magazine* updated its series of articles on Britain's changing geography, the series' editors John Short and Andrew Kirby (1984) noted:

> One of the most notable expressions of public opinion was when young people in certain inner-city areas rioted 1980 and 1981. This was not in itself a reasoned political statement, but in the words of the Scarman report it was the voice of protest whose roots lay in youth unemployment, restricted opportunities and appalling black/police relations. The riots were an indication of some of the social costs of Thatcherism. (15)

## Re-conceptualizations

Early approaches to the issue of race in British academic geography assumed that 'race' was a social category to be measured and mapped. The key theoretical development of the 1980s was the recognition that race itself is a social construction not a biological fact. Race is not a naturally occurring phenomenon: categories of race are produced through 'race-thinking'. The challenge, for geographers and other social scientists, was to understand these processes of *racialization*.

In the postwar period, academic geography sought to shake off its roots in environmental determinism by insisting on a strict separation between nature and culture. Thus, social scientists (including geographers) stressed that what happened in cities, economies and patterns of development were the result of human factors and human agency. The analysis and explanation of phenomena focused on social and economic conditions, not environmental circumstances. Urban geography was a good example of this and has had impact on school syllabuses: for example, the Burgess (sociological) and Hoyt (economic) urban models which claimed to explain land-use patterns in cities.

Geography's closer engagement with the social sciences meant that geographers could no longer present their empirical studies and theories as free from theoretical movements in economics, sociology and cultural studies. For instance, in *Exploring Social Geography* (1984), Peter Jackson and Susan Smith set out the different paradigms current (at that time) within the discipline, to illustrate how each of these might be used to study the theme of residential segregation. Thus, they explored *positivistic* approaches that stressed the measurement of social segregation, including ecological models (e.g. the Burgess model) that used ideas of natural regions, invasion and succession to explain the internal structure of cities frequently on the basis of stereotypical images of different ethnic groups. In contrast, they identified *behavioural* geography, which paid closer attention to the decision making of individuals and institutions in allocating housing, and *humanistic* approaches, which explored the meanings attached by the residents themselves, and finally more *structural* approaches that explained residential segregation as a result of political and economic forces.

The important thing to note about these non-positivistic approaches (behavioural, humanistic and structuralist) is that they focus on human processes, taking care to avoid any ecological (environmentally deterministic) processes such as invasion, succession and the notion that urban residential patterns were in any sense 'natural'. As Smith (1994) later explained, the challenge for an anti-racist urban geography was to account for the socioeconomic and political processes of *race formation*. This would require an engagement with wider developments in political economy to take in issues of labour migration, economic restructuring, social policy and cultural studies. In short, it required human geography's closer relationship to social theory.

Alongside Jackson and Smith's work, there were in the mid-1980s other examples at this time of geographical work coming to terms with the reality of multiracial Britain (see Box 4.1). These include, for instance, John Clarke's essay in *Geography Matters!* ('There's no place like …: cultures of difference' Clarke, 1984), which provides a wide-ranging account of postwar social and cultural change. It stresses the role of *cultural politics* – how the values, beliefs and opinions that shape identity also shape social and economic realities of people's lives. Closely linked to this was Jacqui Burgess's (1985) study of newspaper reports of the disturbances that took place in Britain's inner cities in the early 1980s. Appearing in one of the first books to

**Box 4.1 Robinson, Vaughan. (1989). Economic restructuring, the urban crisis and Britain's black population. In D. Herbert and D. M. Smith (Eds.),** *Social problems and the city: Geographical perspectives.* **London: Routledge.**

Writing at the end of the 1980s, Robinson provided a political and economic analysis of the fortunes of Britain's black population towards the end of a decade of a Conservative government. His account acknowledged that successive rounds of economic restructuring, which had had deleterious impacts on older industrial regions and the inner areas of large cities, dented the optimism of the early years of migration to Britain.

From a political perspective, Robinson suggested that postwar governments paid insufficient attention to the fact that (1) immigrants would have legal rights to citizenship and (2) the likely consequence of introducing black labour into factories and neighbourhoods alongside members of the white working class who had been socialized into regarding black people as inferior. They could not have foreseen that in the thirty-year period in which the black population became established, Britain had undergone an economic and demographic restructuring on a scale not seen since the industrial revolution. The chapter considered how these factors made the black population the unwitting victims of that change.

Robinson argued that the urban crisis stemmed directly from broader changes in the national space economy. These forces, including the decline of the manufacturing base, the spatial redistribution of employment opportunities, selective capitalization of the industrial process, an ageing and deteriorating housing stock as well as selective counter-urbanization, all added to the stress of the black population which were then overlain by racial discrimination and disadvantage.

> It is clear that Britain black population is concentrated into some of those areas which are suffering most from the economic restructuring that has taken place since the 1950s. (257)

The chapter concluded with a discussion of government policy: the reduction of immigration, measures to outlaw discrimination, the combating of disadvantage through non-specific social policy and explanation of the role of local authorities in combating racism to bring about equal opportunities.

Robinson's chapter appeared in the second edition of *Social Problems and the City*. The first edition (Herbert and Smith, 1979) was dominated by the 'welfare approach' and had a very different feel. A decade later, Geography was getting to grips with political economy approaches that explained geographical patterns through reference to changes taking place in economic relations. Robinson's chapter reflected this, but it also took at face value the claims of policymakers to improve the lives of the black population. As such, the chapter raises important questions about whether (and how) geography can make a difference.

link geography with cultural studies, Burgess demonstrated how the popular press located the riots in the mythical 'inner city', an imaginary space that bore little or no resemblance to the actual circumstances of places such as Brixton, Toxteth, and Moss Side. This *displacement* was (and remains) ideological, as the removal of the riots to these 'inner cities' rendered them far-removed from the experiences of the majority of readers: readers were invited to put the disturbances in a box, and to 'other' them. Burgess paid close attention to the ways in which this *representation* worked. The construction of the ideological myth of the 'inner city' was based on four elements:

- a physical environment of run-down houses, abandoned factories and so on;
- a romanticized view of white working-class life;
- a pathological image of black culture; and
- a stereotypical view of street culture.

Burgess's study was one of the first in geography to stress the importance of language, ideology and presentation in the construction of place-myths, and how language such as 'inner city' acted as code for racial meanings. Geographical enquiries, descriptions and analyses could no longer be based simply on taken-for-granted or given sets of meanings or definitions. This was a significant theoretical breakthrough in geography. Place meanings were *constructed* – and that this had to be explicitly recognized.

By the time Peter Jackson (1987) produced his edited book *Race and Racism*, it was clear that many geographers were working with the idea of race as a social construct. Racism could be understood as a component of the inequalities which capitalism both creates and uses, along with class and gender – though it is notable that Jackson criticizes Doreen Massey's (1984) *Spatial Divisions of Labour* because it contains 'virtually no discussion of race' (184).

The challenge then became how to understand and analyse racism as an ideology. For example, Jackson's (1989) analysis of the riots in early 1980s Britain concluded that there was no easy explanation as to why they occurred in some places and not others. The fact that racist attacks and other forms of racism could occur *anywhere* suggested the existence of a dominant ideology of racism in British society. Jackson's solution to this was to turn to the work of British cultural studies, especially in his chapter on 'Languages of Racism' in *Maps of Meaning* (1989). The new 'cultural geography' stressed the importance of the relationship between representation and material practices (see Box 4.2).

### Box 4.2 Jackson, Peter. (1989). *Maps of meaning*. London: Unwin and Hyman.

Appearing in the same year as Robinson's chapter, Jackson worked in the same context, but as his title suggests, his focus was on 'racism as a cultural discourse'. His focus was language and representation – the *idea* of race, rather than of race per se. Whereas Robinson makes much use of census data, accepting categories as collected, Jackson's approach ensures that the focus is on race as a social construction. His title references Gareth Stedman Jones's (1982) *Languages of Class*, which points to the deeply historically located meaning of terms, and also owes much to Stuart Hall's argument that ideologies of race draw upon and modify a reservoir of racist imagery.

Though most of his examples refer to the British context, he suggested that the same method of analysis could be applied to other capitalist societies. His discussion of historical representations of race was linked to empire and ideas of racial superiority and is the prelude to a discussion of how race was represented in the aftermath of postwar migration. Jackson then turned his attention to the representation of Asian migration to Britain which served to highlight the importance of paying attention to the specificities of racialization at different times. The final part of the chapter focused on the geographical implications of Edward Said's (1978) *Orientalism*.

Here, then, is an early geographical engagement with an important postcolonial scholar, and it entails the subtle shift from ideology to discourse. Jackson used Said's work to alert readers to the deep structures of racism – the simultaneous attraction and revulsion that society has to race. The chapter concluded with a discussion of what Jackson called the material basis for racism. Racism is firmly located in state projects, and racist ideologies have severe practical consequences that serve to support the reproduction of a capitalist society. A key challenge was and remains how to theorize the relationship between class and race. Jackson's answer at that time was to follow Stuart Hall et al. (1978) and the idea that in the British case, class is experienced through race. This is not to suggest that race is an epiphenomenon of class but that the two are interrelated. The empirical task ahead, for Jackson, was to work out how this is manifest in practice.

## Widening the Gaze

One problem with these early attempts to put race on the geographical agenda was that the focus was restricted to urban and social geography – to studies of cities and the 'inner city'. This implied that racism was a problem only where black people live, relegating the study of race and racism to the margins of the discipline, rather than placed at the heart of geographical study.

As the economic restructuring described in Robinson's chapter advanced, geographers refocused their gaze on places and localities; so an important move was to examine processes of racialization in a wider range of places and at a variety of spatial scales. Jackson and Penrose's *Constructions of Race, Place and Nation* (1993) developed this approach. If race was a social construction, it was necessary to ask how it was constructed in particular places (and at particular times). This required the examination of the processes of racialization operating in all places and at a range of scales, from the individual (including the body) all the way through to the global. This resulted, from the mid-1990s, in the widespread recognition of *geographies of exclusion* (Cresswell, 1996; Sibley, 1995). The breakthrough from this work was the realization that common-sense understandings of race as a 'black problem' could only work by ignoring the racialization of 'white spaces'. This was starkly revealed through geographical studies of rural areas.

In the mid-1990s, some human geographers were fascinated by the striking images of the black photographer Ingrid Pollard, who took pictures of herself dressed in hiking gear wandering in the English Lake District (Kinsman, 1995). Pollard's pictures provided a striking contrast to the image of the black Briton – whose 'natural habitat' was assumed to be urban. They also challenged the idea of the English countryside as a space of replenishment or transcendence, where people could sense and commune with nature (Young and Pollard, 1995). It was as if black people did not belong there. For Pollard, visits to the countryside were filled with a sense of dread, anticipating 'Walks through leafy glades with a baseball bat in hand' (cited in Jones, 1992: 103). In order for the 'countryside' to remain essentially a *white space*, a complex set of representations and exclusions had to be established and maintained. Julian Agyeman (1989), founder of the Black Environment Network, extended Pollard's work in terms that should resonate with readers of this book: 'Why should I, a black person, … (have felt) uncomfortable when I was a geography teacher explaining glaciation and footpath erosion to thirty white children on a field trip in Cumbria?' (30).

The idea of the countryside as a racialized space that assumed whiteness and acted as a space of exclusion was explored in rural geographies in the 1990s and 2000s (see Agyeman and Spooner, 1997; Neal and Agyeman, 2006). It continues to inform scholarship and has become popularized (e.g. Hayes, 2020), which is unsurprising given the symbolic weight attached to the countryside – even featuring as a theme on the BBC's *Countryfile*. It is interesting to reflect on the imagined geographies of England found in texts as various as James Fairbank's (2020) *English Pastoral*, Anita Sethi's (2021) *I Belong Here*, Paul Kingsnorth's (2008) *Real England* and Vron Ware's (2022) *Return of a Native*, which explores the history of a two-and-a-half acre of land in rural Hampshire. Ware uncovers the ways in which the 'slow violence' of colonialism and industrialism have shaped the landscape, in a way that is similar to the revelation that the National Trust properties have links to the slave trade.

During the 1980s and 1990s, geographical studies of race and racism shifted away from the mapping of 'types of people' to focus instead on the socio-spatial construction of 'race' and racism. These studies highlighted that racism is not confined to urban spaces, but other spaces, such as the suburbs, countryside and urban-rural fringe, are also racialized. The cultural turn in geography, which focused on the so-called *new ethnicities*, highlighted the complexity of meanings attached to people and places. This was in line with 'New Times' arguments (discussed in Chapter 3) about the increased fluidity of social life and the way in which identities were open and fluid. The focus of research enquiry was on agency and contestation and was reflected in the new geographies of youth cultures and young people – notably the 'cool places' created by young people as they negotiated the spheres of employment, leisure and consumption (Skelton and Valentine, 1997).

## Becoming Mainstream

The first decade of the twenty-first century saw growing awareness of the geographies of race and racism to the extent to which it now forms part of the curriculum offered by standard undergraduate textbooks. For example, a geography student who encountered Nayak and Jeffrey's (2011) *Geographical Thought* would learn that 'race' is a social construct. Race is a myth, albeit one with enormous power. Nayak and Jeffrey explain that making generalizations involving difference in human populations is problematic, because the ideas or values we use to make sense of society, economy and the environment are racialized. The result is that 'race' differences appear real, and racism 'presides as a lived reality'. Nayak and Jeffrey inform student readers that although crude biological racism is largely discredited, racism is now prosecuted through cultural means. Thus, the central (racist) idea of the existence of immutable ethnic or cultural differences becomes cemented though the use of language and the ways in which people and places are represented. Having established this, the textbook explores geography's link with Empire, its concern with mapping and the more recent notions of the process of racialization. Recent undergraduate textbooks, written in accessible language and frequently presented in attractive formats, have significant impacts on how successive cohorts of geography students understand the discipline (e.g. Cloke, Crang and Goodwin, 2014; Holloway and Hubbard, 2001; Valentine, 2001).

This goes some way to explaining how, from the mid-1990s, *whiteness* (acknowledging and developing the idea that whiteness itself was an 'ethnic identity') became a focus in social and cultural geography (Bonnett, 1996; 1997). As late as 1997, the report *Ethnic Minorities in Britain: Diversity and Disadvantage* contrasted each ethnic group with a monolithic white category. A focus on whiteness was the direct result of resistance to racism, which drew attention to how whiteness – and all the assumptions that flowed from this – was produced.

While early work focused on the notion of a singular white identity, subsequent studies have pointed to the historical specificity of whiteness and the varieties of white identity. Taking their cue from early studies of whiteness in the United States, social and cultural geographers began to explore the ways in which assumed whiteness underpinned everyday activities such as shopping. For example, Daniel Miller et al.'s (1998) study of the shopping practices in two north London neighbourhoods found that some elderly residents expressed feelings of nostalgia that were based on an imagined idea of Englishness which they saw lost or under threat from social changes related to immigration. This was an example of a localized construction of whiteness (based on something like a yearning for things to return to 'normal').

Once more, this points to the idea that 'race' – in this case 'white' – is a social construct, its particular meaning and performance contingent on time and place. In Chapter 3, we noted the work of Mary Hickman (Hickman and Walter, 1995) and

Bronwen Walter (2001) on the experience of Irish women in Britain and the United States. 'Local' constructions of whiteness are linked to wider national ideologies and global diasporic flows. There are different shades of whiteness, reflected in cases of individuals or groups being 'not-quite-white' (Wray, 2006).

Geographers have been especially attentive to white working-class masculinity. For instance, Anoop Nayak's (2003) studies of white working-class youth in economically deprived parts of England illustrate that such white spaces do not occur 'naturally'. Nayak discerns the 'real Geordies' who are socialized into a habitus with the material symbols of white working-class respectability, such as the availability of skilled labour and home ownership. These young men consider themselves to have a strong identity as the 'backbone of the nation' and distinguish themselves from the 'Charver kids' (chavs) who come from families marked by long-term unemployment or precarious employment and, through their residential proximity to ethnic minorities, are considered not quite white. They distinguish themselves also from the 'b-boys' and 'wannabees' who, through the adoption of symbols of global youth cultures (associated with, e.g. dress, music, basketball and speech patterns), developed a form of whiteness that is associated with 'black cool'. Nayak's categories resonate with those identified by Mairtain Mac an Ghaill (1994) in his study of masculine identities, and again, they show the importance of the place-based making of whiteness (See Box 4.3).

### Box 4.3 Noxolo, Pat. (2018). Laughter and the politics of place-making. In Kamunge Johnson and Remi Joseph-Salisbury (Eds.), *The fire now: Anti-racist scholarship in times of explicit racial violence*. London: Zed Books.

Pat Noxolo makes an argument for geographers to pay attention to the everyday performance of place, which, she suggests, can provide the basis for new forms of identity and sociality. The chapter starts with the observation that, in post-Brexit Britain, place is being made in exclusionary ways. Contemporary Britain is marked by nostalgia, either for the optimism of the 1960s or for a time pre mass immigration. Too often, race and class are treated as discrete and in opposition to one another. Noxolo argues that we should start from a different place, seeing present-day Britain as a shared place. She sees hopeful signs of this in the Runnymede Trust's *Minority Report* (2017) which seeks to explore the similarities between race and class. Race and class do not completely overlap, but they are connected because of the way advantaged groups exercise economic power. Noxolo seeks to try to imagine a more inclusive view of the making of Britain as a 'shared place'.

Noxolo draws upon Homi Bhabha's (1994) *The Location of Culture* which proposes the idea of the narration of the nation – one of which is nostalgia tied up with and based on exclusions. This is counter-posed by the idea of the

> performativity of everyday activities. To imagine a more inclusionary process of place making requires attention to people's lives as they are lived in the UK, to their 'messiness and incoherence'. Noxolo here draws upon Massey's notion of 'thrown togetherness' – it sees place as open and made up of flows of peoples, images, ideas, signs, goods and so on – as the meeting point for strung out webs of social relations. But they are material and immaterial. There are memories and places that are constitutive of the body. People literally wear the places they inhabit.

Despite such critical studies of whiteness, it is rare for geographers to examine their complicity with whiteness and white society – that is, the assumed racial norm that privileges white people at the expense of others. Critical whiteness studies suggest that the epistemology of geography as a discipline is based around an unexamined whiteness: the questions that are asked, what gets studied and the kinds of explanations offered and so on.

In summarizing the state of the study of geographies of race and racism in 2008, Peter Jackson argued that much had changed in geographical research on race and racism:

> While some core concerns remain, in terms of understanding the social and political significance of residential segregation, for example, there are many new areas of interest and new approaches, emphasizing everyday experience and embodied identities encompassing majority groups and definitions of 'whiteness' and the racialization of diverse minority 'ethnic' communities. The context of research shifted significantly, too, with new patterns and sources of migration, new political arrangements in Britain's devolved national administrations and the impact of wider events such as the 'global war on terror'. New theoretical approaches are challenging the previous consensus around the social construction of race. Like racism itself, geographical studies of race are constantly changing shape in response to external forces and internal challenges. (303)

The brief survey of British geography in this section supplements Chapters 2 and 3. It documents how British geography has responded to the changes taking place in the social and cultural landscape of a multicultural society. In the case of Britain, race and racism are linked in complex ways with the challenges faced by the state as it seeks to resolve the recurring crises of capitalism. For example, the policies of austerity pursued by the government from 2010 to 2020 following the financial crisis of 2008 have had differential impact, including shaping the 'hostile environment' policies towards immigration. Of course, there is much more that could be said, but our aim has been to provide a framework into which geography teachers can develop curriculum approaches and resources.

## US-Black Geographies

Our discussion so far has focused on the way in which discussions of race in geography have drawn upon the development of the UK racial state. However, any discussion of race and racism in a British context should acknowledge and draw upon developments elsewhere. One of the most important contributions of geographers to the study of race and racism is to show how these are place-specific. Jackson and Penrose (1993) argued that

> by demonstrating the existence of a plurality of *place-specific* ideologies of 'race' and nation rather than a monolithic, historically singular and geographically invariant racism or nationalism, the constructedness of 'race' and nation is starkly revealed. (13)

Racism in the United States and the UK not only have different histories and trajectories but also share some similar characteristics (not least the deep-seated difficulties society faces in addressing race and racism). In this section, we look to the United States in order to discuss the emergence of 'Black geographies' and how these contribute to an analysis of 'racialized capitalism'.

First, some initial comments. From its establishment as a nation, a major challenge to the image of a unified American space has been the treatment of ethnic and racial groups with respect to social, legal and political rights. Whiteness was a privileged status from the foundation of the United States (many of the Founding Fathers were slave owners) and race-thinking has been embedded within the practices and ideology of American society (Forest, 2002). For instance, it was not until the 1950s that Federal governments made equality of opportunity for racial groups an object of policy.

Key moments in the story of race in the United States are the formal abolition of slavery (Lincoln's Emancipation Proclamation of 1863), the Civil War (1861–5) and its aftermath, and the 'Great Migration' to the northern cities of over six million African Americans. One dominant myth of post–Civil War United States has been the 'melting pot' and the gradual assimilation of different ethnic groups living within the American space (Agnew, 2002). The 'melting-pot' story is more myth than reality. Local police departments, sometimes set up specifically to control 'freed' black slaves, have been in the front line of black oppression (hence, current calls to 'defund' the police). The prison population across the United States is disproportionately black; and on any number of metrics, from poor health and mortality rates to educational achievement and unemployment rates, the United States is a deeply uneven and divided society, and Black geographers argue that the principal division is 'racial'.[1]

---

[1] For instance, in the United States (2014), there are more than 2.2 million people in federal and state prisons, with nearly 3.7 million on probation, 760,000 on parole and 655,800 in jails, which breaks down to one in every thirty-five citizens under the jurisdiction of the correctional system. *But more than 60 per cent of prisoners are people of colour*, with black men representing the majority of those incarcerated. On any given day, one in ten black men is in either jail (where people are held while awaiting trial or sentencing) or prison (where people serve their sentences).

## Changing US Geography

In the United States, much of the impetus of geographical scholarship began in the 1920s and 1930s with the Great Migration, as freed slaves sought refuge from racism and poverty, and sought employment in the booming industries of the north that required supplies of cheap labour. Initial magnets for these migrants were Detroit, Cleveland, New York, Baltimore and Chicago. Thus, in the United States, there is a long tradition of racial segregation research which has focused on the degree to which African Americans and whites share (or more accurately, do *not* share) residential space in contemporary urban contexts. A number of 'tools' were available to urban planners to segregate, and they were used, for example, racialized 'covenants' and racist zoning laws, ended by Supreme Court decree in 1917, only to be replaced by 'single-family zoning', which was expensive and unaffordable to the majority of black residents. More well-known is the practice of 'redlining', the practice by both the government and the private sector of literally putting red lines on city maps where black people lived, classifying the redlined area as 'hazardous' and ineligible for mortgages or other loans (Agyeman, 2020).

Early American geographers assumed the superiority of the white race and explained patterns of settlement and civilization based on environmental determinism.[2] The implications of this view became apparent with the rise of fascist regimes in Europe in the 1930s, and geography fell into disrepute, at best providing ethnographic and anthropological accounts of culture regions. It was not until the 1950s and 1960s that geographers – armed with increasingly sophisticated mapping techniques and statistical methods – began to explore the extent of racial segregation in US cities. Census data allowed geographers to examine residential patterns within and across large metropolitan areas, tracing identifiable segregation patterns. Over time, these studies have become more sophisticated, as researchers developed multiple segregation indices developed to assist in measuring the degree of spatial separation between racial groups.

An important term in the study of segregation in US cities is the 'ghetto'. Black scholars have challenged these ahistorical accounts of the ghetto, and the general move has been away from naturalistic accounts of 'life in the ghetto' towards explaining the way in which space is actively produced and reproduced, both materially and through language and discourse. For example, Schwartz's (2019) *Ghetto: The History of a Word* provides a fascinating account of the way that the term – which began as a reference to distinctly Jewish sections of cities – has changed its meaning, so that, by the 1960s, it became associated with areas of black population. Indeed, Duneier's (2016) book *Ghetto* claims the term as referring to Black areas.

---

[2] With honourable exceptions such as the more recent excavations of the innovative W. E. B. DuBois make plain. See Battle-Baptiste and Rusert (2018).

In opposition to accounts which see ethnic segregation as natural, race and urban planning scholars have revealed how US ghettos, such as Chicago's South Side, have been the product of a series of strategic policy decisions by white people aimed at relegating minorities, in particular black people, to substandard residential areas. Studies have shown that racial violence, binding legal documents ('covenants'), and other strategic means such as 'redlining' have all been used to prevent black people from moving into predominantly white communities (e.g. Freund, 2007). Agyeman (2020) shows how urban planning has been the 'spatial toolkit' of white supremacy.

Any serious discussion of race and racism in school geography classrooms will encounter the word 'ghetto'. Geography teachers will be concerned to ensure that, rather than the natural product of choices or ways of life, explanation focuses on the economic and political racialization of urban space. In order to do so, concepts and ideas derived from Black Geographies will be useful.

# Powerful Re-conceptualization

To preface our discussion of US-Black geographies, we briefly consider three important and powerful concepts. These are *racial formation*, *racial capitalism* and the *white racial frame*.

In *Racial Formation in the United States* (first published in 1986), sociologists Michael Omi and Howard Winant argued that most racial theories fail to capture the centrality of race in US politics and culture. Though acknowledged as significant, race is understood as the manifestation of other relationships such as class or ethnicity. Against this, Omi and Winant argue that the very structure of US society and economy is inseparable from race. The challenge is to study *racial formation*:

> Racial formation theory focuses on the connections between how race shapes and is shaped by social structure, and how racial categories are represented and given meaning in imagery, media, language, ideas, and everyday common sense. Racial formation theory frames the meaning of race as rooted in context and history, and thus as something that changes over time. (66)

Omi and Winant assert that any analysis of the economy, of cities or of issues such as environmental protection, cannot proceed without placing at its centre an examination of the *racial project* it contains. Racial formation uncovers the way in which race is created, used and permeates every aspect of daily life in the United States. The challenge is to think holistically about society.

One of the most important aspects of racial formation in the United States was the idea that such formations are necessarily historical, reproduced over time and space, and therefore subject to change. In *The White Racial Frame*, Joe Feagin (2013) argues that geographical patterns in the present must be explained through a long history of oppression. For example, a substantial majority of African Americans today live in just fifteen of the fifty US states – and very disproportionately in the southern and border states. In these states, as elsewhere, the majority of African Americans reside in relatively segregated areas of towns and cities. In many cities, there are still the infamous railroad tracks, as well as major highways, that divide communities of mostly whites from communities of mostly people of colour (hence, the phrase, on the 'other side of the tracks'). Feagin asks why such segregated residential patterns persist in a nation that sees itself as an 'advanced democracy'. His answer is that the centuries of slavery, legal segregation and contemporary racial discrimination that have set firmly in place and maintained the country's important geographical contours:

> In a great many cases, these racially segregated areas and geographical dividing lines are not recent creations but have been shaped by white decision-makers' actions over a long period of time. (11)

The *white racial frame* operates to assist people in defining, interpreting, conforming to and acting in their everyday social worlds such as the home, in schools, on playgrounds, in the media, in workplace settings, in courts and in politicians' speeches and corporate decisions. This frame rationalizes and structures the racial interactions, inequalities and other racial patterns in an array of societal settings.

The concepts of 'racial formation' and 'white racial frame' are closely linked to the idea of *racialized capitalism*, a term coined by Black Studies scholar Cedric Robinson (1983) as 'a way of understanding capitalism's processes of exploiting who it racializes and racializing who it exploits' (3). We see this through the dispossession of indigenous people from their land, the transatlantic slave trade and colonial enterprise. According to this analysis, capitalism is inseparable from anti-black racism, which is today enacted through neocolonialism and the activities of exploitative multinational corporations. In this sense, the most notable expression of racialized capitalism was apartheid in South Africa, since it highlighted the way in which the construction of racial categories was used to organize the labour process (see Box 4.4).

Robinson's work is an engagement with Marxist accounts of the origins of capitalism, a central element of which was to ask 'How did societies make the transition from feudalism to capitalism?' One answer is that it created a new working class, but Robinson's contribution is to show how capital made use of existing racial structures and ideologies so that from the start capitalism was racialized (here, Robinson was engaging with, and challenging, E. P. Thompson's (1963) seminal *The making of the English working class*). This has important implications for any politics in the present. The argument is that capital has achieved much of its dynamism through creating and exploiting differences between sections of labour, and much of this has been based on race (Jenkins and Leroy, 2021).

## Further Developments

This scholarship, part of the Black radical tradition, has challenged the way in which geography has taken as its reference point an assumed whiteness. 'Black geographies' is an extension of work in critical geography, which flourished as social theory began to acknowledge the role that space played in economic and social restructuring. The reassertion of space in social theory as occasioned by postmodern geographies (e.g. Soja, 1989) led to the realization that it was 'space as much as time that hid things from us'. Neil Smith (1993) suggested how space was used politically to include and exclude, through the politics of scale. The importance of Smith's work was that it allowed geographers to go beyond the idea that space is socially produced in order to show how geographical scales operated to create spaces of inclusion and exclusion, containment and exile, and domination and escape. These processes operate from what Adrienne Rich called 'the scale closest in' – the body, through the home, community, city, nation and global (see McKittrick and Peake, 2005).

Black geographers use *relational perspectives* to understand racism as the result of racial hierarchies within a social system of white privilege, in which whites are the recipients of any number of advantages simply due to their being white. Whiteness is assumed to be the norm against which all other races are evaluated. These privileges are wide-ranging and include access to better educational and economic opportunities, access to better housing than equally qualified minorities and being underexposed to pollution relative to minority groups.

Thus, the production of space is linked to racialization. In *The Racialization of Space and the Spatialization of Race*, Lipsitz (2007) notes that 'the national spatial imaginary is racially marked, and that segregation serves as a crucible for creating the emphasis on exclusion' (10). In *Demonic Grounds* (2006), Katharine McKittrick asserts that 'Black matters are spatial matters'. The body is a *spatial marker* on which race, class, gender and sexuality are imprinted. The faceless and bodiless human associated with economic man or *homo economicus* simply does not exist. The task of Black geographies is to analyse how ideas of geographical organization shape actual and imaginary spaces. Often this racialization of space is so complete, it appears almost natural and is taken for granted, such as in the idea of 'ghettos' or 'white suburbs'.

The challenge for geographers is to understand how such racialized space has been produced, its effects on people and how it might be changed. At the heart of this is a distinction between transparent space and deep space. *Transparent space* refers to what can be mapped. It is concerned with order. It is where all our lives, including black lives, are 'contained'. Traditionally, geography has privileged transparent space and requires blackness to stay 'in place' – so that it *can be* mapped (and literally contained). Black geographies as promoted by McKittrick seek to unsettle traditional geographies by going beyond the empirical. Drawing on Neil Smith's concept of *deep space*, the focus is instead on social, historical and psychological processes that can allow ghettoization to be resisted and challenged.

These arguments, which may at first seem abstract, can in part by illustrated through brief discussions of work produced by Black geographers (see Boxes 4.4, 4.5 and 4.6).

## Box 4.4 Wilson, Robert. (2000). *America's Johannesburg: Industrialization and racial transformation in Birmingham.* Athens: The University of Georgia Press.

Wilson's book represented an important development in US-Black geographies. The title refers to how Birmingham, Alabama, came to known as 'America's Johannesburg' because it had developed forms of spatial division later found in the South African capital. Wilson (2000) developed insights from Harvey's historical-geographical materialism to argue that the built environment can be 'read' to reflect the economic forces that shape it. Drawing on approaches that were common in political economy at the time, Wilson used French Regulation Theory to provide an account of the changing modes of accumulation and how crises of accumulation were resolved through new allegiances and coalitions of interest. It is capital that shapes the urban landscape, but a key insight from Wilson's analysis is how race was a crucial part of capitalism's attempts to secure profitability.

Wilson shows that Birmingham's founding in 1871 represented a continuation of the planter class's power. The planter class, and their new allies, bankers and railroad entrepreneurs drove Birmingham's development as an industrial giant. The city's economic progress was linked, successively, to coal and iron ore mining, iron and steel manufacturing, rail transport and depended upon the existence of a black labour force willing to work long hours for low wages. Industrial capitalism replaced slavery as another but very different form of extreme oppression and exploitation of black people.

Wilson shows that the city's elites built a dual labour system in the factory. White workers held the higher paying skilled positions, while African Americans held hot, dirty, low-paying jobs that were undesirable. This dual labour system minimized competition between black and white workers and confirmed white supremacy and privilege. The use of cheap sources of black labour to drive industrial development also led to the racialization and underdevelopment of black communities, which were marked by inadequate schools, a decaying physical environment, under-resourced institutions, food insecurity and poor health care services. Initially, the city used racial zoning laws to segregate lack people to the most undesirable and inexpensive residential land. Later, after the Supreme Court ended legal segregation in 1917, cities used housing costs and housing values (via 'single family zoning') to continue residentially segregated communities.

These underdeveloped communities reproduced African Americans at the bottom of the economic order by keeping them from acquiring the type of education and training necessary to compete with white workers. *America's Johannesburg* examines race and place in a unique American city.

Wilson's core argument is that the political economy shapes race and place in the American metropolis. Race and inequality are so ingrained in capitalism that one cannot exorcise them. Within this conceptual scheme, the capitalist project forces African Americans into low-wage jobs and concentrates them in development-arrested communities regardless of the form it takes. In Birmingham's case, the combination of blacks' extreme oppression and exploitation as industrial workers and the hardship of living in segregated, development-arrested communities caused Birmingham to be a civil rights flashpoint.

### Box 4.5  Woods, Clyde. (2017). *Development drowned and reborn: The blues and bourbon restoration in post-Katrina New Orleans*. Athens: University of Georgia Press.

The relationship between space and race (and racism) was dramatically illustrated when Hurricane Katrina passed to the south east of New Orleans in August 2005. The storm surge inundated 80 per cent of the city, killing about 1,500 people. However, the costs of the disaster were unevenly distributed, with the city's black population disproportionately impacted.

Katrina was the worst engineering disaster in US history. Although the vast majority of residents were evacuated (significant numbers never to return), black people – who formed the majority of residents living in poverty without the means to escape and with nowhere to go – were, to all intents and purposes, considered disposable. Media coverage quickly shifted from the disaster itself to social control issues. In the process, victims of the disaster were forgotten, concealed by sensationalized reports of gangs of black men looting homes and businesses.

That this was an unnatural disaster is accepted: even President George Bush recognized this at the time, stating that poverty has its roots in racial discrimination. But the disaster was not the result of a culture of poverty or of 'irrational' individual acts. The failure was

> the cumulative result of a long history of institutional arrangements and structures that have produced current realities. We can start with the 250 years of African American slavery and the longer-term effects that status had on wealth creation, family life, and whole attitudes toward – as well as treatment of – blacks. (Hartman and Squires, 2006: 3)

Hurricane Katrina thus provides a 'case study' of racialized capitalism in action, something brought home in Clyde Woods' detailed historical geographies of capitalist development in the New Orleans region.

In his first book, *Development Arrested*, Woods (1998) focused on the Lower Mississippi Delta Development Commission (LMDDC) and its extreme production of social, spatial and economic inequality. *Development Arrested* is a richly historical work concerned with the spatial constitution of the region and sees capitalism as dynamic and in a process of transforming itself. Whereas Wilson (2000) talked of race-connected processes, in Woods, it is clear that this is racial capitalism in which very different conceptions of the world and the region come into conflict. The power of hegemony (drawn from Gramsci) is important here, and one of Wood's key contributions is to show the emergence and development of a 'blues epistemology'. This distinctive way of viewing the world arises out of Black experience and serves to contest the dominant worldviews of the developers.

Woods' work is critical for geographers for two reasons. First, he presents a historical critique of plans for redevelopment that promise racial and economic fairness, but which end up deepening inequity. Second, his blues epistemology offers a rich analysis of the history of counter-mobilizations across the American South that uncovers the possibilities of resistance to racial apartheid. Woods shows how awareness of different ways of seeing and being can challenge planners to create alternative policy frameworks that move beyond white racial frames.

In his second study, *Development Drowned and Reborn*, Woods (2017) focused on the ways in which New Orleans has been redeveloped in the years after Hurricane Katrina. As Jordan Camp and Laura Pulido (2017) argue, Woods wrote in response to the popularization of Naomi Klein's idea of 'disaster capitalism', which focused on how private capital and elites were actively involved in extracting economic profits from the disaster. Though Woods was sympathetic to this argument, he argued that it was also important to emphasize the long history of exploitation in the region. The poor, Woods demonstrates, had been abandoned long before Katrina, and the focus was on the immediate disaster risks, ignoring the deep historical roots of poverty and racial injustice in the city.

Woods' book also points to the important concept of environmental justice and environmental racism, the focus of the powerful environmental justice movement (and its spin offs, climate justice and food justice) in the United States. Vulnerability to natural events such as storms or flooding is structured in ways that advantage some groups and disadvantage others. In this case, the economic and environmental precarity of the poorest residents was compounded by persistent moves to remove welfare safety nets and drive-down incomes. By carefully linking white supremacy and political economy, Woods provides an historical and geographical analysis of racialized capitalism.

## Box 4.6 The Carceral State

An important aspect of Black geographies is to understand how the reorganization of capitalist space associated with neoliberalism has coincided with the growth of the Prison-Industrial Complex (Gilmore, 2007). This is the process by which the US state's dramatic investment in its prison system over the past half century has less to do with crime and criminals and more to do with broader social dynamics in the economy and race relations. This is a case of 'racial capitalism' in action. Prisons are a source of profits, as the state function (law and order) is outsourced to private corporations. Prisoners also provide a source of cheap (free) labour, and create a downward pressure on wages, in the form of a reserve army of labour.

In *Spatializing Blackness*, Rashad Shabazz (2015) examines how the growth of the black population in Chicago was characterized by spatial confinement and a complex geography of exclusion. This was a result of the operation of the housing market, policing practices and the welfare system. Drawing upon ideas first proposed by Michel Foucault (1977), he then documents the rise of the carceral state and shows how together these processes have led to the production of forms of black masculinity. This book details the historical conditions within which the prison state emerged in Chicago, tracing the links between policing, planning, segregation and resistance.

Shabazz's work on black masculinity provides an understanding of the experiences of incarceration and racialization since the progressive (Civil Rights) era. It shows how the modern-day carceral state emerged over time and impacted on specific segments of the population. Shabazz ends his book with an examination of how Chicago is changing, and while in part this is linked to uneven patterns of gentrification, there is hope, he argues, in the emergence of urban green spaces which offer opportunities to break down walls of segregation.

In *Prison Land*, Brett Story (2019) demonstrates how carceral space functions to both produce and manage social inequities in late-capitalist (neoliberal) American life. Story shows that prisons are more than physical buildings where people are 'put away' out of sight from the rest of society. They exert what he calls 'carceral power', which extends into all aspects of society, influencing how economic and social relations are understood. In so doing, Story challenges both the 'common sense' idea of prisons as a reasonable response to the problem of crime and the commonly held emotional attachment to punishment. He argues that despite the fact that the United States has the largest 'archipelago' (a term used by Foucault who borrowed it from the Soviet dissident writer Alexander Solzhenitsyn (1985), author of *The Gulag Archipelago*) of jails and penitentiaries in the world, they are often hard to find, hidden away in remote rural spaces not even viewable on Google Maps. Their capacity to disappear extends to their social role:

> For as well as disappearing people, prisons also disappear the social crises that they are tasked, in practice, with resolving: poverty, unemployment, political dissent, inequality, uneven development, and other social calamities inscribed in the landscape by racial capitalism. (Story, 2019: 168)

This is a concrete case study of the difference between transparent and deep space, and neatly illustrates the ways in which Black geographies develop and extend the basic insight of critical geography that space and society are inextricably linked.

# Summary

This brief discussion of US-Black geographies adds an important dimension to the work of UK human geographers in the previous section. These Black geographies provide examples of the place-specific ways in which race and racism shapes political, social and economic space. They ask whether geographers' representations of economic, social and cultural geographies, as well as their explanations of the processes that shape places and spaces, pay sufficient attention to race and racism as *causal* factors. For example, taking Black geographies seriously raises questions about possible *silences* within dominant geographical investigations of urban America. Stella Gibbons (2018) notes that while geographers such as Ed Soja and David Harvey acknowledge the intense polarization along lines of race and class that are features of cities such as Los Angeles, the long history of Black struggle against discrimination in the city is not adequately addressed. She makes the point that Los Angeles is similar to virtually all cities in sharing a 'history of white discrimination and violence to preserve white privilege through keeping non-whites and above all African-Americans, in their place' (3). By privileging economic processes and explanations, race is relegated to a sub-theme. This 'test' can be applied to other influential work in human geography, such as that of Sharon Zukin (2010), Miriam Greenberg (2008) or David Wilson (2007).

The major contributions of Black geographies in the United States in the past three decades has been to show how the making of America entailed the construction of race – to reveal how American capitalism was and is racialized in ways that are never acknowledged in celebratory accounts of US capitalism (e.g. Greenspan and Wooldridge, 2019). To this end, it is useful to recall David Harvey's comment, made in response to a critique of his 2014 book *Seventeen Contradictions and the End of Capitalism*, that he did not see the protests taking place in Ferguson, Missouri (in August 2014 following the fatal shooting by the police of Michael Brown) as against capitalism. Instead, he thought, these protests were likely to recapitulate "the long history in the United States ... of making sure the anti-racist struggle does not turn anti-capitalist" (Harvey, 2015: n.p.). Harvey insists on the need to focus on the contradictions that are fundamental to capital, even though in practice capitalism may also necessarily involve struggles over racism and sexism.

This is an important argument, and the challenge of teaching in a racially literate way is to ensure that the economic, political, cultural and ideological aspects of racialization are given due attention. They require us to understand the racial frames and formations that contribute to the 'white unseen' (Hamilton, 2020). As Bledsoe's (2021) review of the methodologies used in the study of Black geographies concludes, these studies reveal a commitment to critiquing the notions of being and spatial formations inherent to Western civilization:

> It is this ethic of black struggle that gave birth to Black Studies and this ethic which must continue to animate Geography's engagement with blackness. (1017)

We conclude this section with a challenge, which revolves around the extent to which this notion of political Blackness stretches the limits of what is possible within school geography. Recent calls for 'abolition geographies', based around an uncompromising analysis of the history and geographies of racial capitalism appear as the 'endgame' of Black geographies (Davis et al., 2022; Wilson, 2022). Does the case for abolition extend to school geography? We are reminded of Michael Eliot-Hurst's (1985) argument that geography 'has neither existence nor future'. Given its complicity with the production of racialized capitalism, geography educators should take seriously the question of whether their subject does more harm than good. This is the challenge posed by Black geographies.

## Beyond Development

It is widely acknowledged that geography supported the project of imperial expansion (Harvey, 1984). It gathered together and systematized knowledge of the world's places, peoples and environments. Geography's fascination with adventure and exotic locations, traditions of navigation and discovery, practices of mapping and surveying, classification and display, and creeds of environmental determinism and geopolitics all made it a valuable tool of Empire (Butlin, 2009). As Kearns (2021) states, Halford Mackinder (founder of the Geographical Association in 1893) 'saw geography as a way to inculcate among an informed loyalty to the British Empire ... based on presumed racial superiority' (4).

However, as formal decolonization proceeded in the post–Second World War period, geographical studies of the 'lands of the south' tended to be empirical, descriptive and sought to avoid overt political issues. Generally, geographical literature 'underplayed the reporting and critique of the colonial mission' (Butlin, 2003: 244). The applied nature of the subject meant that geographers addressed questions of agriculture, population, urbanization, health and transport, all within the framework of development geography. Much literature published in this period until the 1960s was concerned with rational description and modelling, but geographers had little to say on 'the deeper and darker political ailments of brutal totalitarian regimes in Africa' (Watts, 1993: 179). The political process of decolonization ran ahead of its intellectual analysis, and decolonization did not make much of an impact in the school geography curriculum.

One way for geography to avoid the taint of colonialism was to align with the growing field of Development Studies. 'Development' emerged as a term to describe the 'process or transformation through which the poorer countries of the world achieve the standards of living experienced in the so-called developed countries of the West' (Jones, 2006: 62). The mainstream approach within Development Studies (and therefore Development Geography) was 'modernization theory', which stressed the importance of developed countries intervening in the economies of developing countries in order to spur growth and modernize their institutions. Accordingly, poverty was understood as a lack of development. Inhabitants of the so-called Third World lacked modern values and lifestyles, and the goal of development was to establish Western-style urban industrial market economies. Geographers' contribution to Development Studies was to describe and explain the geography of modernization, and especially how 'modernization' was transmitted across space through a matrix of cities and transport links (Peet, 1991: chapter 5 provides an accessible account of these theories and their limits).

From the 1960s, modernization theory was critiqued by the Latin American dependency school and neo-Marxian world-systems theory. These stressed how the development of the 'rich world' was built upon the 'underdevelopment' of the 'poor world'. Dependency theory held that Third World nations should resist calls for greater integration into the global system of trade and instead seek to follow their own pathways to self-determination. The salience of this analysis was heightened by the slowdown in the rate of global economic growth and the clear sense that the world was becoming more unequal. In addition, the integration of the global economy and expanding levels of production, trade and transport was giving rise to a new-found awareness of the ecological 'limits to growth'.

All this meant that by the early 1980s, the intellectual 'cutting edge' within development geography sought to go beyond 'applied' studies for the 'problems' of Third World nations and instead seek to analyse the longer term underlying or structural causes of 'underdevelopment' (Corbridge, 1986). This required an engagement with political and economic processes, for example, in the way that prime agricultural land was used to grow cash crops in order to earn foreign currency, with the result that farmers were forced to cultivate marginal land (e.g. on steep hillsides) which was vulnerable to soil erosion.

While dependency theory challenged Western political ideas about Development and the assumption that all societies were embarked on the path to growth and progress, in the 1990s, some geographers came to challenge the very notion of Development itself. Thus, 'Development' came to be seen as new form of colonization that sought to bring about the total Westernization of society: Development really meaning 'they needed to become more like us'. Such a totalizing project imposes a single version of possibility on what are in reality diverse and open historical trajectories. As Porter and Sheppard (1998) argue, Development defines, 'the unquestionable inferiority of two-thirds of the world's people, and also defines their only rational goal to be a project of catching-up with the industrialised societies of the west (111).

Up to this point, what all these approaches to Development had in common was the assumption that there existed a world of singular 'nation-states' which were in the process of developing their economies and societies (Taylor, 1989). There were of course arguments about how to categorize and label these nations (e.g. developed or developing, less developed or more developed, First world or Third World etc.) and how to understand their interrelations, but the capacity of geographers' to *know* something about these places was assumed.

Post-Development focused on how 'Development' was not simply a model or set of economic policies but a product of language and representation. This was linked to the postmodern turn that transformed Western academia (especially the humanities and social sciences). Derek Gregory's *Geographical Imaginations* (Gregory, 1994) examined the ways in which geography had made sense of its object. Importantly he drew upon postcolonial critiques of knowledge. Postmodernism paid attention to the ways in which knowledge was constructed and challenged the claims of geographers to be able to accurately represent their objects of study. Thus, categories such as 'developed', or 'less developed', were seen as constructions, discourses that helped people make sense of the world. They did not represent reality but constructed it through images, words and texts. In this context, geographers focused on the 'texts and words of Development' – on the ways that Development was written, narrated and spoken. For example,

> Little consensus exists around the meaning of this heavily contested term yet most if not all leaders of the world's many nation states and international organisations claim to be pursuing this objective in some way. This book seeks to show that, by contrast, the strength of the term comes directly from its power to seduce, to please, to fascinate, to set dreaming, but also from its power to deceive and turn away from the truth. Development is nearly always seen as something that is possible, if only people or countries follow through a series of stages or prescribed instructions. (Power, 2000: 1)

The language used here – seduction, fascination, pleasure and dreaming – is revealing. It is a far cry from the accumulation of facts about income per capita, Gini Coefficients or levels of literacy. Development is part of an imaginary, a will to power. In other words, research focused on the *discourse* of Development. Geographers took an interest in how Development makes its arguments and establishes its authority, and the manner in which it constructs the world. Thus, Post-Development studies reflected three aspects of critical human geography:

- The so-called textual turn which focused on the idea that *representations* of the world are constructions or texts that are not simply related to the 'truthful' depiction of the 'real world'.
- The rise of postmodern, *postcolonial* and feminist thought which challenged the truth claims of modernism. From this perspective, Development is a modernist project.
- The postcolonial goal to challenge the authority of Western accounts of the world and to foreground *alternative ways of knowing*.

Development then, became part of the 'geographical imagination', constructed as much through the media and popular culture, travel guides and school textbooks as by government agencies or NGOs. From this perspective, discourses of Development have the power to suggest how the world is (or could be) imagined. The idea that Development relies upon 'geographical imaginations' is influenced by ideas linked to French philosophers such as Michel Foucault and Jacques Derrida.

From Foucault comes the idea that Development serves to construct people and places in particular ways. It creates them as subjects and urges them to act and think in particular ways. Thus, nation-states are urged to open up their economies, to adopt particular policies and practices, in order to 'catch up' with the West. In the process, people become units of human capital to be utilized in the project of development.

From Derrida comes the insight that there is always another way to read the world. Thus, there is always something other, or contrary, at the centre of Development discourses that may interrupt or challenge the dominant view. 'Development' then becomes a contradictory term that can be interpreted in unexpected ways.

Post-Development geographies are thus based on Derrida's idea of 'deconstruction'. Categories such as 'First World', 'Third World', developed or developing are seen as ways of imposing certain kinds of order on the complexity of the world. For example, in his book *An Everyday Geography of the Global South*, Rigg (2007) explained how 'I wanted to extract the Global South from the tyranny of the Development discourse and to examine the myriad geographies of the majority world unshackled from such associations' (p. xv). His book seeks to start with the 'personal geographies' of people making a living, working and looking after one another.

This section has stressed the ways in which work within 'Development' geography has sought to remove its association with projects of Empire and colonialism. In the first instance, this involved the adoption of a more theoretical and rational approach to 'Development'. But over time the way in which Development itself is linked to later rounds of capitalist modernity has led to its critique and, more recently, moves to 'deconstruct' the very category itself. Much of this work has pointed to the blind spots of geographical knowledge. The extension of these geographical imaginations is taken up with postcolonial geographies and decolonizing geography.

## The Geographies of Coloniality

The previous section, while admittedly brief, sought to make one important point, which is that academic geography's involvement in the project of 'Development' has been radically reimagined. 'Development' is one of those words that now has to be written with 'scare quotes'. This is not to deny that Development goes on, or to say that geographers are not involved, but any discussion within the discipline must now acknowledge the fact of coloniality, by which is meant the long-standing patterns of power and resistance that resulted from the process of colonization. Although formal colonialism is in the past, coloniality reminds us that its after-effects remain. As William Faulkner famously wrote: 'The past isn't dead, it's not even past.'

We begin with a brief historical note. It was through European colonialism that large parts of the world were made part of the world economy focused initially on Europe and then on the United States. Colonialism sought to spread the European vision of capitalist society and development throughout the world. It maintained economic and political inequality between the 'Third' and the 'First' World, and between European and indigenous social systems within the colonized countries. Colonialism did not end until the end of British and European hegemony during World War Two. The context for acknowledging geography's role in colonialism and subsequently the development of postcolonial geographies was the actual decolonization of much of the world. Between 1950 and 1961 the number of colonized states reduced from 134 to 58. One of the last to gain independence was Namibia in 1990. There were three factors involved. First, following the Second World War, the axis powers (Germany, Italy and Japan) dissolved their empires.

Though Germany and Italy by this point had few colonies, Japan was influential in East Asia. Second, European colonial powers, who were heavily indebted to the United States following World War Two, allowed freer access to their former trading blocs. Finally, geopolitical shifts involved in the Cold War encouraged many states to seek independence. None of this was straightforward.

## Postcolonial Geographies

From the 1970s, geographers explored colonialism and imperialism from predominantly Marxist perspectives. Postcolonial geographies, particularly from the 1990s, adopted a more poststructuralist approach, and in line with intellectual shifts, were concerned to explore the complex meanings associated with space, power and knowledge. The nomenclature is complex. Post-colonial (with a hyphen) suggests the period after colonialism. However, colonial relations did not simply cease with formal colonialism, so postcolonialism (without the hyphen) refers to the ways in which the 'colonial mentality' continues. Colonialism impacted both the colonizer and the colonized, so it is possible to think about countries such as Britain as postcolonial, not least as the empire literally came home in the decades after the Second World War (Sharp, 2005).

It is significant that postcolonialism begins with literature – an important method is 'colonial discourse analysis' derived from Edward Said's (1978) *Orientalism*. For Said, Orientalism was Europe's way of dealing with the difference of its colonies. It was a set of images and ways of looking that set up a series of oppositions between 'the West and the Rest'. Postcolonialism was the empire writing back. It was the culture produced in conversation with colonial power, but which foregrounded the tension with the imperial power, and which emphasized the differences from the assumptions of the imperial centre. This notion of the empire 'writing back' was important in the way that postcolonial geographies developed. (It was the title of a famous text and attributed to Salman Rushdie, whose work represented the experience of living 'between cultures' (Minoli, 2000)). An accessible example of postcolonial geography was Richard Phillips's (1997) study of the geographies of adventure in popular texts (e.g. *Robinson Crusoe*). He clarifies how these texts worked to order the world in particular ways, effectively constructing cultural spaces in which 'imperial geographies and imperial masculinities were conceived'. These texts were not simply ideological, however, because there was space for a variety of readings. The 1990s saw a range of studies of the writing of colonial space in official reports, in travel diaries and in travel literature (Blunt and McEwan, 2004; Blunt and Rose, 1994; Duncan and Gregory, 1999).

At first, geographers were relatively slow to acknowledge this literary link. For example, *Literature and Humanistic Geography*, published in 1981, contained little reference to texts that might be considered postcolonial (except perhaps the chapter on Doris Lessing's perceptions of arriving in London from South Africa). Extending the definition of 'text' a little further, Burgess and Gold's (1985) *Geography, Media and Popular Culture* does not reference to black cultural production at a time when films and texts were providing reflective commentary on the experience of migration to Britain (Young, 1996). Such arguments were beginning to shape the study of literature in schools, but they seemed removed from the field of anti-racism in geography. In a reflection written in 1996, Peter Jackson and Jane Jacobs commented that geography conferences they attended saw almost no overlap between audiences in sessions on racism and those on postcolonialism. Sessions on racism dealt with contemporary political issues, while those on postcolonial geographies focused on analyses of the past. Postcolonial geographies that focus on the ways in which writing is a way of constructing a sense of otherness are of real interest to geography educators. For example, the role of school textbooks in shaping perceptions of colonial societies is ripe for study. Travel writing, too, is a useful genre for analysis. Perhaps most importantly there is a wealth of literature – novels and poetry – that explores the experience of migration, settlement and living in postcolonial Britain. The idea that the landscape is a text (e.g. Barnes and Duncan, 1992; Duncan and Ley, 1993) also shapes the reading of cities (e.g. Ashmore, 2006; Driver and Gilbert, 2003).

Postcolonialism is an inherently geographical concept. Cox (2014) points out that geography was a discipline developed by Europeans, about Europeans and for Europeans. In its interactions through Empire and colonization, it also became concerned with others and in the process established classifications and hierarchies, into the civilized and by inference the non-civilized world. In this sense, geography was based on a series of oppositions that saw the European as civilized, possessed of reason, morally virtuous, Christian, organized and hard working. And non-Europeans as uncivilized, irrational, disorganized and existing in backward, stagnant societies.

Postcolonial debates reshaped the field of Development geographies in the 1990s (Lawson, 2007). Jonathan Crush, whose 1995 book *The Power of Development* was one of the important catalysts towards postmodern Development geography discussed in the previous section, argued that the aim of a postcolonial geography would be

> the unveiling of geographical complicity in colonial dominion over space; the character of geographical representation in colonial discourse; the de-linking of local geographical enterprise from metropolitan theory and its totalizing systems of representation; and the recovery of those hidden spaces occupied, and invested with their own meaning, by the colonial underclass. (Crush, 1994: 336–7).

This statement highlights some of the key features of postcolonial geography. The first point is that geographical knowledge was involved in supporting projects of colonialism. Acts of discovery, exploration, classifying and mapping were all important in establishing colonial domination of other places. Though this was a material occupation, it was facilitated by images and language. Power is exercised through the representations of people and places, and traditional geography claimed that they were applied equally from one place to another: in other words, theories of the economic space or explanations for levels of development were assumed to operate regardless of space. In the process, more local accounts of how to think about and organize space were, at best, ignored or placed to one side, and, at worst, obliterated.

This implies that postcolonial geography should attend to the role that geographical knowledge played in the process of colonizing space. It would look at the role played by geographical texts and images in this process and avoid reaching for easy generalizations. In particular, it would stress the different ways in which landscapes can be interpreted.

These arguments and debates had become so ubiquitous that Barnes and Gregory could state (in 1997):

> It is now unacceptable to write geography in such a way that the West is always at the centre of its imperial geography. (14)

Driver's (2001) *Geography Militant* was a wide-reaching analysis of the geographical imagination during the Victorian era. Gregory's (1994) *Geographical Imaginations* drew upon postcolonial thinking, and there are a number of accessible introductions and collections.

Tariq Jazeel's (2019) *Postcolonialism* represents the most up-to-date and developed introductory text. It provides a detailed account of the history of postcolonialism in human geography and the different strands of study that shape the field. It has at least three implications for school geography. The first of these is that postcolonialism offers a set of methods and concepts that allow for an understanding and analysis of everyday racism and exclusion. Second, postcolonialism is concerned with questions of representation, about who gets their geography talked about and whose geographies are excluded and/or marginalized. Finally, Jazeel makes the case for the importance of postcolonial geographies, focused on material spaces, places and relations, against the tendency to see postcolonialism in literary terms.

Postcolonialism has, to date, made relatively little impact on discussions within the field of geography education. We explore the possible reasons for this in the following chapter, but at this point, note that the fact that Britain is a postcolonial nation means that any geography curriculum that attempts to represent this space should deal with its implications. Since around 2015, postcolonializm has been replaced by a focus on the term 'decolonizing', which we explore in the next section.

# Decolonizing Geography

The growing interest in postcolonial and decolonial geographies represents a significant shift in the geographical imagination. Shurmer-Smith and Hannan (1994) point out that 'many people are drawn to geography by the sheer exoticism' (17), and that the requirement in British universities that geography undergraduates undertake fieldwork in a 'foreign' location can be seen as 'the legacy of geographical exploration and fascination for the exotic' (17). They also note that, when formal decolonization was taking place, geography escaped criticism 'perhaps because it was busy demonstrating that it was a spatial science or because the subject did not have a tradition of self-criticism or political awareness' (18). Geography's subsequent alignment with social and cultural theory means that this is no longer the case. The subject's 'gaze' is now the object of (often intense) scrutiny and self-examination.

Jazeel (2019) suggests that postcolonial geography should be seen as part of a wider intellectual and political project to *decolonize* geography. Again, this is complicated. Individual geographers were actively involved in colonialism. They travelled to places, took up academic and teaching positions, wrote books and played the role of 'expats'. They acted as colonizers. Whatever their individual qualities, they worked within disciplinary frames which ensured that they produced knowledge in particular ways.

There is an important distinction between geographies of decolonization and decolonizing geographies. In terms of the geographies of decolonization, Butlin (2009) provides an authoritative account. He is concerned with the processes through which European powers divested their colonies. There is a complex set of historical geographies in action here. Historical geographers have also recently taken an interest in the geographies of decolonization, with particular attention to the role that geographers played in the process. Decolonizing geography takes a different tact; it is a political and moral project. Although colonialism was declared illegitimate by the United Nations in 1960, and condemned as a denial of fundamental human rights, the term 'coloniality' denotes the continuation of a colonial mindset. This 'coloniality of power' perspective originates in Latin America with the work of the Peruvian sociologist Aníbal Quijano (2000) and cultural studies and literary theorist Walter Mignolo (2000). A helpful statement is found in Mignolo's (2005) *The Idea of Latin America* which accords neatly with Lewis and Wigen's (1997) *The Myth of Continents*. Thus, Mignolo asserts that the Americas only exist today 'as a consequence of European colonial expansion from the European perspective, the perspective of modernity' (2005: 11). It is possible to tell the story of the world in many ways from the perspective of modernity without paying attention to the perspective of coloniality. However, once a Fanonian perspective is adopted, it is impossible to ignore the fact that a colonial wound accompanies modernity, a 'feeling of inferiority imposed on human beings who do not fit the predetermined model in European narratives' (11). This means that it is impossible to separate coloniality and modernity, hence the 'colonality/modernity' couplet.

To get a sense of what changes with a decolonizing perspective, we can look at a relatively recent geographical treatment of Latin America. *Latin America Transformed* was published in 1999 and was edited by Robert Gwynne and Cristobal Kay. Its subtitle is *Globalization and Modernity*. It is a weighty and detailed volume, amounting to a 'realist' account of the transition from economic dependency in the 1980s to the neoliberal model of the 1990s. This transformation was wrought by new ways of linking the nation-states of Latin America to a world economy which was 'globalizing', by which is meant the intensification and extensification of economic activity. This account is clearly located within a political economy approach, and one that stresses the existence of a 'world system'. Neoliberalism favoured multinational elites and local elites and was supported by centre-left governments which heralded a shift from dictatorships to democracy. As always, the costs and benefits of modernization were unevenly shared, and one of the strengths of the interdisciplinary team of authors is that the book offers a range of perspectives or viewpoints.

From a decolonizing perspective, *Latin America Transformed* presents difficulties. To start with the most obvious, there is a provenance of the authors. It is written by 'Latin Americanists', scholars mainly housed in the metropoles of the global economy, and whose capacity to write about Latin America owes much to their privileged academic positions. Next, and perhaps because of this, they tend to write with a totalizing worldview. Though in no sense dominated by a Marxist framework, the book is shaped by political economy. There is little reference to race, and certainly not racialized capitalism. The chapters in the book pay attention to history, but this is largely to provide the backdrop to more recent transformations. It is modernity that is the focus of the volume. Colonialism and colonization play little part in the narrative (receiving only passing mention). But the real difficulty is that the very terms of the volume – Globalization and Modernity – are not interrogated.

From the perspective of decolonizing, these terms are central. It is possible to detect in the volume a sense that changes since the 1990s represent a brand new phase. However, from a decolonizing perspective, recent decades of globalization are the culmination of European-centred capitalism and represent a new form of colonial global power. In the act of colonization, the colonizing powers created a *terra nullius* – an empty space – which enabled them to see the people and landscapes as resources to be catalogued and exploited. This involved the social classification of the world's population around race. Geography as a discipline was from the start linked to this project of race-thinking, which continues even after the formal ending of colonialism.

For decolonizing scholars, to use the concept of modernity or globalization without reference to its 'twin' – coloniality – is to erase the violence associated with these processes. Decolonizing scholars insist on the importance of the 'modernity/coloniality' couplet to remember that the making of the modern world was linked to colonial thinking. The term 'coloniality' signals the fact that the term 'colonial' was present at the 'birth of modernity'. The discipline of geography was implicated in this. Geography actively constructed the world and in doing so, was part of the colonial episteme: in other words, the discipline's ways of seeing the world were themselves colonial, and textbooks such as *Latin America Transformed* continue that legacy. To highlight this, consider the following statement from *Latin America Transformed* in one of its few references to colonialism:

> The roots of Latin America's role as a global resource periphery were laid during Spanish and Portuguese colonization. Initially, colonial interest lay in precious metals such as gold and silver. (Murray, 1999: 128)

Here is a factual and apparently 'value-free' statement, which sees Latin America as a particular type of space (a 'global resource periphery'), which acts as a magnet for rational economic interests. Compare this with Eduardo Galeano's (1973) *Open Veins of Latin America*:

> Latin America is the region of open veins. Everything, from the discovery to our times, has been transmuted into European – or later, United States – capital, and as such has accumulated in distant centres of power. (2)

Here, we see Latin America as an active, living space, with its veins cut open, draining into Europe and transformed in the process, an act of violent accumulation.

To decolonize geography, would be to recognize the hegemony of European knowledge (e.g. that found in *Latin American Transformed*) – the colonial episteme – which erased or marginalized alternative geographical knowledge(s) – and to counter this by seeking out, acknowledging and valorizing indigenous knowledge(s) and scholarship.

The moral case for decolonizing geography may seem clear, but there are important arguments to be had about the political project of decolonizing geography, not least in terms of what that might look like in schools. A decolonizing perspective holds that mainstream geographical knowledge (that which makes up the canon) is *western*, *Eurocentric*, *colonial* or *imperial*. Geographical knowledge comes from *somewhere*, and imprinted with social relations, which are invariably power relations. According to Bhambra, Gebrial, and Nişancioğlu (2018), a decolonizing perspective takes colonialism, empire and racism as its objects of study, and recognizes these as 'key shaping forces of the contemporary world' (2). This gives geography educators pause for thought, as does Kehinde Andrews (2018) argument that 'the neglect of Black knowledge by society is no accident but a direct result of racism' (2). This leads him to conclude that we must 'forever leave behind the idea that knowledge can be produced value free' (4).

In short, decolonizing geography involves not simply recognizing the existence of other geographies but also promoting and valorizing some on the basis of who produced them and where (O'Daley and Murrey, 2022).

It is unclear as to how far decolonizing geographies will reshape geography as an academic discipline. The first 'introductory textbook' in the field was due to be published as this book went to press (Radcliffe, 2022). For some (e.g. Williams, 2017), 'decolonizing the curriculum' carries the risk of promoting the extreme relativism of knowledge; the identity of the knower is what matters most in deciding what should be taught. In relation to geography, Jim Butcher (2020) argues:

> While it is important to study the people, societies and interests involved in the production of knowledge, is also important to see the universal potential of such knowledge, a potential downplayed by the calls to decolonise. For such activists, knowledge and even techniques are tainted by the times in which they were developed and by the individuals who developed them. [3]

---

[3] Butcher's short paper is one of the most succinct attempts to interrupt the arguments associated with decolonizing geography. We always have to look at where ideas come from though, and he is loosely affiliated with the UK organization the Academy of Ideas. Williams, too, is part of this network. We have

There is also a question of how far the adoption of 'decolonizing' as a general term risks glossing over the very different experiences of actual colonization and decolonization. For instance, do theoretical ideas such as the 'colonial episteme' survive the journey from Latin America to say Australia and New Zealand, where very different models of settler colonialism operated?

Perspectives associated with postcolonial geographies and decolonizing geography are important in challenging the unreflective 'whiteness' of geography and addressing the discipline's relationship with the past. It should be clear that the question of where knowledge comes from, how it is produced and in what contexts are at the central of any meaningful geography education and are fundamental to curriculum development in schools. This is true even in relation to that most 'scientific' of approaches –physical geography.

## What Has Physical Geography Got to Do with Race?

In an article titled 'Why Teach Physical geography?' David Pepper (1986) argued that the physical geography taught in schools (derived, of course, from universities) was 'conducive to the stability of the existing economic and political order' (69). His analysis of examination papers showed that physical geography did not encourage students to set knowledge within the context of human society and problems. Students were encouraged to be analytical rather than synthetic, reductionist rather than holistic. However, he argued, without a social purpose, there was little justification for teaching physical geography. Given the argument that knowledge cannot be disentangled from its conditions of production, it is important to consider whether physical geography fails to help teachers and students challenge conceptions of race and racism.

Pepper's article was critical of the clear-cut separation between human and physical geography. This reflected the growing interest in the relationship between society and nature, an interest that has continued to pick up pace (see Castree, 2014). At the time, the most obvious source for this was geographers working in the area of natural hazards and disasters.

In an article in *Nature* titled 'Taking the Naturalness out of Natural Disasters', Phil O'Keefe, Kevin Westgate and Ben Wisner (1976) argued that natural disasters are not created primarily by nature but arise as the result of an unequal distribution of resources. This posed a challenge to earlier forms of research on natural hazards, which assumed that people in societies adapt to natural forces in order to reduce the extent and impact of disasters. The influential Chicago School of Hazard Research

---

written elsewhere about this style of thinking and its relationship to geography teaching (e.g. Morgan, 2012: 9–24).

stressed how this reduction could be achieved through mapping the risks associated with hazards, monitoring natural processes, drawing up evacuation plans and developing new technology. In this managerial approach, the key was knowledge of natural processes and Earth Science, since natural hazards were seen as the inevitable consequence of the vagaries of nature. Such technological solutions were central to the United Nations International Decade for Natural Disaster Reduction of the 1980s, which involved the transfer of Western knowledge and technologies to 'less developed' countries.

This approach to natural disasters research was challenged in the 1980s. A landmark was Kenneth Hewitt's (1983) edited collection *Interpretations of Calamity* which showed that the dominant view of the 'disaster archipelago', whereby natural hazards were bracketed off as exceptional events or accidents, tended to ignore the fact that they were an element of ordinary experience for large numbers of people. Susman et al.'s. chapter in the book was titled 'Global Disasters, a Radical Interpretation'. It noted an increase in the incidence of disasters over the previous fifty years and an increased loss of life per disaster. However, in the absence of any evidence for geological or significant climatological changes over this period, they concluded that the explanation for increased incidence must be sought in people's living conditions, which increase their growing vulnerability to extreme physical events. Vulnerability was more a factor of social processes than natural events. Indeed, as Amartya Sen pointed out in *Development as Freedom* (Sen, 1999), 'No famine has ever taken place in the history of the world in a functioning democracy.'

Thus, natural disasters came to be seen as human-made (and thus avoidable). It is worth noting that this was part of a wider intellectual effort by 'radical' geographers to challenge the Malthusianism that had informed much of the work on cultural ecology (see Felli, 2021; Harvey, 1974b). Such neo-Malthusian accounts attributed environmental degradation to rapid population growth and overpopulation. In 1983, Michael Watts published *Silent Violence* (a phrase that predates Rob Nixon's (2011) idea of 'Slow Violence'). *Silent Violence* was a landmark text in that it sought to question the individualistic and naturalistic models of cultural adaptation to the environment and instead located and explained local responses historically, socially and politically. It was also important methodologically, because, unusually at that time, Watts studied both physical systems and the political economy of West African societies.

Around the same time, Piers Blaikie and Harold Brookfield's (1987) *Land Degradation and Society* developed a method of 'regional political ecology' to examine environmental variability and spatial variations in patterns of land use. This overcame the top-down 'grand narrative' approach to studying land degradation and emphasized the role of local decision makers in land-use policies. Blaikie and Brookfield shared with Watts a shift in focus from the 'exceptional' calamities of natural disasters to focus on the everyday aspects of risk and vulnerability. In later work, Blaikie and colleagues (Blaikie et al., 1994 argued that it is crucial to grasp that disasters, especially natural hazards, are 'not the greatest threat to humanity', and that although they can be lethal, many of the world's poor had their lives shortened by unnoticed events, illnesses and hunger that passed for normal existence in many parts of the world.

The development of critical political ecology was important because it took up Pepper's challenge to avoid seeing physical geographical processes as set apart from society. It shifted the analytical focus towards political ecology. Paul Robbins (2004) summarizes the approach:

> As critique, political ecology seeks to expose flaws in dominant approaches to the environment favoured by corporate, state, and international authorities, working to demonstrate the undesirable impacts of policies and market conditions, especially from the point of view of local people, marginal groups, and vulnerable populations. It works to denaturalised certain social and environmental conditions, showing them to be contingent outcomes of power and not inevitable. (12)

This early work was important in stressing how society and nature are linked. However, such work was largely forgotten as political ecology embraced postmodern, poststructural and post-colonial perspectives (Lave, 2017). These intellectual shifts were a response to, first a perceived over reliance on neo-Marxist explanations for environmental problems (in effect, it was capitalism that, in the last instance, shaped all environmental problems) and second the tendency to emphasize political ecology over physical ecology.

As the field of critical political ecology developed, researchers focused attention on the role of race and gender in the social construction of nature, and in particular to 'local' narratives and the experiences of change. An important part of this involved questions to do with the production and circulation of environmental knowledge, including local indigenous knowledges. The most significant aspect of this is a re-evaluation of some of the dominant environmental orthodoxies upon which accounts of people-environment issues have been based (Forsyth, 2003).

There are four aspects to this re-evaluation:

- First, there has been a move away from equilibrium models of ecological systems to understanding non-equilibrium approaches, and how these may deepen understanding of rapid environmental change.
- Second, and linked to this, it is now acknowledged that theories of environmental change developed in the North and which presumed to operate, evenly and with predictable results in the global South, should be seen as 'local', rather than 'global' theories. Ecology effectively operated as a Western myth and operated on the assumption that local (indigenous) people's understanding of their environments were 'wrong' and that their environmental practices were to be discouraged and replaced.
- Third, there is more attention to the temporal and scale dimensions of environmental change. There is growing knowledge of environmental history, much of which challenges long-established accounts of environmental processes, as well as a recognition that 'local' events may be related to changes at a higher spatial scale.

- Finally, a more critical political ecology has developed which has rejected environmental orthodoxies and paid closer attention to the languages, discourses and ideologies that are involved in construction of environmental knowledge. The result is an approach that is more attentive to difference, context and local knowledges.

It should be clear that his work has strong links with the debates about Development, colonization and decolonization discussed earlier in this chapter. In particular, Western geographical knowledge has been used by government experts and non-governmental aid agencies to impose interpretations of landscapes, environments and resources on local and indigenous people, paying insufficient attention to how such people have managed and maintained resources (often in 'fragile' environments) over long periods of time (Stott and Sullivan, 2003). Attention to these local knowledges, along with a realization that physical environments are linked in complex ways to global environmental processes, have led some physical geographers to examine how their work intersects with human activity (to put it in simple terms, physical geographers studying the mechanics of glacial flow can no longer ignore the socially constructed fact that glaciers are in retreat). This recognition is reflected in the emergence of *critical physical geography*.

Physical geography developed in universities from the 1850s and was inevitably linked with the colonial expansion of the discipline. Lyell's *Principles of Geology* was underpinned by an evolutionary view of landscapes that was then taken up in W. M. Davis's studies of landforms. The development of a more quantitative-statistical geography in the 1950s and 1960s gave rise to process studies and a reduced scale of studies, but Gregory (2000) noted the emergence, from the 1970s, of people-environment studies.

Physical and human geography have gone their separate ways, with different pathways in degree programmes, specialist journals and funding and career trajectories. However, the environmental crisis and the idea of the Anthropocene have brought the fields closer together (Castree, Hulme, and Proctor, 2018), with growing attention to the social contexts in which knowledge of physical processes is produced (e.g. Head, 2000). The editors of *The Palgrave Handbook of Critical Physical Geography* (Lave, Biermann and Lane, 2018) argue that physical geographers have become more sophisticated in their attempts to engage with the roles of human agency, perception, and culture. For example, in hydrology, new kinds of participation with local communities have challenged the orthodox approaches to both flood risk science and flood risk management. In biogeography, the impact of indigenous practices on vegetation and disturbance regimes in the Americas have become the focus of active study and debate. In atmospheric studies, the relationship between climate, climate science, and society has provided new approaches which highlight the 'impacts of climate on culture and culture on climate' (190). The most developed example of such work is perhaps that of Mick Hulme (2008, 2020) leading to a radical reexamination of climate change 'with contributions from the interpretive humanities and social sciences, married to a critical reading of the natural sciences, and informed by a spatially contingent view of knowledge' (5) (see also Mahony and Randalls, 2020). Similar shifts are found in the study of another staple of geographical study, Resources (Himley, Havice, and Valdivia, 2022). Geographers have always been interested in resources, their distribution and the process of exploitation and their implications for people and places. Often, these are termed 'natural resources' and are seen as a factor in economic development. Building on the insight that the discovery, identification, exploitation and use of resources is tied up with the character of economic and political systems (Blaikie and Brookfield, 1987), recent work in the field of critical resource geography (Himley et al., 2022) has paid attention to the processes of 'resource-making', the myriad networks, technologies and economies that turn objects into resources to be exploited, produced and consumed. The emphasis is on political ecology, and how the active construction of resources and their use are linked with racialized capitalism, power and colonization.

The focus on people and the social in this critical physical geography offers the potential to examine how geographical and earth processes are linked with race and racism (see Box 4.7). To the extent that it acknowledges that physical landscapes

### Box 4.7 Yusoff, Kathryn. (2019). *A billion Black anthropocenes (or none at all)*. London: Verso.

Geology appears to be the most natural of all disciplines. Surely it is about rocks? However, in *A Billion Black Anthropocenes (or None at All)*, Kathryn Yusoff argues that geology has played a major part in constituting the environmental crises faced today. Many geographers are exploring the role that colonization and capitalism play as forces that have brought about the epochal shift – now known as the Anthropocene. Geology was crucial in establishing the dominant classifications of human and non-human 'inhuman' matter. White geology provided the basis for colonial modernity's hierarchies, which determined what kind of matter was extractable and by whom. In this way, geological knowledge was fundamental to the racialization that occurred in the making of the 'New World'. It is no accident that areas were named such as 'the Gold Coast' or the 'Copper Belt'. Areas of the world were categorized according to their mineral value, and indigenous lands were classified accordingly. Categories of human and inhuman matter were used to justify the extraction of minerals, and African bodies as commodities. Yusoff argues that the adoption of the term 'Anthropocene' is white geology's attempt to come to terms with the discipline's own role in the current planetary crisis. However, geology fails to recognize its own involvement in producing the crisis.

Yusoff notes that in current arguments about how to accurately date the Anthropocene, much of the concern involves the identification of 'golden spikes': that is, key points in the geological strata that register the impact of human activity. However, in the process of seeking objective, scientific evidence of these spikes – in the process universalizing the human – geologists tend to erase the histories of race and settler colonialism, and the historical violence

> waged against black bodies at the same time. For example, one of the leading candidates for dating the Anthropocene is the detonation of nuclear weapons in the testing programmes of the 1950s. However, it is often overlooked that these took place on Pacific Atolls that were rendered uninhabitable and where the colonized inhabitants bore the long-term impact of radiation. Alternatively, to suggest that the golden spike is the period of the Great Acceleration after 1945 risks downplaying that this was the moment of Development, and a time when renewed rounds of accumulation and incorporation of people into the global economy was taking place. The Anthropocene is, for Yusoff, white geology's revisionist history of itself.

and systems do not exist in isolation from economic and social systems, this work is an advance on traditional physical geography. Physical geographers do not stand as neutral outsiders: what they choose to study and how they choose to study it reflect their own standpoints and interests and perhaps their own unexamined assumptions about society and culture (something that is very evident when geographers reflect on their own work). The results and findings of physical geography research have implications and frequently differential consequences in the world – on real people in real places.

The authors of *Critical Physical Geography* acknowledge that there is more work to be done in this respect, and it remains to be seen whether there can be genuine moves to integrate perspectives from physical and human geography other than the exhortation to 'integrate' with what Johnston (1989) calls 'the obligatory Venn diagram'.

## Conclusion

This chapter has covered a lot of ground. It is the longest chapter in the book, and for good reason. It is a provisional mapping of changing perspectives in geography. We have organized the chapter in a way that identifies distinct sets of literature within the discipline. Though there are overlaps, we think it is important to avoid the tendency to block together 'anti-racist, Black and decolonial geographies'. The advantage of our 'granular' approach for curriculum development in school geography is that it highlights important differences and tensions between such terms that have implications for developing a racially literate geography education. We do not claim exhaustive coverage (indeed, we have barely scratched the surface). What we do offer is an account of a dynamic evolving discipline which, through the processes of research and argument, creates new knowledge that can inform our understanding and actions. By knowledge, we do not mean the accumulation of facts. We mean the creation of powerful concepts and critical ideas which can help to reveal how aspects of the human and physical world can be better understood. It is this we call powerful disciplinary knowledge, and we argue that this disciplinary endeavour provides a vital basis for teaching geography in schools.

In our book, we are making an argument that geography in schools *has the potential* to respond fully to issues of race and racism – and help students to do so. One of the key planks of the argument is that geography as a discipline has responded through the development of theoretical perspectives better to understand societies. In the next chapter, we explore the ways in which race and racism have featured in the teaching of geography in schools.

## Questions for Discussion and Reflection

1. What does it mean to say that geography (including school geography) is underpinned by a 'racial project'?
2. What has race got to do with teaching physical geography?

# Part three

## Remaking Geography

# 5
# Learning to Talk about Racism in School Geography

## Introduction

The previous chapter offered an account of geographical perspectives on race and racism. But, as is frequently noted, a gap exists between university and school versions of geography. This book is published at a time when there are widespread calls to develop anti-racist pedagogy, to decolonize the curriculum and to promote Black geographies. This has, inevitably, provoked reactions. In February 2021, Ofsted issued its guidance to schools on their statutory duty to provide balance and avoid political partisanship. In response, Halima Begum, Chief Executive of the Runnymede Trust argued,

> After the events of the past year, in which Covid has exposed the extent of the structural inequalities facing Black and ethnic minority groups, there could be no more important time to talk about race and racism in the classroom – yet the government proposes limiting these dialogues. Without a clear understanding of racism, pupils will not be taught to become antiracist citizens and will lack vital knowledge of how race, migration and empire have shaped the UK.
> (Begum, 2022)

We agree, and in this chapter, we take a step back from the immediate intensity of the arguments in order to explore how race and racism have featured in the development of school geography in Britain.

## Imperial Past, Racist Present?

It is often claimed that school geography was (and may still be) an imperial subject that taught British children to see themselves as superior or more advanced than the people of other nations. A recent example can be found in Danny Dorling and Sally Tomlinson's *Rule Britannia* (Dorling and Tomlinson, 2018). Tomlinson, a respected researcher of issues of race and racism in education, draws a direct line between geography teaching and Brexit:

> Nostalgia flourishes with ignorance of our imperial past. Many of the people who voted for Brexit were nostalgic for the days when imperial subjects laboured overseas and never came to live in the Mother Country. This should not be surprising. The third edition of a school textbook on *The Southern Countries*, published in 1973, noted the enormous benefit goods from Africa were bringing to Britain, as 'Railways have been built and roads constructed under European guidance', with Africans doing the manual labour. (Tomlinson, 2020)

The argument that the school curriculum is a source of prejudiced and potentially racist ideas gained some acceptance in the 1970s. As we noted in Chapter 3, the Labour government, in its 1977 Green Paper, stated that the curriculum devised for an imperial age was no longer suited to the modern multiracial society. In response, the then Secretary of State for Education, Shirley Williams, commissioned a report on multicultural education, which was published eventually in 1985. The Swann Report, *Education for All*, argued for an approach that would offer all young people a good and up-to-date education for life in Britain and the world as it now actually existed (Department of Education and Science [DES], 1985). It explicitly acknowledged that the school curriculum was influenced by ideas that were a product of the age of empire.

The Swann Report was seen by many educationalists as 'a landmark in pluralism' (Verma, 1989). It officially acknowledged the existence of the failure of the education system to meet the needs of black and Asian children in school and argued that multicultural and anti-racist education was a matter for all schools, regardless of their racial mix. It highlighted the need to change curricula and to develop resources to support the curriculum. However, by the time the report was published in 1985 the politics of race had changed dramatically. Conservatives rejected its multiculturalism, and anti-racist educators saw it as too moderate, failing to develop an overtly political approach to race and racism.

In an excellent chapter on the origins of the 'ethnocentric curriculum', Tomlinson (1989) explained that, as the British Empire went into a final stage of expansion, many aspects of what came to be seen as typical of British culture were reflected in the school curriculum. Democracy, tolerance and social and racial justice were seen as uniquely 'British values'. This world view was one in which imperialism, militarism and racial beliefs based on social Darwinism fused to 'create a popular consciousness that the British "race" had a particular superiority vis-à-vis the rest of the world' (27). As Tomlinson noted, there was nothing innocent or natural about this world view. It was promoted by, and served, dominant social and political elites.

Tomlinson's analysis was underpinned by the work of John Mackenzie (1984), whose *Popular Culture and Imperialism* argued that colonialism dominated British popular culture for much of the nineteenth century. The values of the social and political elite came to influence mass education through the public schools. Indeed, Mangan (1986) asserted that the British Empire was run by public schoolboys and that schools were the place where imperial cultural values were inculcated. Head teachers spread imperial cultural values through sermons, prize-giving speeches and school magazine editorials. This filtered down to the schools attended by working-class children. The public schools were the model for the elementary state schools, as described by Roberts (1971) in *The Classic Slum*. School textbooks for history and geography played their part, as did children's literature (Phillips, 1997). Tomlinson (1989) argued,

> The intensity of ethnocentric beliefs in the glories of Empire, white superiority, and a militaristic 'patriotism', were uncritically reflected in textbooks and other literature; and were reinforced by pedagogic techniques which encouraged simplification of complex moral issues, and unthinking acceptance of value-laden content. (37)

Geography was widely taught in the 1890s (the Geographical Association (GA) was formed in 1893), and a 'single ideological slant' was introduced into school texts. The slant was towards ideas of patriotism, militarism, respect for the monarchy, support for imperial expansion and dominance and racial superiority. The values implicit in these texts were 'passed on to a receptive white majority in Britain' (Tomlinson, 1989: 34). Tomlinson was in little doubt about the difficulties of challenging these ethnocentric ideas, not least because the parents and grandparents of children were influenced by this world view. She cited Mackenzie's (1984) view that 'the values and beliefs of the imperial world settled like a sediment in the consciousness of the British people' and concluded that 'disturbing the sediment will be one of the major challenges to the education system in the future' (37).

There are other sources to support this view. John Ahier's (1988) *Industry, Children and the Nation* set out to explore the images represented to pupils in history and geography texts. He argued that the links between British school geography and imperialism are most explicit in the way early texts merely listed countries, their physical features and their place in empire's history. At times, these texts read 'like an imperial, military shopping list' (46). The most important imperative was to show young British readers how they were more advanced than people in other places. This was achieved through pedagogical devices such as imaginary journeys in the form of 'travels through the British Empire'. However, merely visiting these places could not convey to children the connectedness of their lives to people and places elsewhere, which was achieved through studies of 'what they send us' in the form of food and clothes. Other places were portrayed as sources for English suburban consumption:

> It was a world in which our food was produced by willing, happy natives in far-off lands; in which Britain had a guaranteed superiority; a world full of people of an imperial nation who could appreciate the natural, elemental existences of their simple charges. (Ahier, 1988: 169)

Ahier concluded,

> The places offered to white children in the 1930s and 40s and 50s were comfortable ones, but for others they were very difficult to accept. The problems were most obvious for certain racial minorities who began entering the schools whilst many of these books were still in use. (171)

These arguments about the ethnocentricity and racism in school geography textbooks may appear as obvious and common sense to present-day readers. This is because, in contemporary culture, there is an increased willingness to accept that any text of this period reflected (knowingly or unknowingly) an imperialist world view. This idea has gained influence since the publication of Edward Said's *Culture and imperialism* (1993), which revealed imperial traits not only in the obvious literary canon (Kipling and Conrad), but also in earlier authors (Austen, Charlotte Brontë, Dickens). Said was not the first to make this point (see e.g. Raskin's (1971) *The mythology of imperialism*), but his work has led to a growing awareness of how imperialism was whitewashed out of domestic British history. The implication of this is that we should re-read the geography curriculum and its supporting texts and resources as sources of ethnocentric and racist ideas.

However, according to Bernard Porter's (2004) *The absent-minded imperialists*, we should be careful about drawing too straight a line between texts that supposedly contained these values and their reception. Whereas Mackenzie and Said tended to see imperialism as saturating the whole of British society and culture, Porter disputes the evidence for this. For the majority of Britons, imperialism was not overtly part of their world view (which is not to argue that they did not benefit from it).

Porter argues that, until the 1880s, there was little evidence for imperial propaganda and its effectiveness. He notes that although many hundreds of textbooks were published, and that this alone can give the impression that they were influential, such texts were rarely used in state schools. At best, such textbooks were evidence of how the empire was presented to *some* mainly middle-class children. But, Porter concludes, few textbooks written before the 1880s devoted much space to empire, and almost none of them held up the empire as a source of pride. A geography textbook of 1863, for example, tells readers that British colonization has 'not been an unmixed good – oppression, corruption and even devastation having been in many cases the consequence to the savage races (sic) of the approach of the whites' (Bray, 1863, cited in Porter, 2004: 69). Porter even argues that most geography schoolbooks prior to 1880 made a conscious effort to be non-racist. The reason is that empire was not (yet) a central theme in these books: the main narrative was the growth of peace and freedom in Britain from feudal times to the present day.

Working-class children were never exposed to the ideas found in these textbooks. Patriotism was never taught, since the subjects that could have supported it were absent from the curriculum. Where geography was taught, it was 'deliberately parochialized'. Geographical Readers felt no need to inform children of life beyond the rural scene. Even London – the imperial capital – was presented as a place best avoided. Porter (2004) summarizes,

> Some schools may have had globes or maps, but we have seen that those great world maps with empire proudly marked out in red that are supposed to have hung on nearly every classroom wall in Victorian times are a myth. (208)

Porter does acknowledge that, from the 1880s, as Britain sought to maintain its empire, there was a heightened 'jingoism' reflected in both popular and educational texts. The 'Mackenzie–Porter' debate has some important implications for how we think about the production and dissemination of geographical knowledge in recent calls to decolonize geography. As Sanghera (2021) comments, 'Just because something happened in 1787 and 2019 doesn't *prove* that the former caused the latter' (emphasis in original; 21). The 'Mackenzie–Porter debate' reveals the challenges in being able to make sense of 'difficult history'. Even though we could never prove that school geography teaching caused racist imaginaries or behaviour, it is highly likely that it was one part of the cultural climate in which it was assumed that Britain had a right to dominion over people in other lands. Ploszajska's (2000) study of the visual imagery used in school geography textbooks and sources in the teaching of Australia is useful methodologically. It highlights the fact that, on its own, any single resource is unlikely to prove imperialist ideology, but when viewed as part of an ensemble of imagery and signs, and part of a larger set of cultural discourses, the overall effect of school geography was to promote British superiority. What we cannot know is how such texts were actually read (Driver, 2001).

On one level, this may seem like an archaic debate. However, it has important implications for any understanding of how race and racism are reflected in school geography. In *The white man's world*, Bill Schwarz (2011) works backwards from Enoch Powell's incendiary speech in Birmingham in 1968. He shows how the reaction to this speech drew upon a structure of feeling that was rooted in memories of empire. These were part of an informal culture shaped by the period of imperial expansion and particularly the settlement of white Britons in places such as Canada, Australia, New Zealand and South Africa. What is particularly interesting for geography teaching is that at the very moment when these arguments were coming to the fore in the national political sphere – 'the end of empire' – school geography was busily involved in ridding itself of its association with imperialism. This was not an explicit 'policy', but one affected through the move away from regional geography and descriptive accounts of areas and nations, towards a new 'scientific' geography concerned with patterns and measurement. It is therefore ironic that, as the empire came home, and in the midst of migration to Britain from its former colonies, geography teachers appeared to avoid studying these places. Avoiding this difficult history and politics was possible because of the adoption of a more technocratic geography and an abstract view of geographical space. This is explored in the next section.

## Unmasking Technocratic Geography Education

Tomlinson (1989) concluded that the imperial view persisted in many history and geography textbooks 'until changes in approach, content and methods in the subjects developed in the 1960s' (34). Similarly, Bill Marsden (2001) noted that grotesque stereotypes of foreigners have a long history in geography education and that although by the 1960s the more pernicious stereotypes had generally been excised, more subtle ones persisted. This suggests a qualitative shift in representation occurred as a response to curriculum change, reflected in broader themes addressed earlier in this book, such as

- the growth in the amount of and organization of knowledge;
- new understandings of the processes and consequences of teaching and learning; and
- rapid social and cultural change.

Rational curriculum planning, imported via the United States and drawing upon developments in educational psychology and theories of learning, ensured that curriculum selection was to be informed by the needs of the child (albeit a 'universal' child, assumed to be growing up in a white, middle-class, nuclear family). At the same time, many geography educationalists and teachers were keen to apply the insights of the 'new geography' associated with the statistical and quantitative revolution. These innovations dovetailed neatly, and resulted, in the mid-1970s, in three books that defined 'modern school geography'. These were Norman Graves's (1979) *Curriculum planning in geography*, Bill Marsden's (1976) *Evaluating the geography curriculum* and David Hall's (1976) *Geography and the geography teacher*. They condensed approaches that were informing the curriculum projects reshaping school geography teaching and given official recognition in publications such as *New ideas in the teaching of geography* (DES, 1972).

Thus, geography as a school subject was being remade during the 1970s through the twin processes of intellectual developments in the discipline and curriculum theory. During this optimistic, technocratic period, there was a strong commitment to a liberal humanist perspective on knowledge and the curriculum (we discuss this in more detail in Chapter 6). Geographical knowledge was regarded as politically neutral. It was assumed to describe – and explain – the world as it was. In many of the 'new' geography texts of this period, we encounter little *overt* racism, just the strong urge to be modern and rational. Positivism, associated with the 'quantitative revolution' and the new geography, was readily adopted because it was aligned with the scientific method that appeared to provide geography with objectivity and intellectual weight. As Brown (1985, cited in Dale, Robinson, and Fergusson [1988]) noted, 'In a world where British influence is conspicuously waning it might not be in the interests of a secure national identity to throw it open for young Britons to gaze on' (222).

The combined belief in science and liberal humanism of many leading geography educators ensured that geography education offered a particular ideological view of the world. This enabled the world of geography education to insulate itself from the wider strains of progressivism and radicalism that came to play an important role in educational debates in the 1970s and early 1980s (Jones, 1983). In school geography, the various Schools Council projects of the 1970s had led to the emergence of a technocratic elite within university departments of education and the GA (Huckle, 1985). This was evident in the establishment of a serious geographical education research community which sought to provide teachers with a sounder rationale and method for teaching geography.

In a later reflection, Marsden (1995) remarked on the fact that his 1976 book was written without any reference or acknowledgement of the so-called Black Papers[1] which were reorienting educational debate at the time. It is also hard to find, in the body of literature around geography teaching, any sustained engagement with the changing ideas about race and education we discussed in Chapter 3. Thus, at the moment when the Notting Hill Carnival was erupting into violence, and relations between Black youth and the police were at a low ebb, geography educators appear to have had little to say. For instance, John Hall's *London: Metropolis and region* was published in 1976 and left it to the very last paragraph of its 1978 reprint to make this elliptical remark:

> The profit and loss account of London's mood shows wide variations: an estimated 20 million visitors during Jubilee year, 1977; ugly scenes as carnival turned pillage in Notting Hill in 1976.

His later book, *Metropolis now*, written with sixth formers in mind, hardly expands on this observation (Hall, 1990).

It is unfair to single out any one text. Hicks's (1981b) survey of geography textbooks on the British Isles confirmed the reluctance of geography's gatekeepers to deal with the reality of a multicultural society. Hicks suggested three ways such textbooks might attempt to reflect the development of multicultural Britain. First, in dealing with ports, there could be reference to the ways in which the growth of Bristol and Liverpool were based on the proceeds of the slave trade and Britain's colonial past. Second, in terms of studying areas of the country, minoritized groups should be mentioned when dealing with West Yorkshire or the Midlands, whether

---

[1]The Black Papers were a series of articles on British education, published from 1969 to 1977 in the *Critical Quarterly*. They attacked the supposed excesses of progressive education at the time, and their name was intended as a contrast to government White Papers.

talking about employment or housing patterns. Third, as part of population studies, there could be reference to the migration of peoples into and out of the country.

Four of the fourteen textbooks Hicks analysed made no mention of immigration, and of those that did, only two dealt with the issue at any length. Thus, one had a section titled 'Immigrants from Overseas' that looked at phases of immigration into Britain, at population figures and distribution in relation to the major conurbations. The section finishes,

> In these areas, a linked series of social problems is to be found, not only questions of colour-prejudice, but also of language difficulties, cultural differences, multi occupation of houses, educational disadvantage and unemployment. In times of boom, unskilled coloured workers 'fill in the gaps'. In times of slump, they are the first to be made redundant. (Marsden, 1978, cited in Hicks, 1981: 67)

The other text stood out in having nearly two double page spreads on 'Migration into the UK'. These discussed why in-migrants often settle in places where previous migrants have settled. Population figures were examined for the country as a whole and in particular for the wards of Bradford and Ealing. Students were asked to find out the meaning of words such as 'culture' and 'integration', and it was pointed out that where people live is a geographical reason that contributed to racial tension.

The section finished,

> There are differences between people, it is no use pretending there are not. But the differences of each group from white English people, and from each other, are very valuable. They need to be preserved and used for the development of society as a whole. And remember, 'society' is not all the same. It is now, and has long been, culturally, racially and socially mixed. This mixture can be both a strength and a weakness. It is up to you to see that it is the strength that is encouraged. (Turner, 1976, cited in Hicks, 1981: 67)

Hicks concluded,

> Such is the total contribution of these books on the geography of the British Isles to multicultural understanding. They largely reflect the view of traditional geographers who see multicultural Britain as outside the boundaries of school geography. (Hicks, 1981: 67)

There were some 'outliers'. In an article in *Teaching Geography*, David McEvoy (1983) recommended a field work exercise in which students identify 'Asian' surnames in order to map the distribution of migrant groups and measure levels of segregation. Despite the obvious difficulties and issues raised in such an exercise, this was an attempt to recognize the UK's changing social geography:

> It is appreciated that discussion of such issues among teenagers could easily escalate into ill-informed allegations of a racist nature. The teacher will need to carefully consider his or her own position before broaching the subject. However, geography has reached a stage where ethical and value judgements cannot be

avoided. This is as true of purely urban issues as it is of environmental concerns. If geography avoids contentious areas it will suffer justifiable encroachment by other disciplines. (102)

Notable outliers notwithstanding, our discussion so far suggests that 'new' school geography was contained within the 'white racial frame'. In all these texts, it was assumed that the reader is a white, 'indigenous' Briton. The main approach was to ignore race; but if it could not be avoided, race was constructed as a 'problem' to be solved (Leach, 1973).

If, in geography texts, race was confined to a view of 'problem people' living in 'problem places' within Britain, a similar view was extended to the ways in which school geography represented 'distant lands'. The twenty-five years after the Second World War had seen the publication of numerous bulky, regional geographies of the non-Western world. These were related to Britain's own histories but there had been little methodological advance in these 'colonial geographies', which, apart from anything else, were often 'dreary' (Power, 2000). As we have seen, in the 1960s, geography underwent the shift from regional descriptive approach to a systematic scientific subject. Fundamentally, regional approaches were seen as focusing on unique 'features' and thus failed to identify more general rules and processes, such as those governing economic development, for example. In the face of these criticisms, geographers became increasingly interested in advancing general models of development underpinned by ideas of modernization.

Despite these changes, the claim that geography was the 'world subject' was hard to sustain. For instance, the GA convened a working party on teaching about the geography of the 'Third World' in 1974.[2] It reported that it was very hard to identify schoolteachers who were much involved in teaching critically about the 'Third World'. Those who did were likely to do so as result of their own experiences and travels. David Wright pointed out that at 'O' Level (the examination taken by sixteen-year-olds which was replaced by GCSE in 1988), the University of London Examination Board required that students study either North America or Europe, or what Wright termed 'rich, white areas'. The Cambridge Board had introduced a unit with the title 'Africa south of the Sahara', which attracted less than one percent of candidates. Of students studying geography at Goldsmith's college in 1970, most students had studied only 'rich, white countries', and only one of twenty-three booklets in the GA's *Teaching Geography* series focused on the so-called 'Third World'. The working party report concluded that geography teachers should give thought to the implications of being in a multicultural society. It noted that the Schools Council had been funding and supporting projects on this theme but that the contribution so far of geographers to this major issue has been minimal.

All this was occurring while much of the 'developing world' was undergoing significant changes and, in many cases, political turmoil. However, geographers had

---

[2] One of us (Lambert) was invited to serve on a subsequent group convened in 1981 (Bale, 1983) by which time the GA was concerned to investigate the relationship between geography and development education.

little to say about these issues, and school geography failed to respond to the challenges posed by the formal process of decolonization and critiques of Development. This was part of a wider problem: geographers working in the so-called developing world tended to operate with an atheoretical 'empiricism'. They were adept at providing detailed descriptions of features of individual societies, but less inclined to link what was happening to broader models of an uneven and unequal world. Thus, geography teaching about the so-called Third World suffered from two main problems. First was the tendency to approach places as 'exotic', with a focus on the colourful, the bizarre and a tourist's eye view. Second was the tendency to descend into various forms of encyclopaedism, with the tracing and colouring of maps, the copying into exercise books of large amounts of reference material and the listing of towns, products and population statistics (Storm, 1975).

School geography appeared to be unable to accommodate itself to important global shifts, notably the existence of an interlinked global economy and the end of the long post–Second World War economic boom, which had promised to level up economic growth but which had faltered and led to acknowledgement of 'rich world and poor world' as an issue (Merriam, 1973).

These issues presented challenges for school geography. The field of World Studies was expanding (supported by a Labour government that sought to convince the public of the benefits that would come from increased overseas aid). This movement encouraged the development of issues-based approaches to teaching and experiential learning techniques. The work of non-governmental organizations lobbying for change in the curriculum and producing resources for teachers was increasingly influential. In short, alternative approaches in the form of Third World Studies, global education and World Studies challenged the tendency of the academic curriculum to avoid questions of politics (Dufour, 1988). An important strand of this work was multicultural and anti-racist education, and this came to a head with the eruption of a bitter argument about racism in school geography textbooks and examination syllabuses. We address this in the next section.

## Racist Society: Racist Geography?

Throughout the 1970s, school geography slowly responded to the changing social and educational contexts. Approaches to teaching and learning were modernized, and attempts were made to ensure curriculum content was 'relevant'. However, the subject was quite resistant to attempts to reform the curriculum to reflect contemporary political issues. As the political mood shifted to the right and the post–Second World War social settlement disintegrated, there were moves, in some parts of the education system, to respond. The rise of the National Front (which sought to use schools to recruit members), the continued stand-off between Black youth and the police, racism on the football terraces and the urban disturbances of 1980 and 1981 provided the backdrop against which some teachers sought to 'challenge racism' in schools. In 1981, the Inner London Education Authority (ILEA) began consulting about school achievement and found evidence that the black communities demanded unequivocally anti-racist policy.

This was the backdrop for the GYSL (*Geography for the Young School Leaver*) affair (as it has come to be known), which was a defining moment in the development of arguments about race and racism in school geography. It came at a time when the UK state was seeking to deal with the fact of immigration and the rise of a strong Black political formation (Troyna and Carrington, 1990). The government-funded Schools Council sponsored a project called Education for a Multiracial Society between 1973 and 1976, but in 1978 rejected the project's report on the grounds that it 'made too much of racism and was unnecessarily critical of schools and teachers for their inaction' (Jeffcoate, 1984: xi). The Schools Council eventually published a version of the report in 1981, which *omitted the section on racism*.

Dawn Gill, a geography teacher, had written an MA thesis on textbooks used at O Level in Geography syllabuses. Subsequently, she was commissioned by the Schools Council to enquire into how the assessment system at sixteen could be improved for ethnic minority students. She argued that

> examination courses which ensure better grades for non-whites will not necessarily have any effect on discrimination in employment. Unless there is an attempt in schools to educate against racism the result of ensuring that examinations better serve the needs of ethnic minority candidates could be an increased percentage of overqualified, unemployed or poorly paid non-white people. (1982: 5)

She argued that racism, not formal educational qualifications, was the main determinant of life chances for black students. She concluded that the geography syllabuses she studied, including the Schools Council's flagship qualification, the GYSL, were racist. Her report pulled no punches:

> If the National Front wants a training course which fosters racist attitudes amongst its new recruits, it could be argued that it need look no further than the geography curricula in [London's] schools. (Gill, 1982:16)

Gill argued that anti-racist educators should uncover the extent to which school syllabuses and resources incorporate and perpetuate racist assumptions.

Gill located her work firmly within the theoretical framework of anti-racist education (as opposed to multicultural education) as set out in Chapter 3. The following passage might still be used to test geography's commitment to addressing racism:

> It [Geography] tends to use explanatory frameworks which fail to mention the trade relationships between first and third world as a reason for the relative poverty of the latter; it presents the notion that third world peoples are responsible for their own poverty and thus implicitly supports the view that they are ignorant or stupid; population growth, if mentioned in the texts at all, is rarely linked explicitly with

levels of economic development – more often with hints that the uneducated are failing to use contraceptives; developing countries are presented as places which are important only because they provide us with certain commodities; urbanization is considered a major problem – its cause, immigration into cities; immigration is presented as an important cause of inner city decline. (Gill, 1982: 16)

The Schools Council declined to publish Gill's report. However, the Institute of Education produced two 'working papers', and the Commission for Racial Equality (CRE) sponsored a conference (held in 1982) titled, 'Geography Education for a Multicultural Society', which was used as a launch pad for a new journal, *Contemporary Issues in Geography and Education*. One of the reasons that Gill's report caused controversy within geography education was that it challenged many of the 'progressive' new directions in geographical education discussed in the previous section. The GYSL 14–16 framework was a flagship syllabus because of its mix of relevant and contemporary content, rational curriculum planning and progressive pedagogy. Indeed, it was seen as the Schools Council's 'jewel in the crown' with widespread take-up in schools.

The GYSL project was strongly informed by developments within the subject as a whole, particularly the critiques that were made of positivist approaches. The titles of the units for the GYSL indicate what 'relevance' meant in the minds of the curriculum team – *Man, Land and Leisure*; *People, Places and Work*; *Cities and People*. Behavioural and humanistic geographies, which offered ideas about individuals' mental maps, perceptions and values, chimed well with many teachers working in schools in urban and suburban settings experiencing economic and demographic change. There were radical new ways on offer such as (urban) 'streetwork' developed by Fyson and Ward, members of the Town and Country Planning Association's Education Unit (Fyson and Ward, 1973), rather than (rural) 'fieldwork'. Later iterations of GYSL materials incorporated ideas from 'welfare geography', concerned with the question of *Who gets what, where, and how*? (Parsons, 1987).

To date, the most extensive published commentary on the 'GYSL affair' is found in Rex Walford's (2001) *Geography in British Schools*. This response points to some of the ways in which issues of race and racism in school geography were interpreted by influential individuals and organizations. Rather than acknowledge and address an inconvenient or uncomfortable challenge, legitimate arguments were discounted from a lofty position of 'authority', drawing on mature experience and established wisdom.

The first tendency in Walford's account is *puzzlement*. In a number of statements, Walford seems to imply that he doesn't quite grasp what is being argued, despite accepting that there were some 'constructive' elements to the report. Similarly, he found that the cartoon on the cover enigmatically 'seems to make a sharp comment'. We have reproduced that cartoon here (Figure 5.1), and it makes a direct and clear point: that geography in schools had failed to make the link with Britain's imperial past.

Figure 5.1 Front cover of the conference proceedings

The second tendency is to focus on *style of argument*: style rather than substance. All the controversy, Walford implied, was unnecessary, as Gill's final conclusion was 'quite moderate'. Her main concern was that poor published teaching resources were being used without question, a point 'which might well have been acknowledged and accepted' if it had been offered in a 'less confrontational' way. This is an attempt to take the heat out of the argument and maintain the status quo of rational and reasoned debate. After all, the GYSL team had acknowledged 'gauche errors' of language in their early worksheets.

Thirdly, there is the charge of *politicization*. Walford argues that the GYSL affair was complicated by the wider issues with Gill and colleagues brought to the analysis of materials. A set of six newer textbooks from GYSL were criticized because they presented 'the current system of power relationships – globally and nationally ... as natural and inevitable'. The effect of this was to widen the educational arguments beyond an in-house debate about teaching resources to include political ideology. For Walford, this 'heavy political baggage' was counterproductive in producing educational change.

Finally, Walford's commentary sees the approach adopted by Gill as misguided, taking some 'curious' strategic directions such as the establishment of an alternative association and journal. He suggests they would have been better to become involved with the well-established GYSL project (as they were invited to), and with the GA, whose much larger membership and substantial infrastructure of committees and salaried administrators could have provided fertile ground for Gill and colleagues, armed as they were with 'enthusiasm and purpose'.

In response, the GA set up a 'working party' on multicultural education which reported in 1985. According to Walford (who led the working party), the report *Geography education in a multicultural society* brought 'a calmer tone to the rather frenetic arguments' which characterized the GYSL affair, bringing us back to a framework of progressive liberalism:

> When the working party began its task, it was already aware that there was no lack of source material on the topic of multi-cultural education in general. The field was crowded, not to say confused, with many voices, and even at the level of semantics (for example 'multi-cultural or multi-ethnic education?', 'racism or racialism'?) there was disagreement ... The Working Party read and considered a range of this material before embarking on this work. (Walford, 1985: 6)

Thus, although the working party acknowledged the controversies taking place as it was doing its work, it did not focus on the *actual debate*. For example, it did not explain *its* choice of terminology: this is a significant omission for, as we argued in Chapter 3, the terms chosen reflect underlying theories of race and education.

The report was an attempt to close down the issue of race and racism in geography teaching as quickly and fully as possible. There was self-interest in this. The Conservative governments of the time were planning the introduction of a national curriculum, and it was far from clear that geography would be included. Downplaying controversy and avoiding politics would have appeared sensible to those involved in creating *A Case for geography* (Bailey and Binns, 1987).

Writing in 2022, the GYSL affair seems like a classic case of 'institutional racism'. It was part of a long-standing tendency for influential geography educators to avoid the politics of school knowledge and the curriculum. For example, Boardman (1985) cites Gill's work, but only to reproduce figures on the number of schools and students taking up the course. He saw no need to acknowledge Gill's arguments about the need to educate young people about race.

It is also worth considering that there was a 'geographical' element to this. Bonnett's (1993) study of anti-racist education suggested that there was a distinct geography of anti-racism in Britain in the early 1980s, which was linked to the differential experience of 'crisis'. Teachers always have to work within a set of contradictions. They are responsible both for the progress of individual students and for the collective reproduction of society. They work within institutions that may talk about equality of opportunity but in practice operate in ways that discriminate. At moments of crisis, these contradictions may present themselves as challenges to the professional image of the teacher. In teacher interviews, Bonnett found that those working in inner London schools were more likely to adopt more radical forms of anti-racist practice, whereas those teachers working in 'white' areas were more likely to accept the ideas of multicultural education. This, Bonnett suggested, was a response to the depth of the crisis, and it helps us to understand something of the GA Working Party's response: racism, and the politicalized response to it, was seen as a 'London thing', far removed from the experience of the vast majority of members of the GA. Anecdotally, we can agree with this, and it forms a telling backdrop to the reflections Lambert provides on his time as Chief Executive on the GA (see Box 5.2).

## After GYSL

Following the arguments about multicultural education and anti-racist geography teaching in the 1980s, the issue largely disappeared from the agenda. The final act in the 1980s was Peter Jackson's article in *Geography* in 1988, 'Beneath the headlines: racism and reaction in contemporary Britain'. Jackson attempted to tread a pathway between the GA's 'liberalism' and Gill and colleagues' 'radicalism'. He proposed a strategy for anti-racist teaching through the analysis of media representations. This paper accompanied his chapter on the 'Languages of racism' in *Maps of meaning* (see Chapter 4, Box 4.2). The paper recognized that newspaper articles were an important source for the study of contemporary issues in geography classrooms but that there was a need to read 'beneath the headlines'. For this we need theory. Jackson stressed the importance of recognizing the historical basis of racism in Britain. In particular, how race relations have tended to be framed by the idea of black people as a 'problem', as a 'pathology'. He asked how representations of the black presence have changed in light of the urban 'riots' of 1980, 1981 and 1985 (see Box 4.2).

Jackson's article appeared in the same year as the Education Reform Act (1988). Brought in under a Conservative government, it was shaped in part by concerns to restore tradition and fears about a perceived loss of social order and control. The new national curriculum was one part of this. Kenneth Baker wrote in the *Times Educational Supplement*,

> I see the national curriculum as a way of increasing our social coherence. There is so much distraction, variety and uncertainty in the modern world that in our country today our children are in danger of losing a sense at all, common culture and a common heritage. The cohesive role of the national curriculum will provide our society with a greater sense of identity. (Baker, 1987, n.p., cited in Sarup [1996: 140])

Critics saw the national curriculum as reflecting an imperialist and Eurocentric concept of a static Anglo-Saxon culture – which in fact no longer existed. They worried that a national curriculum would become a nationalist curriculum (e.g. Sarup, 1996). This is a theme that continues to reverberate through discussions about the school geography curriculum, from the School Curriculum and Assessment Authority chief executive Nick Tate's calls for a British geography in the mid-1990s, through the Ajegbo report of 2007, to the Sewell Report's (2021) call for a common curriculum.

## The False Dawn of 'Cultural Understanding and Diversity'

The National Curriculum sought to ensure common practice across schools. The subject working groups were instructed to ensure that a focus on cultural diversity permeated their work. Multicultural education was one of five cross-curricular themes. We do not revisit the arguments about the National Curriculum, other than to note that there were concerns that the content would seek to reinstate an imagined geography of former national glory. In line with the 'official' policy set down by the Swann Report, the 1990 'National Curriculum for Geography' contained a relatively benign statement about geography education for all students irrespective of their ethnic background. The main concern at the time was that the curriculum risked underplaying the UK's role as part of Europe. Indeed, Rabbett (1993), in his role as a local authority advisor, considered that

> history and geography have, traditionally, made a significant multicultural contribution to the curriculum, but they have both fared badly in the process of drafting NC subject reports. It is curriculum content which is at stake and the desire to re-establish a greater focus on Britain and its history … produced a sharp division between European and non-European areas of study. (13)

This assessment came in an edited collection that sought deliberately to move beyond what its editors saw as the acrimonious arguments and debates of the 1980s and use the national curriculum as a means to provide education for cultural diversity (Fyfe and Figueroa, 1993). This tone was adopted by geography teacher Geoff Dinkele (1993) in his chapter 'Geography and Multicultural Education'. Dinkele saw the Final Report for National Curriculum Geography (DES, 1990) as a culmination and distillation of a series of official curriculum documents that pointed towards the importance of multicultural education. The purpose of multicultural education must be to increase pupils' understanding of other people, places and cultures – the assumed key to overcoming prejudice. To this end, Dinkele (1993) welcomed the emergence of humanistic geography in which the focus is on 'people's feelings, perceptions, experiences and fear – in other words, personal and private geographies' (170). He took his cue from John Fien's (1983) elaboration of 'confluent education', in which attention is paid to both the cognitive and affective domains, an approach advocated by Frances Slater in her influential book *Learning through geography* (Slater, 1982). Interestingly, one of Fien's examples was of the St Pauls riot in Bristol in 1980:

| Cognitive domain | Abstract cognitive | Ethnic segregation in the inner city and the problems of living in such areas |
| | Straight cognitive | Case study of the geographical background to the St Pauls riot in 1980 |
| Affective domain | Abstract affective | How did the people of St Pauls respond? What made them respond in this way? Were their actions effective? To what ends? |
| | Straight affective | How would I have responded if I lived in St Pauls? How would I react to situations in which I feel the system had trapped me? |

The idea of confluent education is to acknowledge and develop both the cognitive and affective domains of learning. For Dinkele, it was important to stress the humanistic elements of teaching about themes and places, and his chapter provided examples of teaching about values and beliefs. This was similar to Johnston's (1986) formulation of geographical knowledge contributing to 'mutual understanding'. The goal of such knowledge is to break down purified identities and stereotypes by making people aware of people with different experiences and backgrounds and helping them to understand how the world looks from their standpoint.

However, while Johnston deemed mutual understanding a desirable part of geographical education, it would not necessarily lead to emancipation and social transformation. That would involve 'revealing to individuals, and thus to societies as a whole, the forces that underpin how their own and other societies operate' (Johnston, 1986: 121). This is what makes geography teaching such a challenge, since these forces are not directly observable. For example, you cannot observe the laws of capital accumulation (just as you cannot observe the law of gravity). The challenge is to construct adequate theories of how the world works, and perhaps the first task of education for emancipation is ideology critique and an analysis of power. We discuss these issues in detail in the following chapter.

## Macpherson and After

The New Labour government reviewed the national curriculum in 1999, leading to the introduction of 'citizenship' as a foundation subject at Key Stages 3 and 4. Citizenship sought to promote students' political and economic literacy through learning about the economy and democratic institutions, 'with respect for its [Britain's] varying, national, religious and ethnic identities'. In the same year, the MacPherson report into the murder of the black teenager Stephen Lawrence concluded that the London Metropolitan police force was institutionally racist. As a result, the issue of race and racism – and equalities education more generally – appeared to be back on the educational agenda (e.g. Hill and Cole, 1999).

Many of the texts written to support these goals were organized thematically rather than by curriculum subject. Dave Hill and Mike Cole's (1999) *Promoting equality in secondary schools* was an exception. Dawn Gill wrote the chapter on school geography. It was effectively a restatement of her work from the 1980s. Gill continued to see potential racism at almost every point of the national curriculum. Because of Britain's history as a colonizing power, geography was inextricably linked with the history of racism and the white exploitation of black people in the developing global economy.

> If we were to study the global distribution of infant mortality [for example] and to examine the processes ... we would [find] exploitation of the poor by the rich, unequal trade relationships, racism, sexual oppression, the exploitation of children ... where racism, class inequalities and sexual oppression are woven into the very fabric of the global economy. (Gill, 1999: 161–2)

Gill's approach in 1999 shows strong continuities with her 1980s work. It is firmly set in Johnston's idea of education as emancipation. However, at the time we were preparing our 2001 article on 'Race, education and geography' for *Geography*, we found this theoretical approach seemingly out of step with developments in the study of the geographies of race and racism. Gill's analysis tended to see geographical patterns as reflective of social power, as if there were a one-way relationship between society and space. Gill insisted that such patterns could only be explained through an understanding of social processes, which requires 'theory', and she was critical of what counted for theory in school geography. However, when it came to providing alternative theories on which a critical geographical education might be constructed, Gill's chapter came up short. This is principally because the complexity of what human geographers called the 'sociospatial dialectic' was missing. As we suggested in Chapter 4, in the late 1980s and into the 1990s, British human geography had developed a more nuanced account of the racialization of space. Note, this is not to criticize Gill, but to make a more general point that, during the 1990s, geography educators in schools had made few advances in moving beyond 'rationalist' approaches to anti-racist education that saw racism as a matter of 'false consciousness'. Late-twentieth-century anti-racism seemed attached to the assumption that anti-racism was rational in comparison with the racist individual or subject (deemed to be irrational and wrong-headed). This is tantamount to saying that racism can be *corrected* simply by introducing an alternative set of images and ideas (see Rattansi, 2007). In the absence of theory, the tendency was to fall back on calls for geography teachers to adopt a moral stance in their teaching (e.g. 'geography teachers should …' or 'geography teachers must …'). Such an approach leads to charges of propaganda and indoctrination.

In many ways, Gill's 1999 position was reflective of a wider debate about anti-racism on the British political left. One approach is represented by the work of Phil Cohen, an educator working at the intersection of cultural studies and cultural geography. Cohen argued that

> presenting the true historical facts about Empire, explaining the different structural causes of unemployment and immigration, demonstrating the processes of unequal exchange between European countries in the Third World, all this is supposed to enable students to break with racist commonsense and adopt more enlightened positions. (1998: 157)

The result, he suggests is that

> antiracism is therefore all too easily recruited to the traditional remit of the civilizing mission of education. This can lead to a kind of blindness about how young people themselves make sense of the anti-racist message, how its hidden curriculum is read and reworked through young people's own cultural understandings. It is as if what was taught was entirely transparent, and simply presented an alternative, better and more enlightened view of the world. (1998: 157)

The danger, Cohen argued, is that a 'common-sense' understanding of racism (i.e. that it is a form of irrational prejudice, ignorance or superstition) can lead to the assumption that it is a defining characteristic of the more backward, deprived and less-educated members of society. Another widely held assumption was that some white working-class children simply echoed their parents' beliefs, which were in turn a reiteration of what they got from the mass media (here we are reminded of Tomlinson's comment about 'disturbing the sediment' and the role that such 'images' played in the Brexit vote). Cohen argues that what underpins both accounts is the idea that reason and progressive values are the prerogative of the educated classes and that unreason is a lot of everyone else. The political and pedagogical implications of Cohen's position are not straightforward, since they appear to suggest that 'simply' presenting the 'facts' about racism is unlikely to change attitudes and behaviours. This is because these are complex psychic investments. This was a position that interested the late Stuart Hall, leading him to engage with the complex cultural geographies of race and nation. Against this, commentators associated with the Institute of Race Relations such as Ambar Sivanandan and Jenny Bourne were concerned that this ceded too much to racism (and that the prospects for anti-racist practice were limited if racism was locked up on the mind).

It is important to note that there was little evidence of these debates and arguments in school geography in Britain at the time. In our attempt to engage with these issues (Morgan and Lambert, 2001), and in the subsequent booklet in the GA's *Theory into practice* series (Morgan and Lambert, 2003), we stated from the outset our commitment to 'the idea that "race" and "nation" are social constructions rather than naturally occurring phenomena' (9). This work sought to develop some of the ideas contained in the publication of *Constructions of place, race and nation* (Jackson and Penrose, 1993). Our book took this as its starting point and attempted to 'deconstruct' racial categories in common geographical texts and topics. In Box 5.1 we provide an illustration of this. We present this material not as examples of 'finished work', but as an attempt to reorient debates within the field.

## Box 5.1 Examples of Deconstructive Pedagogy

In our 2003 book, we stated, 'Adopting a social constructionist position in geography teaching suggests that we need to resist any form of teaching and learning that leaves students with the idea that patters of segregation or inequality based on "race" are fixed immutable and unchanging' (9).

http://www.geography.org.uk/download/GA_TIPPlaceRaceandTeachingGeographySample.pdf. This is what we mean by adopting 'deconstructive pedagogies'. Here is an example of the implications of this approach.

### Does Britain Have Ghettos?

A useful way into developing knowledge and understanding of issues of 'diversity' is for teachers to explore the question 'Does Britain have ghettos?' This was the title of an article by Ceri Peach in the *Transactions of the Institute of British Geographers* (1996). One of the advantages of this approach is that it allows for a consideration of the 'facts' of ethnic concentration in Britain. Teachers can be encouraged to seek out more recent treatments of these issues in the light of the 2001 Census. (Note: There have been two Census years since we wrote this – in 2011 and 2021.)

The 'measurement' of ethnic diversity can form the basis for discussion. For instance,

- What are the limitations of using statistics to gain an overview of issues of 'diversity'?
- Does possession of the 'facts' necessarily lead to changes in pupils' perceptions of issues of diversity?
- How do teachers handle the 'objective' knowledge alongside the 'subjective' experience of diversity?
- How might the 'voice' of diverse groups in society be heard in geography classrooms?

### Unsettling Geography

The previous activity allowed teachers to develop their knowledge and understanding of a 'social scientific' approach to issues of race and racism. This activity was designed to help them explore the implications of different ways of understanding diversity. (Note: Writing the materials now we would be a lot more circumspect about the language: 'diversity' is a term that needs to be problematized, at least in the way it can be used in a way that dilutes or diverts attention away from racism).

Teachers undertake readings of the representation of issues of 'race' and ethnicity in school geography textbooks. Examples of the types of approaches they can use are found in 'Theory into practice: place, "race" and teaching geography' (an extract can be downloaded at http://www.geography.org.uk/download/GA_TIPPlaceRaceandTeachingGeographySample.pdf).

### Black Britain: A Geographical Perspective

A final activity that will allow geography teachers to explore issues of race and racism is suggested by Paul Gilroy's book *Black Britain* (2007). This is a pictorial history of black settlement in Britain, based on photographs published in British newspapers and magazines. Because these photographs were taken for commercial purposes (to inform a largely white public of the 'problem' of black settlement in Britain), they provide a fascinating index of the changing attitudes to 'diversity'.

Stuart Hall's introduction to the book (and Gilroy's accompanying essay) raises interesting questions about representation. In particular, Hall asks readers to think about the places and spaces that frame the people in the photographs. This is a useful way to read the photographic record and leads to questions about the changing geographies of settlement.

Hall's introduction to the book was published as an article in *The Guardian* and can be accessed at http://www.guardian.co.uk/uk/2007/oct/15/britishidentity.race

Looking back, we can discern that our approach was a reflection of a wider intellectual mood in geography and beyond. Throughout the 1980s and 1990s, it was clear that the economic, social, political and cultural contours of 'the UK space' were changing and that geography as an academic discipline was coming to terms, albeit in uneven and complex ways, with the 'transformation of Britain'. Although we now know that this was a failed transformation (signified by the Brexit vote and its aftermath), there was at the time a sense that school geography would be compelled to come to terms with the new perspectives that were being touted. Things seemed more fluid, provisional and open to change. This was reflected in our co-authored (Morgan and Lambert, 2005) book *Geography: Teaching School Subjects 11–19*, which opted for Peter Jackson's (1996) call for geographers to stop policing their own disciplinary boundaries in an 'embattled and defensive mood' (92) rather than Peter Haggett's (1996) call for a return to the 'central and cherished aspects of geographical education'

(17). We acknowledge that 'race' and racisms were absent from that book. However, the inclusion of cultural understanding and diversity as core concepts of the 2008 revision of the national curriculum ensured that we discussed race in our 2010 book *Teaching geography 11–18: a conceptual approach*.

There is little reference to debates about race and diversity in the geography education literature at this time. The appearance of the Ajegbo Report in 2007, clearly rooted in a multicultural framework and focused on 'diversity' as a virtue, was welcomed by the GA (after all, it was unusual for an official report in that it placed a novel and original priority on the school *curriculum*). Ajegbo addressed the GA annual conference and wrote an article for *Teaching Geography* (Ajegbo, 2011). However, by this time, the political mood was swinging away from diversity towards integration. As noted in Chapter 2, the early 2000s were marked by arguments that multicultural calls for diversity had 'gone too far' and that ethnic groups in Britain were leading 'parallel lives' rather than integrating into society, signalled by the Chief Executive of the CRE, Trevor Phillips's controversial statement in 2005 that Britain was 'sleepwalking to segregation'.

The argument was that British society had been too liberal, and too willing to embrace 'multiculturalism'. Policy goals focused on promoting cohesion and fostering 'British' core values, shared mores and national allegiance. These shared values would foster a sense of national identity. Schools, and the official curriculum, would be inclusive, based upon shared, fundamental values: 'Britishness' would be taught to children through the national curriculum.

## Why Is Geography So White?

This account of how the issues surrounding race and racism have waxed and waned in geography education suggests that there have been important moments when geography teaching has been subject to racialization. For most of the time though, the attention of geographers in education has been elsewhere: technology, enquiry, assessment for learning, thinking skills and so on. Thus, Eleanor Rawling's (2001) study of the changing fortunes of geography as a school subject between the 1980s and 2000 makes no reference to developing national education policy on race, multiculturalism or anti-racism. The so-called 'new agenda' for geography in the late 1990s chose citizenship, Personal, Social and Health Education (PSHE) and sustainability as its main cross-cutting concerns (GA, 2000). Acclaimed texts such as Margaret Roberts's *Enquiry through Geography* (2003, 2013) show little engagement with how race could be incorporated as part of the curriculum.[3] The latest edition (Jones, 2017) of the *Handbook of Secondary Geography* (published by

---

[3] Roberts's book encourages student teachers to find out about the demographic and ethnic composition of children in geography lessons in order to recognize and acknowledge their geographies. This is a start, but a long way from placing race and racism at the centre of curriculum development.

the GA) does not mention race and racism. Finally, Butt's (2020) exhaustive account in *Geography education research in the UK* is silent on race and racism. In making this list, we are not looking to apportion blame. However, it does suggest there is a problem. In Box 5.2, David Lambert provides a reflection of his own time as Chief Executive of the GA.

### Box 5.2 Reflections of a Former Chief Executive (David Lambert)

I was appointed Chief Executive of the GA in 2002. I was the third appointment to the role, a position which was created only in 1997. The first century or so of the GA's existence, it had been run by elected, volunteer officials and administered by a small office.

As a former secondary school geography teacher, researcher and teacher educator I was in a position to bring a broad range of perspectives to the job. This included perspectives on race and racism. Indeed, those matters in particular were on my mind:

- For example, in 2001 I had an article published in *Geography*, co-written with John Morgan (Morgan and Lambert, 2001). In this article, we attempted to review the question of racism in school geography, discussing the socially constructed nature of 'race' and drawing from geographers such as Peter Jackson and Alistair Bonnett. It was an attempt to stimulate debate.
- Furthermore, in 2002 I had a follow-up article published, based on a lecture given at the Annual Conference. In this article, I sought explicitly to discuss the space provided by geography for educating students about racism and about society scarred by the deep-seated injustices of racist outcomes. I also explicitly acknowledged that the GA itself was grossly and persistently under-representative of Black and Asian people – in its membership, its volunteer force, its trustees and leadership.
- In 2003, John Morgan and I published a booklet in the GA's *Theory in practice* series. This was an attempt further to support the debate we fervently believed the association *had yet to have* on race and racism.

If our intention really was to stimulate discussion, debate and action, we can safely say that we failed. And this was despite my influential position within the association.

### It Is Important to Identify Some Reasons Why

This does not require deep and detailed analysis – so long as it is accepted that structural racism and subtle racist practices exist and persist. For it is then clear that good intentions alone count for very little. The institution has to accept that even though it can declare that it is not racist, that it is inclusive, that it promotes equality and social justice, that geography itself is a subject that can claim to have shaken off the yoke of imperialist assumptions and practices … this all counts for nothing, if nothing changes. So, to repeat, the association (its members, its volunteers and elected leaders, those who run the journals, the quality marks, continuing professional development [CPD] and conferences) needs to *learn to talk about race and racism*. This will not just happen. It will happen only though deliberate intent.

Looking back on my ten years as Chief Executive, I conclude,

- publishing articles, reports, declarations … is necessary, but on its own insufficient to bring change;
- the right kind of articles (etc.) need to be written that challenge, engage *and* inspire action;
- questions need to be addressed:
  - What kind of issue is race and racism considered to be by the leaders of the institution (the trustees of the GA)? Is it 'core' or 'periphery'? That is, is racism a central concern in geography education, or an 'add on'?
  - What are the issues and challenges that can and are allowed to supersede race and racism, and why does this happen?

In relation to those questions, it is important to note that 'curriculum making', the valuable and now familiar concept which was developed by the GA through the Action Plan for Geography (APG) and the 2009 Manifesto (*A Different View*), failed completely to take issues of race on board (maybe, implicitly, it was considered 'periphery'). Furthermore, the enduring, core priorities of the association are 'existential' – concerning the very presence of geography in the official curriculum. It is as if this silences issues of race and racism (even though taking race seriously may ultimately be integral to the continued health of geography in the school curriculum).

As we say in Chapter 1, we hope this book will help geography education, embodied by the GA, *turn the page*. Tackling race and racism intentionally in geography will bring changes to what geography is taught (curriculum) and the way it is taught (pedagogy). In the longer term, the way geography as a school subject is perceived may also change, as will the profile of geography teachers and those who choose to study it at higher levels in school and at university. The make-up of the GA itself, through its elected officials, will also change.

All this might take some time. But such changes have to happen for geography to remain current, relevant and engaging.

It may be that we are in one of those periodic moments of racialization, with recent calls to decolonize geography teaching and recognize Black geographies. A decade of austerity in Britain since 2010, which has disproportionately impacted Black and Minority Ethnic communities, has pointed to society-wide failures to challenge institutional racism, including in geography. Black Lives Matter, formed in 2013 in the United States, has gathered momentum and been taken up in the UK through calls to 'decolonize the curriculum' (see Chapter 7). There is interest in Black Studies and scholar activism. Continuing campaigning on race and education in a series of publications from the Runnymede Trust have renewed interest in race and education and calls to teach Black history.

This has filtered into discussions of geography teaching. It is evident in the GA's conferences and publications where there is now an increased focus on questions of anti-racist approaches. Articles in *Geography* and *Teaching Geography* talk of racial capitalism, white privilege and white supremacy. The group titled Black Geographers (https://www.blackgeographers.com/) and the *Routes* journal (https://routesjournal.org/) run out of Queen Mary's (London) feed into and draw from wider discussions, such as the work of the Runnymede Trust and developments in the academic discipline. There are also cross-subject links, with, for example, the call for the Black Curriculum in history. Christine Winter (2022) has argued recently for the acknowledgement of white supremacy. In 2020, the GA itself issued a statement[4] in which it proclaims the strategic objective to 'promote greater diversity in geography education and the Association' (but interestingly, barely mentions race and racisms).

Recent moves to address issues of race and racism in geography education stress that geographical knowledge is produced in ways that are exclusionary. Thus, for example, the Decolonizing Geographers state that

> We aim to challenge the reproduction of colonial practices of knowledge in our classrooms. The Decolonising Geography website contributes to developing curricula that challenge 'universal truths' and 'objective knowledge' in geography by offering: *pedagogical techniques* to empower students to co-create knowledge and build critical geographies; a space for *critical reflection* on the content we teach in geography education; and *practical teaching resources*. (https://decolonisegeography.com/about)

Black Geographers, too, focuses on the curriculum:

> If geography teaching is not engaging with the issues Black pupils care about, including through discussing how the subject intersects with race and inequality, then it follows that few choose to continue studying it. (Black Geographers website)

Gillian Rose, writing in *Routes* in 2020, reiterated the argument about the lack of diversity in geography as a discipline. She refers to the development of feminist geography, which, in the 1980s, challenged the ways in which most geography was researched and published by men:

> The same argument applies to other kinds of social diversity, including race. If geography is being written overwhelmingly by white folk, then it's unlikely to be sufficiently attentive to issues that are felt especially keenly by many black communities. And as a result, it's not going to be very good geography. (Rose, 2020: 1)

---

[4] https://www.geography.org.uk/Announcements-and-updates/black-lives-matter (accessed 23 September 2022).

These excerpts illustrate the context in which calls to decolonize the geography curriculum have emerged in higher education and in schools. In summary, it is possible to see this moment as a potential turning point, the moment when leaders and institutions in geography education begin seriously to talk about and address issues of race and racism. It is important to note that Black in this moment is generally assumed to refer to people who are 'dark-skinned' and of African descent (Noxolo, 2022), or part of the African diaspora (Andrews and Palemer, 2016). The focus is on the process of 'learning whiteness' and how this excludes black people. To paraphrase Zara Bain (2018), geographers are being challenged to answer the question of whether the subject promotes 'white ignorance':

- The white geography curriculum *excludes* or marginalizes Black, brown and Asian scholars' perspectives. White scholarship constitutes the majority of compulsory material in courses. Textbooks tend to be written by white authors and reflect their white *normalized* view of the world.
- There is little or no acknowledgement of the significant contributions made to geography by Black geographers.
- The geography curriculum *whitewashes* and erases the role of British and European colonialism and imperialism. If colonialism and imperialism are not entirely absent from geographical narratives, their presentation tends to be framed as a project of benevolent improvement of inferior peoples. Similarly, the richness and sophistication of civilizations that the British destroyed is rarely acknowledged, let alone instances of enslavement and genocide.
- Black people are *under-represented* in academic posts at all levels of education. White, as opposed to Black, epistemic authority thus remains normalized within geography. Black scholars are forced to navigate the whiteness of geography's disciplinary communities, practices, norms and canons.

Movements such as the 'Why is my curriculum white?' campaign from UCL[5] assert that to be educated in a racialized system is to be educated into a partial world view featuring white ignorance. This must be confronted – through decolonizing the curriculum – and anything less is a capitulation to white supremacy.

## Conclusion

This chapter is a contribution to the history of knowledge of geography as a school subject. We have identified those moments when ideas about race and racism have focused the gaze of geography educationists, including teachers in schools.

---

[5] http://www.dtmh.ucl.ac.uk/videos/curriculum-white/ (accessed 23 September 2022).

We conclude this chapter as we started, just as the government presented its guidance to teachers on teaching politically controversial issues.[6] This guidance was nothing more than a restatement of existing laws and regulations on teachers' political impartiality. The Secretary of State, Nadhim Zahawi, prefaced the guidance with the comment that the curriculum offers 'an important way in which schools support pupils to become active citizens who can form their own views, whilst having an understanding and respect for legitimate differences of opinion'. While we might question what is meant by 'legitimate' – is this a coded warning that some views are out of order? – he states candidly,

> It is also important to remember that nothing in this guidance limits schools' freedom to teach about sensitive, challenging, and controversial political issues, as they consider appropriate and necessary.

So, it is 'official'; there is no reason why race and racism cannot be part of a challenging and rigorous geography education. The final section of this book focuses on the question of how geography teachers can construct the curriculum in ways that make race a continuous thread in a rigorous geographical education.

## Discussion Points

1. How important is geography's past for addressing racism in the present?
2. Has your geographical education to date prepared you to teach about race and racisms?

---

[6]https://www.gov.uk/government/publications/political-impartiality-in-schools/political-impartiality-in-schools (accessed 23 September 2022).

# 6

# Knowledge and the Geography Curriculum

## Introduction

Since this book is about how school geography can contribute to student's knowledge and understanding of race and racism, the curriculum is central to our argument. We are interested in how we can make progress towards an anti-racist school geography, but also to recognize that what such 'progress' looks like is, as Young and Lambert make clear, always open to question:

> Powerful knowledge is precious. It is not made up of accumulated lists of 'facts'. In the form of subjects, powerful knowledge is continually evolving as new and tested concepts and explanations are introduced. (Young and Lambert, 2014b: n.p.)

The questions raised about representation, about inclusion and exclusion and about the status of powerful knowledge, including that of Black geographies, strike at the heart of the curriculum question facing schools and teachers. We cannot fully resolve these questions. Instead, the aim of this chapter is to set out – in a clear and logical way – how questions about the *nature of geographical knowledge* have important implications for the construction and teaching of the geography curriculum. A key theme in our discussions of race, racism and geography education in previous chapters has been that the knowledge that makes up the school curriculum is problematic: for example,

- the idea that subjects are alienating because black children do not recognize themselves in the curriculum, or that the curriculum offers negative views;
- the idea that there exists important knowledge that is excluded and could form the basis for an alternative curriculum;
- the idea that the curriculum should reflect the reality of a multicultural society;
- the idea that knowledge is power – that knowledge could be used to exclude and that the curriculum is ideological; and

- the idea that knowledge is powerful – that knowledge can elucidate, liberate and emancipate, but at the same time can obscure and be used to maintain ignorance.

These statements are about knowledge, its status and how it is organized in the school curriculum. They challenge the assumption that curriculum is a technical matter, concerned with selecting the appropriate mix of knowledge, concepts, skills and values and organizing them in a sensible and logical sequence. Such an approach to the school curriculum is peppered with jargon such as 'curriculum delivery', or 'operationalizing the curriculum', or even curriculum 'coherence' and 'intent'. In contrast, as Michael Apple (1979), working from a critical perspective, pointed out many years ago, curriculum is also a political matter, one that involves understanding who gets to select the content of the curriculum and on what basis. As we saw in the previous chapter, when it came to making *its* selection from the culture, school geography has often sidelined issues of race and racism.

However, changing the curriculum is not simply a matter of deciding we are now going to teach an anti-racist geography or challenge white supremacy in our geography lessons. Curriculum change is one of the most complex questions faced by teachers and policymakers, and Box 6.1 reminds us of some of the issues discussed in Chapters 2 and 3 that need to be addressed. Not only are these issues complex, but they are enduring: we should at least try to learn from earlier struggles and attempts at making progress through, for example, the introduction of Black studies in the school curriculum.

### Box 6.1 Struggles for curriculum change

In the 1970s, as the children of migrants found themselves in schools catering for the white majority, some parents sought to challenge the way the curriculum represented their experience. As Jackson (2016) states,

> Black children encountered a curriculum, teachers and classmates largely ignorant of the world from where their parents emigrated. (117)

Black students complained of how the places from which their parents originated were represented by geography teachers. Much of the school curriculum contained negative references to Black experience(s) – or ignored it. In response, Black parents organized to create counter-narratives about British history and culture. One place for this was the system of Supplementary Schools that operated outside the state education system, but there were also changes in state schools, where, in line with the policy moves towards multicultural education (Department of Education and Science, 1985), it was slowly acknowledged that the curriculum itself needed to change. For instance, an early project in Lewisham in South-East London found evidence that black children held negative self-images due to bias and inappropriate material. Teachers against Racism was formed in 1971 and campaigned for Black studies as a new subject in state secondary schools. Tulse

Hill Comprehensive School in Brixton, South London, established a Black studies course, arising from Black students' demands to recognize their experience. It was open to both black and white students because 'Our society is a multicultural, multiracial one and all of us need to understand it better.'

This was not without controversy (Waters, 2020). Black radicals argued that Black studies in schools was an appropriation of a radical initiative. Indeed, at Tulse Hill, it was argued that Black studies was adopted by teachers to dampen the threat of student activism. Students resisted what they saw as its co-option by white teachers. Others pointed to the danger that it confined Black experience to one part of a timetable and worse if, as we saw in Chapter 3, it became a holding ground for black students whilst the white students got on with studying for the high-status knowledge associated with public examinations.

In the early 1980s, Maureen Stone (1981) challenged the view that black children developed a negative self-image through their encounters with the formal curriculum. She concluded that black students need to be taught the formal curriculum, implying that the formal Western knowledge that made up the school curriculum is high status, available to all and neutral. This debate continues in curriculum studies to this day. In the United States, it is associated with the cultural literacy advocated by E. D. Hirsch Jr., whose 1987 book *Cultural literacy: What every American needs to know* became a bestseller). Hirsch's argument has been explored at length by Buras (2008) and in Britain it has been conflated, unhelpfully we think, with arguments about 'powerful knowledge' (although curriculum theorists such as Deng (2022) are careful to make important distinctions).

This example demonstrates the complexity of questions around who controls the curriculum, how decisions are made and which knowledge is of most worth. Whereas Stone worked from the epistemological assumption that we can find a neutral standpoint, Black studies assumes that there are distinct positions, or standpoints, from which the world is experienced and known.

Recently, there has been a renewed interest in Black studies in British universities, building on acknowledgement of the intellectual contributions of black people to science, the arts and culture and recognizing that these contributions continue to be overlooked, obscured or ignored (Warmington, 2014). This is the result of institutional racism within higher education and reflects deeply entrenched Eurocentric assumptions governing the production of knowledge. The British academy remains an overwhelmingly white space and has remained largely resistant to the scholarship produced by Black intellectuals to address social problems.

The editors of what is billed as the first book about Black studies in Britain argue for the knowledges produced within and beyond the university being a lens through which to examine the complexity and multiplicity of black experiences (Andrews and Palmer, 2016). This is not just knowledge about and for Black people. Writing in 1969, C. L. R. James was quite clear that he was not an advocate of the idea that Black studies should only be of concern for black people. Instead, Black studies is an epistemological world view that centres on the experiences of black peoples in providing perspectives on the formation of Western civilization (James, 1969).

These debates are directly relevant to this book. Calls for Black studies have appeared in major geographical journals (Andrews, 2020), and there are also wider curriculum initiatives. For example, arguments for 'The Black Curriculum' in history teaching[1] reconsiders the temporalities that underpin the National Curriculum. There are also debates about the ways in which the nation is represented and performed in English literature that eschew any simplistic division between included and excluded (Bromley, 2019). An enquiry recently reported on the teaching of Africa in the UK school curriculum (Royal African Society, 2022). These all have relevance for the geography curriculum, although, as we noted in Chapter 5, debates about how Britishness functions in geography curricula are arguably less advanced than those in history or literature. But what is to stop an awarding body from introducing a Black geography option (along with a sponsored textbook)? Or schools holding an annual 'Black Geography Week'?

At the beginning of this chapter, we asked how we are to 'make progress towards an anti-racist school geography'. Short (1998) distinguished between *progress of geographers*, *progress of geography* and *progress in geography*. In our current context, *progress of Black geographers* might be measured in the numbers of black students and teachers studying the subject at higher levels of the education system, the receipt of awards or the citation indices of Black scholars. *Progress of Black geography* could be seen as the chance for geography to steal a lead and show itself to be leading developments in the school curriculum and opening new opportunities for students. And finally, *progress in Black geography* could be defined as the ability of geographers to make the world more understandable and more socially just or to reveal more fully the processes that shape the world. This last question itself suggests the need to clarify the relationship between understanding and explanation. Indeed, we think it is possible to argue that ever since the publication of David Harvey's (1969) *Explanation in Geography*, the curriculum question has become one of selecting knowledge and organizing it in ways that help us to provide better explanations of the 'ways of the world' (Harvey, 2016). This task never stands still of course, as new theories and perspectives come to the fore (see Chapter 4)

In summary, when it comes to making decisions about curriculum content and selection, there are no clear-cut answers or procedures. But just as we should pay attention to earlier attempts as making progress towards anti-racist geographies, we should also examine previous work on curriculum planning in geography. This serves to clarify the links between what counts as geographical knowledge and what gets taught in schools.

---

[1] https://www.theguardian.com/commentisfree/2020/jun/13/equal-britain-teach-black-history-empire (accessed 30 September 2022).

## Modern School Geography and Curriculum Planning

In this section, we set out three different views of knowledge that have informed geography teaching in schools. These are broadly

- 'liberal',
- phenomenological, and
- critical.

While the first of these rests on the possibility of the objectivity and universality of knowledge, the latter two have given rise to the idea that geographical knowledge is partial and situated and therefore (especially when it comes to critical perspectives) linked to concepts of power and representation. One of the features of geography education as it has developed since the 1970s is that it has become more focused on *questions* of knowledge – what exists in the world and how it is possible to know it. As we hope to show in this chapter, this has important implications for curriculum planning in geography and in particular in relation to race and racism.

It is striking to find that Norman Graves (1996), perhaps the person most responsible for helping geography teachers to take seriously the issue of curriculum planning, could remark that

> I am not sure that in the 1950s we really understood what curriculum development was about, though it was evident that no subject and its teaching could stand still for long. (72)

Thus, curriculum innovation was slow and piecemeal, confined to the gradual updating of curriculum content and refinement of conceptual frameworks to guide teaching. If there was a theory of knowledge in underpinning school geography, it was *naïve realism* (in contrast to critical realism – see Appendix 1). As Gibson (1981) explained it,

> Geographical facts of observed phenomena and changes within them can be objectively established and any question of unseen entities, problematics, abstract forms or subjective impressions are irrelevant. With due precaution ... we can know a place as it really is, as the topography looks, as the soil feels, as the water tastes and so on. (152)

There exists a world, out there, beyond the classroom, and the role of the geographer is to study it, systematize it and describe it, in as neutral a language as possible. This led to the naming of phenomena, objects and processes and to various types of causal explanation. In the 1960s and early 1970s, a different type of realism came to dominate geographical studies, *scientific realism*. The methods were different, but the goal was the same: to describe and explain the world *as it is*. The geographer's goal was no longer to produce clear and detailed descriptions of the uniqueness of places and regions, but instead to search for order, patterns and spatial correlations.

Both these views of geographical knowledge sat comfortably with the dominant approach underpinning the school curriculum advocated by British educational philosophers Paul Hirst and R. S. Peters. In a series of important books and articles, Hirst and Peters argued that human beings have slowly differentiated out different types of knowledge. They distinguished between *forms of knowledge*, *fields of knowledge* and *practical theories*:

- *Forms of knowledge* refer to seven kinds of conceptual structure (mathematics, the natural sciences, the human sciences, moral knowledge, religious knowledge, philosophical knowledge and aesthetics). Three points are worth noting. First, each form of knowledge has its own concepts. Second, the concepts within a form of knowledge are logically connected. Third, each form of knowledge has its appropriate evidence, its test of validity. Peters and Hirst argued that everything we know lies within these forms of knowledge. These forms are autonomous, though of course, they are transferrable. For example, scientists make use of mathematical concepts. Although knowledge may be interlocking, each form of knowledge is distinct and autonomous.
- *Fields of knowledge* refer to domains where several forms of knowledge constitute a subject. Geography is a prime example of this.
- *Practical theories* include law, medicine, engineering and teaching.

## Assumptions of 'Liberal' Education

The liberal view of education advises that all children be introduced to the forms of knowledge. Understanding means learning to recognize the difference between these forms, and schools exist so that young people can be initiated into them. To be educated is to have mastered one or two forms of knowledge and so embody the ideals and some of the principles of rational argument. Disciplined understanding is the key to rationality, and rationality is the means towards full personhood. This is the logical basis for the school curriculum.

This philosophy was attractive to geography educators interested in developing and implementing rational curriculum planning in schools. First, knowledge was objective. This fitted very well with the strong traditions of naïve realism within the subject. Second, there was an assumption that education was politically neutral. The curriculum should change students' minds, but it should not seek to change society. Finally, selection was a matter of the trained geographer making reasoned and rational choices from their expert field of knowledge. Rational curriculum planning was logical and sequential. There was a nod towards the aims and purposes, but it was assumed that there was broad agreement and consensus about what these were, and once established and agreed, teachers could get on with the practical activity of preparing geography lessons.

An illustration of how this type of approach to knowledge and planning could be applied is found in *African Geography for Schools* (UNESCO, 1974), which was part of the UNESCO programme to improve planning, teaching and content of the school curriculum (and in which Norman Graves was closely involved). The volume had as its aim to give suggestions 'for the development of geography teaching about Africa in accordance with the current conditions and needs of that continent' (vi). These conditions and needs were to be met by a scientific approach that would be directed towards planning for a more rational use of the natural and human resources of countries, regions and continents. Geography had a special responsibility for the economic development of the whole continent and teaching should create 'attitudes favourable to economic growth and social development' (4). This was to be achieved through an overview of the economy of Africa, study of the regions of the continent and specific case studies. This approach embodies geography as a field of knowledge in Hirst and Peters's sense. It is a rational, ordered scheme that can contribute to 'international understanding of the peoples of Africa, their ways of life and their problems'.

# Phenomenological Challenges

It was not until the 1970s that this dominant ('liberal') view of knowledge in education was challenged by radical sociologists of education, notably Michael Young (1971), who reacted against the functionalism of the disciplines and rigidities of an elite curriculum. The 'new sociology' drew upon social phenomenology, which placed emphasis on the mental conceptions that people held in their heads. According to this analysis, school knowledge was a social construction and tended to reflect the interests of the most powerful groups in society. School knowledge tended to favour the written over the oral, the theoretical over the practical and the individual over the collective. The radical sociologists pointed to sociological and anthropological studies that showed that such patterns were not universal.

This 'phenomenological' approach to school knowledge appeared about the same time as some geographers were reacting to the limitations of positivist science and 'spatial-quantitative' approaches to geography. The goal of humanistic geography was to develop an understanding of how people experienced the social and natural worlds. This was popularized through the idea of a 'sense of place' and was attractive to geography teachers because it acknowledged and recognized children's experiences. Teaching through a humanistic approach could be an active attempt to develop a shared – or inter-subjective – understanding of people's lives. Whereas positivist attempts to plan and manage people and environments involved experts imposing their mental conceptions of the world, humanistic knowledge accepts the impossibility of separating facts from values, aiming instead for mutual understanding.

This is reminiscent of Pat Noxolo's 'politics of laughter' discussed in Chapter 4 (Box 4.3), and it is perhaps through literature and oral histories that the meanings of terms such as 'migration', 'home' or 'exclusion' might be developed in geography classrooms. There is a great deal of potential material available for geography teachers to help students develop a 'sense of place'. Cultural geography has widened the range of texts to go beyond the recreation of landscapes in great literature to include a routine focus on movies, television and popular music.[2]

There are dangers associated with humanistic geography, of course. The focus on shared feeling or mutual understanding, coupled with a strong sense of choice and agency, can divert attention from the harder economic and political structures in which human experience is lived (and crucially, how these are produced). And this is before we question how to avoid tokenism and the adoption of the 'exotic' or 'tourist gaze' of people and places. All too often, geography lessons that adopt a humanistic stance risk concluding with the trite observation that, deep down, we are all the same. However, the main point, that geography teachers can and should seek to construct and examine 'maps of meaning' with students, is important to acknowledge.

But we end this discussion with an important reminder (as noted in Chapter 5) that influential curriculum planners in school geography – steeped in the liberal approach of Hirst and Peters – looked at Young's work, noted it, but decided that it was not applicable to geography curriculum planning in schools. In doing so, they ensured that school geography remained committed to the idea of realism based on the distinction between objective and subjective knowledge. Marsden (1976) mounted a strong defence of Peters and Hirst; Graves (1975) considered the ideas in Young's new sociology of education 'interesting' but not relevant to the practical work of curriculum planning; and Hall (1976) was so concerned with highlighting the benefits of the new geography – drawing on scientific realism – that he failed to mention the new sociology altogether.

## Critical Views on Knowledge

Phenomenology (which gave rise to the insight that school subjects are social constructions) and humanistic geography (which sought for the meanings about places and environments held by individuals) were part of a critique of 'scientific' knowledge. By the late 1970s, the new sociology of education had adopted 'radical', Marxist-informed critiques of school knowledge, pointing to the ways in which school knowledge represented the world views of dominant groups in society (Whitty and Young, 1976). School subjects were seen as ideological in that they hid the real forces and processes that shape the world. Geography, especially as a school subject, was vulnerable to this critique.

Thus, further intellectual shifts within the academic discipline took place, enormously assisted by the work of David Harvey and Manuel Castells. Space reflected social process, they argued. Therefore, a society dominated by capitalist

---

[2] In order to develop a sense of place in this way, there is a rich resource in the BBC series *Small Axe* (which takes its name from a Bob Marley song), described on its website as 'Love letters to black resilience and triumph in London's West Indian community, directed by Oscar winner Steve McQueen. Vivid stories of hard-won victories in the face of racism' – we would add with a very strong sense of both time and place. https://www.bbc.co.uk/programmes/p08vxt33 (accessed 30 September 2022).

relations would tend to reflect this in its spatial organization. From a radical, critical perspective then, the task of the geography teacher is to reveal these processes and show how what seems natural is in fact the product of historical and social processes.

This critical approach led to a series of ideology critiques of *the exclusions* found in school geography. These were around sexism and racism, its use of selected concepts and language, and ideas supportive of capital. As we indicated in Chapter 5, this was the basis for Dawn Gill's widely cited review of geography syllabuses and textbooks, which found that geography textbooks remained influenced by a colonialist perspective. As Gill showed, many textbooks presented Europeans as people who have organizational ability, as scientific and efficient business people who get on with building roads and railways. Non-Europeans, on the other hand, were presented as dependents who have houses and roads built for them and need to be 'given jobs' that enable them to survive. The problems faced by so-called Third World countries were viewed as internal to those countries. Most textbooks took the Western model of development where the (no need to be stated) goal was for poorer countries to emulate Britain and the United States. This approach is ideological because it suggests to students that this relationship is both natural and inevitable rather than a social and political creation. Critical school geography was needed to cut through this ideology to reveal the real forces shaping the world.

## Discussion

By the mid-1980s, it was accepted that there existed different approaches to geographical knowledge and that knowledge could serve different interests or purposes. Ron Johnston's (1983, 1986) work identified three paradigms that had shaped Anglo-American human geography – positivism, humanism and realism. These gave rise to three different types of applied geography (and by extension, approaches to geography education) – geography as technical control, geography as mutual understanding and geography as emancipation. These categories are aligned with the philosopher Jürgen Habermas's (1971) theory of 'knowledge interests'. Geographer Tim Unwin (1992) provided a useful summary of this work. He argued that that there is no such thing as a world of objective facts waiting to be uncovered. What are commonly accepted as neutral geographical facts are socially constructed. The important implication or consequence of this is that students should be offered opportunities to question the truths they are presented with because, Unwin concluded, education must have as its goal emancipation rather than conformity.

Although these debates about geographical knowledge and the *interests* that it serves were not ubiquitous or even widespread within the world of geography education at the time, the idea that there was one true approach to geography was no longer tenable. The notion of the geographer as objective or neutral observer of the world was now a problematic assumption. Values were understood to be important in the selection of what we chose to study and teach, and why: for example, the classical models no longer worked, if they ever did, and the ways in which certain ways of seeing were excluded (e.g. women's experience of the urban environment, the child's view). These arguments about the nature of geographical knowledge came at a time when the social and spatial fix that had characterized the post-war welfare state and economy was in the process of breaking down. The result was that geography was now understood to be political, and any discussion of the geography curriculum would inevitably raise questions about 'whose geography?'

Put simply, teachers could no longer assume that the school geography curriculum was based on a secure, defined body of knowledge, or a logical sequence of concepts (even though some still insist on this, e.g. Standish, 2017), or that the 'curriculum problem' was basically a technical one of selecting things and putting things in the right order (e.g. Gardner, 2021). However, it is important to stress that all of the approaches to geographical knowledge considered so far broadly agreed that it was possible to ascertain *truth* about the world. In this sense, they were all 'modern' in that they sought out orderly and general principles in order to describe and understand geographical reality. That goal became more problematic with the postmodern challenge in geography and education.

## The Postmodern Challenge

> In a general sense, postmodernism is to be regarded as a rejection of many, if not most, of the cultural certainties on which life in the West has been structured over the last couple of centuries. It has called into question our commitment to cultural 'progress' (that economies must continue to grow, the quality of life to keep improving indefinitely etc.), as well as the political systems that have underpinned this belief. (Sims, 2000: vii)

From the late 1980s into the 1990s, postmodernism had a profound impact on the humanities and social sciences. In geography, one of the first major statements was Michael Dear's (1988) article, 'The Postmodern Challenge: Reconstructing Human Geography'. This was followed by Ed Soja's (1989) *Postmodern geographies* and David Harvey's (1989) *The condition of postmodernity*. These (white, male) authors were ambivalent about the political implications of postmodernism. Whilst the focus on difference and diversity with the possibility of 'other spaces' was to an extent appealing, they worried that postmodernism seemed to revel in surface over depth. The 'playfulness' of postmodernism seemed frivolous to some, and many geographers were reluctant to give up the Enlightenment project of progress and commitment to the creation of a 'better world'. Of course, readers of this book will be quick to point out that the so-called postmodern condition was a decidedly 'Western' concept (see Ahmed, 1992; Sardar, 1998; Radhakrishnan, 2003). The reason we focus on the 'postmodern' moment in geography and education is that many of its assumptions about knowledge, positionality, situatedness and the role of power in geographical representation have become widely accepted in critical human geography.

Early concerns about the excesses of postmodernism gave way to a more open (if still tentative) embrace of the progressive potential of postmodernism, acknowledging the importance of the idea of a 'crisis of representation' (see Teresa Ebert (2009) for a useful discussion of 'ludic' and 'critical' postmodernism in education). Trevor Barnes and James Duncan's (1992) *Writing worlds* was one of the first truly postmodern texts in geography in the sense that it took seriously the crisis of representation and its implications for the discipline. Postmodernism challenged the very idea that it was possible to gain access to 'truth', since all such truths are human constructions. A little earlier, Derek Gregory and Rex Walford (1989) drew upon the crisis of representation to state that 'our texts are not mirrors that we hold up to the world'(2). Geography had previously been about *mimesis*, but now this was not the case: geography was better understood as a form of 'earth-writing'. This statement, coming from an eminent and influential geography educator (Rex Walford) had important implications. As Barnes and Duncan (1992) stated,

> To take issue with modernist representation in late twentieth-century human geography is to adopt a radical stance on a number of grounds. (248)

First, adopting postmodernism was to set oneself in opposition to the goals of the vast majority of researchers in the field, whose work aspired to a realistic representation of places, regions and environments. Secondly, it was to take issue with the history of human geography, which was narrated in terms of the gradual advance of knowledge, expressed as geography and geographers' increasing ability to describe and explain the world.

To reiterate. According to postmodern thinking, the three approaches or paradigms so far described in this chapter – positivism, humanism and realism – shared the common goal of accurate description of the world. In this sense, they were all instances of modern geography. Postmodern geography challenged the idea that there could be any neutral or disinterested representation of people and places. Michael Curry (1996) provided a succinct statement:

> First, language is rethought. The traditional notion that some language is literal and some figural, or figurative, is discarded; all is now seen as figural. The image of the text as a neutral and transparent representation of the world is abandoned; the written word is now seen as inevitably partial, obscuring just as it represents. Second, knowledge is now taken fundamentally to derive a particular point of view and the products of knowledge are therefore taken to be relative to that point of view. Third, the world is now seen as resistant to a reduction to a simple set of constituents. (5)

Reading this, it is perhaps obvious why postmodernism challenged the very basis of the school geography curriculum. Geographical writing and texts are no longer 'scientific', but rhetorical. The idea of unproblematic representation is abandoned. Furthermore, anything that geographers write is partial, in both senses of that word.

Finally, the notion of cause and effect, and of finding clear explanations for geographical objects, is rendered impossible. The world is hopelessly messy or entangled. If taken seriously, these arguments have profound, and possibly destructive, implications for the work of geography teachers in school: teaching becomes 'impossible', shifting the emphasis of classrooms onto learning. But learning what?

> ### Box 6.2 Versions of powerful knowledge
>
> 'When I was an undergraduate in England in the early 1970s, there were courses available on Africa, South America, and South Asia but, like most of my contemporaries, I did not elect to take them. The fault was in large measure my own; but the other, supposedly more general courses in spatial science seemed to promise so much more. Theirs was not the instrumentalist language of the 1980s, with its characteristic emphasis on the marketplace and the cash register, but it put in place an economy of power-knowledge of the most emphatic (and no doubt masculinist) finality. Its generalisations were not only "rigorous" and "objective", I learned, but "powerful". I now realise just how particular those generalisations and how insidious their powers. But to a working-class kid at Cambridge this seemed highly seductive' (Gregory, 1994: 203).

Derek Gregory's (1994) *Geographical imaginations* mediates between 'modern' and 'postmodern' perspectives (his doubts about the 'powerful knowledge' of scientific realism are shown in Box 6.2). In the first of two long introductory chapters, Gregory charted the rise of what he terms 'geography as world-expedition', which recounts the discipline's encounter with anthropology, sociology and finally spatial science. Each of these encounters promised the power to know and represent the world in new ways. In a sense, therefore, geographical knowledge became more and more powerful. However, in the second chapter, Gregory suggested that, from the 1980s, geographers experienced 'cartographic anxiety' – confronting the crisis of representation and the growing doubt about geographers' claims to be able to know and represent the world. Powerful geographical knowledge seemed to be problematic.

Throughout the 1990s, the general consensus was that postmodern geographies had little to offer geography teachers, and influential figures in the field of geography education lined up to downplay postmodernism's significance. For instance, notwithstanding his 1989 comment (cited above) on language, Walford returned to the 'world-as-exhibition' that underpinned spatial science, albeit with a common-sense educational humanism at its heart. Thus, his 1995 *Geography* article on the future of geography (co-authored with Peter Haggett) imagines a world awash with information just waiting to be taught by a new generation of 'keen' geography graduates. To the geography educationist Gwyn Edwards (1996), this was an idealization and a fantasy, but it was echoed by Haggett (1996) in his later discussion, which itself was approvingly cited by Rawling (1997):

> We need to conserve and re-emphasise some central and cherished aspects of geographical education, a love of landscape and of field exploration, and fascination with place, a wish to solve the spatial conundrums posed by spatial configurations. (Haggett, 1996: 17)

However, as we have seen, when Haggett was writing this, human geographers were busy questioning the possibility of any unproblematic notion of landscape; places were now being seen in terms of inclusion and exclusion, and geography's spatial fetishism (its love of patterns and 'conundrums') was being replaced by a focus on the social–spatial dialectic. Nevertheless, Rawling (1997) insisted on the need to be 'absolutely clear' about what constitutes the core of geography. Meanwhile, Marsden (1995) correctly identified postmodernism as an attack on rationality, enlightenment and the promotion of individual autonomy, locating his attempt to 'rekindle good practice' in geography as underpinned by a humanist slant. Thus, commentators such as Marsden, Walford and Rawling united in calling for geography teachers to avoid the pitfalls associated with postmodernism.

Our own book (Morgan and Lambert, 2005), *Geography : Teaching School Subjects 11-19*, was shaped by Gregory's scheme and appeared at what was perhaps the high-water mark of postmodernism in geography. It was the moment when the idea of the *constructed* nature of geographical knowledge was widely accepted. Postmodernism opened the discipline to new ways of thinking and understanding, not least because knowledge was now understood to be specific to place and time. All the inherited body of concepts, categories and metaphors in geography were now considered suspect, capable of obfuscation and open to deconstruction. Knowledge reproduces identities and therefore underpins and reproduces a hierarchical ordering of the world (Cox, 2014).

It may seem odd to spend time discussing the concept of postmodernism in geography. It is no longer in vogue (though see Jeffries's (2022) recent reassessment). However, there is a real sense in which contemporary geography is shaped by the 'posts', and its influence has inspired ways of thinking that have become widely accepted in school geography. It is, for example, no longer automatically assumed that teachers can teach from the position of the neutral, detached observer. Geographical knowledge is one of many forms of knowledge, and it is widely accepted that geography teaching is inescapably 'partial'. There is a strong focus on representation and the idea that we are shaped by 'discourses'. This is itself part of a longer-term shift in both geography and in education. What has been jettisoned from the postmodern toolkit is the idea that we cannot seek to develop a 'better world' or that geography can 'make a difference'. Thus, around the turn of the century, human geography undertook an 'ethical turn'. This was registered in books that set out to explore, for example, dissident geographies, moral geographies and environmental justice. This is part of the discipline's shift from being an explicative science to a normative one. Since around 2005, partly in response to this turn, the search has been on to explore the *powers of powerful knowledge* in geography education. In the next section, we explore two ways to think about powerful knowledge, before providing an example of what this might mean for curriculum planning.

## Two Approaches to Powerful Knowledge

# Knowledge Is Power

Following the realization that rather than objectively or neutrally representing reality geographical knowledge is a social product, many geographers quickly accepted that knowledge reflects the interests and world views of those who produce it. This is captured in the idea of 'positionality', which holds individuals responsible for acknowledging the position from which they speak. Thus, individuals speaking from certain privileged positions (e.g. white, Western, male, straight) have used this power to define the concerns of academic disciplines such as geography. The result is to deny or marginalize the geographies of other less well-positioned interests and groups. This applies to the curriculum taught in universities and in schools. It quietly, and perhaps insidiously, results in a curriculum of erasure. As we explored in Chapters 4 and 5, there is a realization that that geography is a white subject, largely studied and taught by white people. We also referenced moves to redress this, primarily through prioritizing 'Black' perspectives and Black geographies.

According to this analysis, knowledge is powerful. The dominant culture imposes its world views and ideology on subjugated or subordinate groups. The curriculum is organized in such a way as to ensure continued dominance. The question then is whether it is possible for teachers to teach from the *standpoint* of the least advantaged.

The notion of a standpoint provides the basis for the construction of an emancipatory curriculum and an inclusive approach to teaching and learning. Standpoint theory stresses how the notion of disinterested, 'objectively produced' knowledge is a myth that serves to *obscure* power relations. The knowledge produced by dominant social groups tends to reproduce their world view(s), while knowledge produced by marginalized people produces alternative outsider perspectives. Indeed, outsider perspectives may improve the possibility of more 'objective' knowledge because it brings to attention things that dominant groups are unlikely to see. Standpoint theory therefore offers a critique of any academic field such as geography – including ideas about what the discipline should look like; what type of theory, methods and research belong to the discipline; what rules the discipline should abide by; and how different knowledges are valued or devalued (whereby some become dominant, while other standpoints remain marginalized).

According to this critique, geography has worked with a Eurocentric standpoint: this a particular way of looking at the world, often characterized by *Orientalism* (Said, 1978), a process producing ideas about the non-Western world as being backward or less civilized than 'the West'. This Eurocentric standpoint relies upon a binary distinction in which the West is seen as being different from the rest of the world. In practical terms, this enables geographers to study the West independently from its relation to 'the rest' and to develop 'universal' theory on this basis. An example of this can be found in the case of studies of urban growth. Myers (2011) argues that as

African societies urbanize, they do so in ways that challenge prevailing theories and models of urban geography, but most urban studies are built on theories utilizing US or European cities as the universal models.

Against this orthodoxy of normalizing the West (also expressed in terms of Northern as opposed to the Southern standpoint), arguments have been made to reject Orientalism in favour of recognizing and valuing the agency of people and knowledges from the Global South. But it is not simply a matter of changing representations of people and places. Southern standpoints also tie processes of Western capitalism and modernity to the processes of colonial and imperial exploitation and expropriation. This is the basic premise of the concept of 'modernity/coloniality' pioneered by Walter Mignolo (2000) and discussed in Chapter 4 – the idea that modernity happened in the West not because of Western internalist exceptionalism, but because of the West's external (colonial) relations with the rest of the world built through their empires. Furthermore, even though the moment of formal colonialism has passed, we still live in the colonial present (Gregory, 2004).

Approaches to geographical study based on standpoint theory are closely linked to arguments about representation. Language is no longer assumed to offer a neutral representation of the world. The categories and concepts we use are part of discourses, which have the power to shape the world. This gives rise to the claim that all claims to truth are claims to power. Taking its cue once more from Edward Said (1993), geography is a discourse that constructs the world in the interests of the powerful.

Understanding that knowledge is power has important implications for any attempt to develop an anti-racist geography. The first task is deconstruction (e.g. Winter, 2006, 2018). It is assumed that any representation of spaces, places and environments found within the curriculum and its resources are likely to be based on the world views of the powerful, and thus (knowingly or unknowingly) marginalize and exclude other ways of making sense. One of the important skills of the geography teacher is, therefore, ideology critique and the ability to construct other representations which are more inclusive or prioritize alternative geographies. Black and minority students can be empowered if they see their identities and histories reflected in the curriculum and the resources used to teach it. Students from more privileged and advantaged groups may also come to recognize their own powerful positions and seek to develop solidarity with others. This is a strong element in the discipline of ethnic studies in US universities, which is increasingly being introduced into the school curriculum in some states (Lambert and León, 2023).

As we argued in Chapter 5, the implications of these arguments in school geography have not been fully explored. There is a long-standing acknowledgment of the need for multicultural diversity (for instance in textbooks or teaching materials), but the more radical implications have been downplayed. More recent moves to decolonize geography have largely revolved around changing the nature of representation. Thus, categories such as rich and poor, developed and developing, First and Third World are deconstructed. The ideas behind environmental and economic determinism are challenged, as is the notion of a uniform space. The goal is to assert the agency of marginalized people - a pedagogy of the oppressed. It is also to place colonialism at the centre of any discussion of space. An important part of the argument is around who produces geographical knowledge. Thus, we should identify indigenous producers of knowledge and give priority to the voices of actual people on the ground.

## Powerful Knowledge as Enabling

Powerful knowledge is a term that has become closely associated with the later work of the sociologist of education, Michael Young (2008). It is 'controversial' because it posits the existence of knowledge that stands alone, outside the conditions of its own production. All knowledge is social because it arises out of human study and reflection on the world, but once it has been produced, it exists outside of the conditions in which it was produced. To give an example familiar to geography teachers, Walter Christaller's theories of settlement patterns were in part derived from his work for the Nazis in the 1930s in imagining an ideal settlement pattern once Poland and Ukraine were occupied by Germany. Is the fact that Christaller was a member of the National Socialists inseparable from his theory? Is Central Place Theory an example of racist knowledge? Or do the concepts Christaller came up with have validity irrespective of his views and social location?

Powerful knowledge suggests that we judge knowledge according to its power to explain reality, rather than who produces it. This means that we assume that there is a 'real world' which is capable of description and explanation and that we can distinguish between the 'knower' and the 'known'. This is what *we* mean by powerful knowledge. It is something we began to develop through our 2010 book and have attempted to apply in our subsequent work (Lambert, 2018; Morgan, 2012; Morgan and Lambert, 2018; Young and Lambert, 2014). It is worth elaborating on how we arrived at this.

As geography teachers, we were both socialized at a time when the goal of geographical education was for better explanations of the social and natural world. The search was on for 'theory'. As Harvey (1969) wrote in *Explanation in geography*,

> We are not content to describe events in a random manner. We seek, rather, to impose some coherence upon our descriptions, to make them rational and realistic, to try to bring out what we understand of a situation by patterning our descriptive remarks in a particular way. (336)

As students and teachers, we experienced the 'new' geography in which 'techniques' seemed to offer the promise of discerning 'some semblance of order in life' (Toyne and Newby, 1971: ix). However, by the time we were teaching the subject in schools, actually existing geography seemed to be falling into *disorder* as the 'spatial Keynesianism' of the post-war years was breaking down. A new generation of geographers (many of whom had been trained in and pioneered the new techniques) was therefore beginning to explore alternative ways of thinking about space, reaching the conclusion that space was a reflection of society, but also that space acted back on social relations. As Doreen Massey (1984) famously said, society's production does not take place on the head of a pin: that geography matters. A key feature of this work was that it was marked by a search for abstraction – that we seek to find concepts that help us to make sense of geographical phenomena. One of the examples we often return to in our teaching is Peter Taylor's (1985) discussion of the politics of scale. A shipyard closing on the River Tyne is a local event (people *experience* losing their jobs and the economy suffers), but the event is also relevant at a national scale, the scale of national *ideology* where governments can act to support the industry, or not. The 'real' cause of this event lies elsewhere, in how global capitalism operates – the scale of *reality*. As geography teachers then, if we want to explain this event, we have to use concepts such as capitalism or division of labour, and, with the theme of this book in mind, we should reflect upon why we come back to this example in our writing and teaching. The north-east of England with its history of shipyards and coal mines is a repository of images of a 'white working class', and the region's involvement in Britain's industrial revolution and empire is significant (John's earliest memory of primary school was copying out John Masefield's 'Cargoes').

A moment's thought reveals that, when it comes to explaining human geography, there is nothing final about the concepts we use. For instance, capitalism is a useful shorthand, but of course the concept has its own history, and arguments rage about its use. A feminist geographer might look at the closure of the shipyards and be interested in how the gender relations in this place are changing and introduce concepts such as patriarchy. But whatever the source of the conceptual abstraction, the way in which explanation proceeds is by relating the surface appearance of an *empirical* event to the actual processes taking place *behind it*. This is what we mean by *powerful knowledge*. When we wrote our 2010 book, we were influenced by Roger Lee's (1983, 1985) important (but seemingly little read) contributions to discussions about geography teaching in the 1980s. These were 'realist' and drew upon the work of Andrew Sayer who, in geography, did most to develop the framework of critical realism (Sayer, 1985, 2000).

Critical realism, which we have attempted to summarize in Appendix 1, was a response to the limits of positivist explanation in geography, the type that provided 'surface' geographical explanations for geographical patterns. An example would be the assemblage of data to test the hypothesis that the prevalence of measurable racist attitudes is related to spatial proximity. This would suggest that there is a relationship between the levels of racist incidents and the density of black settlement in an area (which conveniently assigns 'the race problem' to black people themselves). Of course, even when we put to one side the problems of definition, measurement and ideology, this law does not hold true. There is no necessary relationship between racist incidents and the pattern of black settlement. We need a *different type* of explanation, and this is where critical realism comes in.

Powerful knowledge has taken as its theoretical basis the tenets of critical realism. This creates some challenges for geography education though, because critical realism was relatively short-lived as a methodological approach in human geography. One of the problems was that it became associated with complex procedures, and the language of contingency and complexity seemed to some to be needlessly obfuscatory. However, as geography educators working with young people in schools, it seems to us that the spirit of critical realism is more important than the letter. The need to maintain the sense that as geography teachers we can gain understanding of the real forces shaping the world has become even more important as the discipline has abandoned its claims to explain reality in a 'once and for all' manner. We find it disconcerting that, by 2005, a book written to introduce advanced students to important debates in the field could write,

> It is no longer possible to take for granted that academics produce 'objective' knowledge, knowledge that represents reality 'more accurately' than lay knowledge. Indeed, the success of all knowledge has been fundamentally called into question. (Hannah, 2005: 151)

We quote this as a reminder (to ourselves and to readers) that as the undermining of realist claims in geography has gained ground, it has become simultaneously harder to argue for a common curriculum experience for students in schools. Critical realism helps us with this question, mainly through its challenge to simplistic notions of cause and effect. In order to understand what happens in the world, you need to be aware of underlying *structures*. For example, let us consider the concept of 'division of labour'. The division of labour in those parts of Africa still subject to pre-capitalist forms of land tenure is very different from what you would find in a Western capitalist society or indeed in the ancient world. But the concept 'division of labour' reveals a *structure* as a necessary part of the explanation of how economies work in these contrasting localities (for instance, the types of work, how these are valued and renumerated, who does each type and so on). Exactly how the division of labour plays out in one place may be different from another based on different geographical and historical conditions (influencing, for example, how gender roles are understood). One of the best ways to grasp this remains Doreen Massey's (1984) *Spatial divisions of labour*. The patterns of industrial change on the UK landscape, she argued, could only be explained with reference to underlying social structure, and this was different in say Cornwall in comparison to South Wales. But the concept of divisions of labour was a powerful element of understanding both settings. It is a small step to move towards thinking of racial divisions of labour.

There are two sets of curriculum issues here. The first concerns concept selection: How do we know we have concepts that are helpful ('powerful') in explaining the events we are seeking to explain? And then there is the more obviously geographical aspect: How exactly do these concepts change and work within specific situations and contexts?

## Discussion

Even though critical realism's influence was relatively short-lived, at least in human geography where it was superseded by postmodernism, it performed, and still performs, a useful role. It sensitizes us to the complexity of the world and guards against reductionism and overgeneralization. The most important element of critical realism for geography teachers is that it urges us to question *which are the most powerful concepts (the 'building blocks') for making sense of the world*. Critical realism encourages us to identify concepts that may apply across the world, but which have no clear or predictable outcomes – because we must look at how they operate in specific contexts, situations or geographical settings.

There is another part to this, which is that the world is not static. The world does not stand still and is always in the process of becoming. As such, critical realism is part of an open and dialectical method, whereby we continue to move between the empirical and theoretical, asking questions that can lead us to a better set of explanations – of how and why things happen.

To conclude this chapter, we provide an example of how our assertion of a 'continuing move between the empirical and theoretical … leading to a better set of explanations' may work out in practice. What we offer is a worked example that draws upon the ideas set out in this chapter.

## How and Why Things Happen: Case Study of Urban Change in Liverpool

In this chapter, we have set out a discussion of geographical knowledge in a formal way. Geographical knowledge does not just exist in a given or predetermined way, waiting to be found and written up. It has been made, revised and remade – it comes from human intellectual effort. Our argument is that expert, specialist teachers of geography in schools, while not necessarily philosophers or epistemologists, nevertheless need to have a handle on the nature of geographical thought, where it has come from and how it continues to develop. This we argue is a prerequisite for designing and enacting an anti-racist geography curriculum based on enhanced racial literacy.

Thus, we now go on to show how discussions about the nature of knowledge have important implications for practical curriculum making in geography. We do this through a case study of urban change in Liverpool. We seek to clarify how different approaches to geographical knowledge have different implications.

## An Orthodox Approach

The starting point for this discussion is a series of lessons on 'Urban Change in Liverpool' produced by the Oak Academy.[3] These reflected the requirements of

---

[3] https://classroom.thenational.academy/units/urban-change-in-liverpool-uk-a425.

GCSE specifications within a framework of 'opportunities and challenges' for urban areas. The materials certainly didn't represent the limits of what can be done in a series of lessons – they illustrated, in effect, a rather minimalist 'call and response' pedagogy.

The sequence of lessons was as follows:

Location and importance of Liverpool
Impacts of migration on Liverpool
Opportunities of urban change in Liverpool
Challenges of urban change in Liverpool
An urban regeneration project in Liverpool: the Anfield Project

This is an issues-based approach, amenable to enquiry learning, that geography teachers will readily recognize. The approach to geographical knowledge is realist because the lessons assume that there is a real world and that these processes of urban change can be observed and recorded. In other words, there are ways to match up data to demonstrate geographical concepts such as counter-urbanization, urban sprawl, conurbation and commuter zone. The purpose of the case study is to demonstrate some key generalizations and how these play out in a specific location. Although not formally emphasized, the 'opportunities and challenges' structure offers space for students to evaluate the success or failure, or even the desirability of the changes taking place in Liverpool. It would also be possible to bring in the voices of various groups of people to explore the subjective elements of urban change in Liverpool, thereby adding a more humanistic dimension to the study. For example, were there winners and losers? What would it feel like to live in Liverpool? There is plenty of scope to interpret and develop this scheme of work, and implicit in this approach is the need for the teacher to ensure balance and to act as a guide to the geographical inquiry.

## Crucial Critique

Interestingly, this series of lessons was critiqued in a blog post by the 'Decolonizing Geography' (DG) group.[4] DG argues for the need to 'focus on how places have been shaped by competing dynamics of power, resistance and agency'. We summarize their critique of the Oak Academy materials here:

> *First*, the DG argue that the lessons fail to present a rounded picture of the relationship between urban change and processes of racialization. Although the lesson on the 'Location and importance of Liverpool' notes the historical significance of the city when it says 'the ports played a role in the growth of the British Empire', it understates the centrality of the city to slavery. Liverpool derived great public and personal wealth from the slave trade, but the Oak

---

[4]https://decolonisegeography.com/blog/2021/04/the-commission-on-race-and-ethnic-disparities-report-and-the-geography-curriculum/ (accessed 31 October 2022).

Academy lesson does not mention this. By the 1830s, Liverpool was the financial centre of the global slave-cotton industry and in *Empire of cotton*, Sven Beckert (2016) argues that the city was the true centre of the (commercial) world in the nineteenth century. Underplaying this role means that the lessons misrepresent the urban history of Liverpool.

*Second*, the DG point out serious omissions, and here we use their words almost verbatim. The failure to reference slavery is evident, again, in the migration lesson. The slave trade played an important part in the build-up of early Liverpool's black community. The lesson states 'The UK's oldest black community is found in Liverpool with roots dating back to at least 1730.' However, it fails to mention where members of the black community came from and why. Early arrivals ranged from freed slaves and black servants, to the student sons of African rulers. Neglecting to mention the slave trade as the key driver of flows of people presents the migration of the black population as independent of the events of the time.

Another omission is the history of conflict between the black population and the white working class. The lesson on 'The challenges of urban change within Liverpool' references the urban riots of 1981, but stresses that the causes of this were economic and social deprivation. This neglects recent scholarship that points to the discriminatory policing of black communities. DG argues that 'to reduce the causes of the riots down to material deprivation is not only a gross misrepresentation but also fails to equip students with the knowledge to navigate the urban landscape of Liverpool today'.

*Third*, the lessons present too many moments in the history of urban change in Britain in a 'race free' manner. There is a lack of reference to ethnicity and data concerning social and racial inequality in Liverpool. Thus, whilst the lesson on urban change considers challenges faced by Liverpudlians across education, housing, unemployment and health, the DG note that at no point do the lessons engage with how these impact differently on racialized groups. The inner city in the 1980s was increasingly seen as a racialized space where 'riots' and 'race' were linked, and this paved the way for increasing policy intervention. The inner city was seen as a 'problem' area that needed to be controlled. The Oak Academy lessons fail to include the vital role ethnicity played and continues to play in urban change in Liverpool.

Overall, the Oak Academy's lessons on urban change in Liverpool are said to be unable to provide students with the tools to be critical. Students do not have access to the full range of perspectives available in the current stock of knowledge and, as a result, are left with a 'post-racial' geography that 'inadequately explores the entanglements of race, power and place'. The DG article goes on to argue that 'favouring cheerful stories of cultural exchange without also facilitating understanding of the uncomfortable context which shaped these stories devalues the historical and continuing marginalization of ethnic groups in the UK and former colonies and their place within it today'.

It should be clear the basis of the DG critique is a very different view of geographical knowledge from that found in the Oak Academy materials. It adopts a *standpoint* approach, whereby urban change in Liverpool is linked to race, racism, colonialism and imperialism. The city's wealth was generated through the profits of the slave trade. This past reverberates in the present. In terms of the discussion in the previous section of this chapter, this account stresses the relational element involved in taking a Southern standpoint. It stresses how past and present are connected and how the development of the modern West was linked to the colonial relations.

A decolonizing approach demands that we do not treat slavery as an unhappy historical incident that was dealt with, but instead draws attention to the ways in which power was central to the production of space. This is an important correction to earlier accounts. Too often, for example, historical geography downplays or obscures such power relations. For instance, Perry's (1975) *A geography of 19th century Britain* refers to cotton as 'the most important of the great consumer-oriented industries of the nineteenth century' (22), but makes only tangential reference to its global links, and Lawton and Pooley's (1992) *Britain: an historical geography, 1740–1950* is focused on the internal development of the space economy. We find it in academic texts such as Couch's (2003) *City of change and challenge* (which, focused on Liverpool, makes only passing reference to race) and books written for students and teachers, such as the GA's book on Liverpool in the *Discovering cities* series (readers might compare the book on Bristol in that series).

The ultimate task of the DG critique is to understand the link between space and blackness. This is achieved through an historical–geographical analysis of society, which overcomes the apolitical and 'natural' account of urban patterns. This standpoint epistemology demands that we teach geography from the 'standpoint of the least advantaged'. This is an important advance on the apolitical and ahistorical accounts found in the Oak Academy materials, but, as we now go on to suggest, it is important to consider whether still more powerful accounts are available.

## Critiquing the Critique

As already noted, academic studies have tended to neglect Liverpool's 'inconvenient imperial past' (Haggerty, Webster and White, 2008). In much of the literature, 'Liverpool is contextualised as a port with global commercial links, especially with the America's, an image which subtly aligns the city with notions of free trade and cosmopolitan liberality, rather than the aggression, protectionism and oppression of empire' (Haggerty et al., 2008: 3). For instance, it is perhaps significant that the title of Tony Lane's popular book on the city changed between editions from *Liverpool: gateway of empire* to *Liverpool: city of the sea*, because the 'economics, politics, cultures and attitudes of British imperialism are not ... recognised as ingredients in the recipe for Scouse' (Haggerty et al., 2008: 4–5). Similarly, Marriner's (1982) geographical account of the economic development of Merseyside is relatively silent about Liverpool's involvement in the imperial project, and her roll call of the region's contribution to the cultural life of the nation is decidedly 'white'.[5] Finally, the magisterial *Liverpool 800* (Belcham, 2006), written to mark the city's 800th anniversary, emphasizes the city's global or 'cosmopolitan' character rather than its imperial side.

These references point to one of the key methodological insights of critical realism – namely, that it is important to examine the concepts used to explain geographical events and patterns: are they up to the task? In other words, are the concepts selected to frame our practical curriculum making capable of providing powerful explanations?

For instance, as geography teachers, we may decide that concepts such as 'conurbation', 'sprawl', slums or 'counterurbanization' do not in themselves *adequately* explain urban change in Liverpool. However, they may be useful when linked to more powerful concepts, such as, for example, 'economic development' or 'spatial inequality'. All the time, a critical realist stance assumes that the powerful concepts chosen to explain reality, such as imperialism or cosmopolitanism, are building blocks for explanation – they lead our explanations in particular directions. We can see this in the DG critique, which uses racialization as a key concept. Whilst this enables us to recognize some previously hidden or ignored aspects of urban change in Liverpool, it may also risk an under-examined acceptance of binary terms such as white and black. One of the problems with that is how, ironically, it therefore accepts 'race' as an essentialized category. In order to overcome this possibility, it is interesting to see how the explanation of urban change might be different through adopting an expanded concept such as racialized capitalism. This reminds us that powerful disciplinary knowledge is inherently dynamic and in a constant state of becoming.

## Revisiting Liverpool

One way to frame Liverpool is as an example of a world city. Liverpool came to the centre of the world stage in the 1850s. This prominence was based on the vast profits made from the slave trade. Its role as an imperial port city led to massive population growth as it became a centre of immigration and emigration. With the Irish potato famine of the mid-1840s, Liverpool became the first port of call for refugees fleeing oppression, crop failure and starvation. It is estimated that two million people came to and through Liverpool within the decade. In addition, the city also gained

---

[5]Thus, Merseyside has made a

disproportionate impact on national television through Z-Cars, the Liver Birds, the Onedin Line, Ken Dodd's Knotty Ash ... in sport its soccer players and their fans carry its name beyond national boundaries; its rugby league teams frequently feature in national cup finals and to steeple-chase enthusiasts it is the home of the Grand National. The Beatles have indelibly imprinted it in the annals of pop music ... as a source of famous comedians its reputation is unrivalled – Tommy Handley, Arthur Askey, Ted Ray, Jimmy Tarbuck and Ken Dodd, to name but a few. (Marriner, 1982) the reputation as the 'capital city of Wales', the result of economic migrants (a reminder of the internal colonialism that often occurs within nation-states). These population movements profoundly impacted the city's culture. Certainly, the city was cosmopolitan in that it drew people from all over the globe. The main black population came from the African seamen who worked on the docks and stayed in the city, but there were few slaves.

A key part of the story of capitalist development for Liverpool was the fact of class division. To say (as decolonizing arguments tend to suggest) that 'Britain' held all the power is simply wrong – more accurately, certain economic classes did. The city's impressive architecture was a product of the wealth created through trade, including the slave trade, and reflected the power of the merchant classes. The public buildings that grew up to support welfare and health were part of the process of managing a large and potentially unruly working class. The struggle of black Liverpudlians is one of competing with other groups for scarce resources, particularly when the city's economy grew more slowly by the end of the nineteenth century. The 1919 riots were an example of the struggle to build a Black British working class in the context of many firms seeking to divest their black workers because white workers refused to work with them. These were the origins of the Aliens Act of 1919, which set the tone for twentieth-century immigration policy.

The nature of racial capitalism changed after the Second World War. Even before this, the city and its region were designated as one of the UK's Special Areas, eligible for state assistance to attract firms and create jobs. This was a period of state-building projects aiming at national full employment through regional economic policy. It represented a period of accord between capital and labour during which a national Keynesian–Fordist settlement sought to 'manage' the changing spatial divisions of labour. It was facilitated by the post-war economic boom, based on the continued expansion of the global economy which led to the affluent society. Liverpool itself had a series of Labour administrations, which in this context of economic adjustment sought to downplay the city's role in empire.

All this had important cultural implications. In the 1960s, the US 'beat poet' Allen Ginsburg considered Liverpool (which, of course, gave us the Beatles) to be 'at the present moment, the centre of consciousness of the human universe'. More prosaically,

> While Liverpool's cosmopolitanism and ethnic diversity were to be celebrated, and the sins of the slave trade acknowledged, the preferred image of the city focused upon its cosmopolitan proletarian character and its role in the development of British popular culture and music. (Haggerty et al., 2008: 6)

Meanwhile, the post-war Merseyside development plan focused on the decentralization of population and industry. 'Slum clearance' was central to 'renewal', with the shift of people to municipal suburban housing estates and New Towns such a Skelmersdale (designated in 1961). We can understand these processes in terms of a 'spatial fix', designed to secure capital accumulation and profits through rising land values and construction. These processes were themselves racialized, as the benefits of outer-city branch-plant prosperity and the affluent, new housing estates of the 1950s and early 1960s was not shared by the black community. Furthermore, the post–Second World War economic boom was over by the mid-1960s, causing Liverpool (and other cities from Newcastle upon Tyne and Glasgow, to East London and Bristol) to be ravaged by de-industrialization and attempts at 'restructuring'.

The impacts of these changes were unevenly distributed. In 1977, over half of those unemployed in Liverpool were aged sixteen to twenty-four, and for a young black worker living in 'Liverpool 8', the prospect of even an unskilled job was virtually nil. The proportion of the city's population made up by black people was comparatively small (less than 2%), more than half of whom had been born in Liverpool. Nevertheless, segregation in housing was at high levels and existed in the workplace too. In the late 1970s, black employees represented just 0.75 per cent of workers in shops and factories and 0.9 per cent of jobs in the city council and had virtually no presence in 'white collar' occupations. The Toxteth riots of 1981 were not simply about poverty and deprivation. They were certainly also about race and the policing of the black community.

The American scholar Jacqueline Nassy Brown's (2005) *Dropping anchor, setting sail: geographies of black Liverpool* gathered together and narrates the ways in which blackness was constructed in Liverpool. One mode was to establish a racial identity through the figure of Liverpool-born black people. Such an identity looks back to the roots of African seafarers – and others such as loyalist fighters in the American Revolutionary War – who had settled the city (in a few cases up to ten generations ago). However, this identity was itself quite exclusionary and not always welcoming of other, more recent, migrants. Another approach to constructing 'Liverpudlian blackness' was to invoke 'the Liverpool that was': a reified, authentic multicultural Liverpool belonging to all. These narratives feed into both the city's exceptionalism and its sense of apartness as a 'renegade outsider'. They clash with some of the ways in which geographical studies generalize about urban change.

Such local detail is important, for there are aspects of most localities that are unique. Liverpool's black community took a different trajectory from that found in other large industrial cities in the UK. For example, in the 1970s, newly arrived immigrants from the New Commonwealth and Pakistan constituted just 0.4 per cent of the city's population, with the result that by 2007, Liverpool had become one of the least ethnically varied cities in Britain, with the proportions of Hindus, Muslims and Sikhs falling well below the national average for England and Wales.

# In Conclusion: Towards Powerful Geographical Knowledge

In our account of Liverpool's development, race is an *integral* part. The crucial element of our historical account of urban change in Liverpool is that it places emphasis on the flows of capital in the remaking of urban space. Added to this is an understanding of how this story is racialized – of racial capitalism. Racial capitalism is the process by which the key dynamics of capitalism (e.g. accumulation/dispossession, credit/debt, production/surplus, capitalist/worker, developed/underdeveloped, contract/coercion among others) become articulated *through race*. Indeed, this list of conceptual binaries gives us clues as to how we could develop this case study further so as to think about how the operation of capitalism shapes race and racism.

Whereas DG's account sought to centre 'colonialism as the driver of urban change and cultural change in the UK', our account frames the narrative in slightly different terms. It prompts us to ask broader questions that take us to a potentially richer array of explanations than 'colonialism'. We seek to build a broader base of powerful disciplinary knowledge, rooted in geography. From this geographical point of view, there is an important set of questions about the nature of the Liverpool story. For example, what is unique to this particular locality? How does Liverpool relate to a broader story of geographical change? How are local, national and global dynamics worked through in this story of urban change?

## Conclusion

We have covered a lot of ground in this chapter. We hope it is becoming clearer why in this book we have focussed our discussion of race and racism on the *geography curriculum*. This is not the curriculum seen as a technical device for delivering prescribed content, but the curriculum as a space in which questions of knowledge and values can be addressed. We hope that this chapter has clarified our argument in Chapter 1: that any geography education that ignores processes of racialization is partial (in all senses of the word) and incomplete.

What we have been describing is a continuing and deepening engagement with *explanation in geography*. This is how we define *progress* in geography. Thus, we have discussed how school geography has handled debates about knowledge and attempted to illustrate how these relate to arguments about race and racism. This is linked to our vision of the aims, purposes and value of geography education. Geography, like any social science, is concerned with how and why things happen. We have been at pains to stress that this endeavour at the level of the discipline is not easy. But teaching good explanations in school geography is, if anything, even harder. In addition to understanding, explaining and communicating the geography, it also entails a theory of learning. In essence, we think our approach is about developing the cognitive depth of geographical understanding. School geography is concerned with providing students with cognitive (conceptual) maps – these are 'building blocks', 'handholds' or 'pegs' with which to make sense of a changing world.

Note that we have no wish to engage in a competition to produce ever more sophisticated case studies or examples. We do think it is imperative that teachers clarify their own position as they produce curriculum knowledge. In the case study example of urban change in Liverpool, we sought to stress the importance of the changing fortunes of the city in terms of the international division of labour *and* the specificity of the place itself. We recognize that this analysis is incomplete: we also acknowledge the way in which the scale of analysis we adopted does not shine a light on the lived experience of people in the city. What we are modelling is a thought process, not the final word.

In the end, our discussion of knowledge and curriculum stresses that curriculum thinking starts with theory, rather than teaching methods, and that theory requires conceptual clarification. It is not an exaggeration to say that before we can teach about race and racism in geography, or teach in a racially literate manner, we have to clarify the conceptual basis for our teaching.

## Questions for Discussion and Reflection

1. To what extent should the school geography curriculum seek to promote a common and shared understanding of the world?
2. Are standpoint theory and powerful knowledge able to coexist in classrooms?

# 7

# Changing the Geography Curriculum

## Introduction

It should be clear that addressing race and racism in the geography curriculum is not simply a matter of 'colouring the white spaces', in the form of new case studies or extra topics. The contents and methods of geography teaching, together with geography teacher education, are set within a white framework. It is time to change therefore, on the basis of deep and critical reflection, on how to place race and racisms at the heart of a better geographical education.

We have argued throughout that thinking about school geography without reference to wider contexts is inadequate. Thus, although reading the critiques and arguments in the academic literature (some of which we introduced in Chapter 4) about race and representation is important, this alone will not conjure an anti-racist geography curriculum. This is because the curriculum as a whole, and geography's particular role within it, is wrapped up within the trajectory of educational change and the state policies of which this is part. That explains how we have arranged the chapters in this book, to study:

- first, the politics of immigration and racism;
- second, changing ideas (theories) about race and education;
- third, evolving perspectives (theories) on the curriculum enactment;
- fourth, the responses of the academic discipline to understanding race and racism; and
- finally, the way in which race has been handled (or not) in school geography.

Developing racial literacy is challenging because it requires thinking about all these dimensions at once and together.

So, in this final chapter, we focus on the geography curriculum and the prospects for teaching a racially literate school geography. Our interest is with the geography curriculum as a whole, acknowledging that this is a part of a continuing conversation on how schools and teachers respond to and contribute to social change. We are concerned with how those involved in geography teaching in schools (subject associations, policymakers, departments and teachers) can *approach* their curriculum making so that race and racism becomes central to teaching and learning.

Our starting point for analysis is an article written by John Huckle in an edited collection called *The Future of Geography* (Johnston, 1985). It provides an historical account of the making of school geography, but for our purposes, it is the methodology that is important. Huckle insisted that the content of school geography can only be understood in relation to wider social and political changes. Though this sounds rather obvious, in practice, discussion of school geography in the literature rarely explores the implications of this view. As Huckle (1985) argued:

> Contrary to the beliefs of many geography teachers, changes in the nature of schooling, curriculum content, and methodology are not simple a response to the growth of knowledge or the changing preoccupations of geographers and educationalists. (294)

This chapter therefore re-visits and expands on the 'politics of multiracial education'. Without a robust understanding of the macro context of curriculum change, we argue, any claims for racial literacy in our own curriculum making (the meso and micro context of curriculum) will be superficial. Although we stress that there are limits to the impacts of curriculum change, we nevertheless recognize that schools and teachers have some autonomy to interpret and shape the curriculum – and more than they sometimes want to acknowledge. This is reflected in the idea of curriculum making, which invites teachers to make better choices about what and how to teach in their particular settings.

## Changing Capitalism, Changing Racism

It is a widely acknowledged truth that going to school in Britain today is preparation for life in a capitalist society. A capitalist society is one in which market relations dominate (Streeck, 2016). Crucially, this is not the only set of relations in operation. However, the important thing to realize is that 'the market' seeks to extend its influence over society. The increasing commodification of the social and natural world, and the expansion of the ideologies and practices of consumerism, require an educated, socially mobile and ideologically encultured population.

The state operates to smooth the process of accumulation for capital. Again, this is not all it does. But in relation to assisting capitalism, it performs two roles. First, it sets the rules for accumulation, and second, it provides legitimation for the system as a whole (Offe, 1984). Those who work in the welfare state (e.g. most teachers) occupy a space of some contradiction, and many teachers feel this acutely. They must promote equality but *also* (because this is the system that has been set up) help sort the school population into 'winners' and 'losers'. The egalitarian aims of the welfare state must coexist with the successful development of the capitalist economy, and so education provides two functions. It prepares children and young people for their future role in the labour market, and at the same time, it plays a role in socializing them into the norms and expectations of society. At times of crisis, the nature of education systems is prone to change or reorganization, and teachers' work is redefined: this frequently involves curriculum reform.

Chapters 2 and 3 portray the postwar story of race in Britain and the evolving role of the state, especially in relation to education. Box 7.1 provides a summary sketch of the development of state education in Britain and how this came increasingly to impinge on curriculum matters and the landmark Education Reform Act (ERA) of 1988.

## Box 7.1 The Emergence of 'Curriculum' as a State Concern

Universal state education was a response to the changes wrought by industrialization and the growth of towns and cities and the need to socialize children into the norms of a modern society. In the twentieth century, debates about the curriculum in the interwar period focused on the question of access to schooling for working-class children. As the Second World War approached, it was clear that schooling needed to accommodate the working classes. The 1944 Education Act established a three-tier system with curriculum responsibility going to local authorities and teachers enjoying levels of relative autonomy to handle matters of curriculum, pedagogy and assessment. This was a moment of modernization in education facilitated by historically high rates of economic growth. Capital faced acute shortages of labour, and official reports were concerned with what they saw as a 'wastage of talent'. The focus of much of the educational research at this time was on establishing the extent to which working-class children had equality of opportunity and whether education was genuinely a means to social mobility. Modernization coincided with the encouragement of international migration in order to fill growing labour shortages. In the case of postwar migration to Britain from its former colonies, this was a clear example of the state acting on behalf of the capitalist class as a whole.

The expansion of education in the 1950s and 1960s took place at a time of economic growth and provided the basis for the relative autonomy of teachers. Another way of saying this is that the Fordist capitalist economy was supported by a Keynesian welfare state that was driven by goals of inclusion and equality. Teachers working in state education were socialized into a view of their role as compensating for the relative deprivation of working-class and 'immigrant' children. There developed a strong ethos of equality of opportunity. As the state sought to integrate black and Asian children, curriculum reformers sought to overcome the Eurocentric images of 'despised places inhabited by savages' (Williams, 1979), and to this was added the assumption that such images would impact on the self-concept of black children and their educational performance (Milner, 1975).

Reading that last sentence, it might be tempting to conclude that such curriculum reform was simply a response of teachers and educators to a genuine and perceived problem. However, moves to develop multicultural education (as we saw in Chapter 3) were also part of the state's response to political activism on the part of the Black community. Mullard (1984) insisted that the rise of multicultural education was state constructed and state sanctioned. But the state was reluctant to intervene at first, beyond the assumption that schools would help the children of immigrants to assimilate the norms and values of British society. As late as 1971, government advice was that there was no need for a coordinated national policy response – on the grounds that the scale and permanency of migration was unclear.

This 'hands-off' policy (generously described by Kirp (1979) as 'doing good by doing little') was in line with the terms of the social-democratic settlement that granted schools, teachers and teacher unions control over educational decisions. The emergence of welfare capitalism, the licensed autonomy of teachers and modes of professional socialization created a space where more progressive and even radical ideas about society and its organization could be explored. Hence, moves towards a multicultural curriculum. However, broadly speaking, recently arrived migrants occupied a subordinate place in the class system, marked by a divide between the white working class and the black working class.

As long as the economy was buoyant, and there was political consensus around the role of the welfare state, these struggles were muted. But between the mid-1970s and the mid-1980s, working-class youth went from 'learning to labour' to 'schooling for the dole'. A series of moral panics emerged around Black youth and criminality and the political mood shifted as part of a sea change in thinking about the welfare function of state education. Across the advanced economies, the school was in question (Husen, 1979). The so-called Great Debate of the crisis ridden mid-1970s, which culminated in the ERA of 1988 and the introduction of the national curriculum, constructed schools and teachers as somehow promoting an 'anti-industrial spirit', and sought to ensure that schools and teachers met the needs of industry – a case of blaming teachers for the underlying crises of capitalism at that time.

In 1983, Sally Tomlinson summarized the early piecemeal and often locally inspired multicultural curriculum development work mentioned in Box 7.1, posing questions that endure to the present day:

> Proponents of multicultural education assume that changing the curriculum will lead to wider acceptance of cultural diversity and an enhancement of the self-concept of minority children as they see their cultural values reflected in the curriculum. They also see it as leading to an improvement of the chances for equal opportunity for minority children. But it is difficult to test any of these assumptions empirically. Anxieties centre around how far minority cultures can be reflected in a common curriculum without becoming too divisive, and whether the majority

society controllers of curriculum may use multicultural education as a means of containment of minority pupils. How far antiracist teaching should be specifically included is also an issue. (Tomlinson, 1983: 101–2)

So, from the 1980s, the UK has seen an almost continuous restructuring of state education. First, there was an attack on teachers wrapped up in debates about education, followed by a re-culturing of schools and an appeal for a 'new professionalism'. The tensions between two different versions of conservatism were played out. The National Curriculum was the culmination of this, but there was also a move to ensure that this was capable of technical interpretation via a national assessment/testing regime. It could be seen as ideology free, and teachers were encouraged to get on with the task of 'delivery' for all students. It gave birth to the 'school-improvement' movement and technocratic instruments to raise the 'effectiveness' of teaching and schools.

The curriculum has been viewed by successive governments since ERA as a tool to be tweaked and refined in order to increase the productivity of state schooling – perhaps epitomized by the New Labour slogan 'Every Child Matters'. The Swann Report of 1985 remains a key document, when the UK state became officially 'post-racial' in its approach to education. Box 7.2 provides a summary of this period during which 'colour-blind' globalized neoliberal economics held sway. Despite the claims that British society was 'post-race', in the years since the 2008 financial crisis many questions have arisen including subtle yet important shifts in racial discourse. We conclude this section with an account of how race and racism feature in the present moment, most visibly in the highly publicized Commission on Race and Ethnic Disparities (CRED) or Sewell Report released in April 2021.

## Box 7.2 The Rise of 'Post-Race' in the 'Neoliberal' State

The Conservative governments of the 1980s and 1990s harboured deep tensions between tradition and modernity, and between heritage and enterprise. On the one hand, there were moves to shore up the boundaries of the nation, with a common history, understanding of landscape and culture. This was reflected in the subject-centred 1988 National Curriculum. On the other hand, there was an acceptance that the world was changing and that opening the nation to the market would require new approaches, new technologies and new 'neoliberal' subjects, reflecting new school subjects such as IT and Business Studies.

Thus, in a whole range of areas, the conservative governments of the 1980s and 1990s sought to 'nationalize' education, defining and policing the boundaries of the nation (Donald, 1992). These sought to re-establish particular highly conservative versions of history, geography, English literature and music (Ball, 1994). Moves to develop multicultural and anti-racist practices in education were challenged by the development of a national curriculum that sought to tell a singular story about the nation. Religion, too, became a site where the unity of the nation was contested, and in response, the 1988 Education Act legislated for schools to ensure that there was a daily act of worship of 'a broadly Christian nature'.

By the end of the century, it was clear that the curriculum modernizers had won out. Modernization found its apogee under New Labour, which from 1997 saw the school curriculum as a place where ongoing social challenges could be addressed. It actively promoted ideas of sustainability, well-being, diversity and citizenship and reshaped the curriculum accordingly (still with subjects, but stripped of much of the official content, thus giving teachers more choice). It saw educational success as important to all and introduced metrics for how to measure performance and assess school effectiveness. The more relaxed view of school knowledge at the turn of the century, bolstered by a 'postmodernism' which asserted the relativism of knowledge (see Chapter 6), paved the way for the shift from curriculum to pedagogy in the New Labour years.

As noted in Chapter 3, almost immediately after coming to power, New Labour's attitude towards multiculturalism changed. The goal was now integration, prompted by Trevor Philips's perception that Britain was 'sleepwalking to segregation'. The years following the Macpherson Report at the turn of the century saw a series of studies which pointed to continued institutional racism. In practice, there was little progress on the curriculum, so that the Ajegbo Report of 2007 harboured a tension between multiculturalism and integration.

The global financial crisis of 2008 and the years of austerity that followed led to a conservative renaissance and the re-establishment of curriculum politics dominated by Michael Gove's reforms as Secretary of State for Education (2010–14) and his ministers, who had sought a return to the 'rigour' of traditional subject knowledge. This was accompanied by a rhetoric on 'the importance of teaching'. However, the autonomy of teachers remained limited, tethered by the notion of effective 'delivery' of the authorized curriculum.

---

The ascendant moment of neoliberalism (the economic aspects of which were dissected in Harvey's 2005 book, *A Brief History of Neoliberalism*) stressed the colour-blindness of economic rationalism. Neoliberalism, after all, was concerned with removing the barriers to global capital and labour flows. But since 2010, policies of austerity have had uneven social and economic impacts and consequences. As part of the neoliberal attempt to shift the costs to individuals (part of the state's changing role – from 'caretaker' to 'traffic cop'), a suffocating and oppressive discourse has emerged which argues that race is less and less relevant – that Britain really is a 'post-race' society. An early example of this can be found in a 2010 issue of *Prospect* magazine in which four commentators (reflective of what Warmington (2014) calls 'Black conservative social thought') argued that although race was no longer so important as a social determinant in British society, increased monitoring associated with the Race Relations Act of 2000 had created a climate of suspicion and fear. Munira Mirza, the Director of Boris Johnson's No 10 Policy unit (2019–22), wrote that while old prejudices have faded, new paternalistic stereotypes are growing. To engage minority students, particularly if they are disruptive and struggling with the mainstream curriculum, teachers are encouraged to focus on 'their culture' or 'their history.' Black artists are encouraged to explore their identity but are then pigeonholed according to their ethnicity. We may have seen the decline of old racism, but we are witnessing a new kind of racializing. (Mirza, 2010)

The 2011 riots in English cities provide another example of this post-race framing, with Prime Minister David Cameron claiming that these were quite different from the 'race riots' of the 1980s. In this way, racism was presented as a regrettable but long-gone aspect of British life. The 'trick' of post-race framing is to suggest that racism itself is diminishing. There are four elements to this (discussed more fully in Chapter 3):

- abstract liberalism – the idea of equal opportunity, and benign meritocracy (as in 'Every Child Matters');
- naturalization – the idea that where differences exist, these are the inevitable result of cultural distinctions (e.g. the growth of 'ethnic communities' – not 'ghettos' – (as a natural, positive choice);
- cultural racism – the idea that certain groups do not help themselves because of their lifestyle characteristics – and that change has to come from within; and
- minimization – the argument that claims of racism are overblown or overstated.

All aspects of this post-race ideology are present in the 2021 CRED Report, which looks to provide a positive narrative about the direction of change around racism in British society. In relation to education, it suggests that educational opportunity is open to all (abstract liberalism) and uses the example of 'model minorities' whose educational success 'proves' that institutional racism does not exist – and that failure must be the result of some internal characteristic of the cultural group (cultural racism). It is evidence based and seeks to minimize the existence of racism, especially through the idea of progress over time (things are better now than in the past). In addition, the CRED Report looks forward to a positive, unifying sense of Britishness. The government's plan to implement the recommendations of the Report (published in March 2021) includes the sentiment that 'all children should grow up feeling a strong sense of belonging to this country' (89–92), which becomes a *de facto* curriculum aim.

It is at this point that the present-day educational struggle over race and racisms becomes clear. The CRED Report takes the position of arguing for progress – with educational failure seen as a feature of cultural 'backwardness'. It argues for a unified curriculum that narrates the nation's colonial past in relatively benign terms. It identifies its enemies as 'critical race theorists' and 'decolonizers' who wish to dig out the bones of Britain's imperial past (and thus, erroneously in our view, undermine a 'strong sense of belonging to this country'). This is framed by what the CRED Report calls a 'white majority nation', resonant of Eric Kaufman's argument in his 2018 book *Whiteshift*. In doing so, for the Conservative government who commissioned the Report, there appear to be remnants of Powellism in this (see Chapter 2 of this book), designed to appeal to a constructed political constituency, the so-called left behinds who face economic instability and uncertainty.

This section reminds us that the curriculum is shaped by wider forces. We are now in a position to better understand Huckle's statement (quoted at the beginning of this chapter) about geography teachers not being in full control of their work. It also requires us to acknowledge the fact that any attempt to teach about race and racisms in school is unavoidably political. The next section considers geography's part in all this.

# Capitalism, Race and Geography Teaching

## Where We Have Come From

School subjects find their place in the curriculum according to their capacity to support broad economic and societal agendas. In this way, the curriculum is a reflection of the culture. It would be hard to imagine an anticapitalist school geography being sanctioned in a capitalist society (which is not to say we cannot teach about capitalism in schools!). School geography contributes both to the practical ideology or hidden curriculum of schooling, and a more specific or overt ideology through its curriculum content selections (Huckle, 1985). In terms of the latter, Huckle (1986) argues that

> [school geography] … clearly acts as ideology supportive to capital. … The resulting costs and inequalities are largely ignored in the benign image often presented, and … change is generally presented as a rational consensus activity, free of conflict, racism, sexism or class struggle. (9)

This statement requires some elaboration. In Chapter 5, we encountered the argument that geography was part of the propaganda of empire. It served to support a geographical imagination that divided the world into 'them' and 'us', and 'home' and 'abroad', all of which was underpinned by a moral hierarchy. Exposed to this propaganda, it became 'natural' to see Britain sitting at the head of a vast Commonwealth. It is important to restate that this empire was geared to supplying the needs of British capital. It was the desire for raw materials and food that prompted the expansion of trade and the activities of Royal companies overseas. Textbooks tended to wash over this, setting out instead the regional and local diversity of 'people at work', resting on appeals to tolerance, charity and a desire to know more about 'people in other lands'. However, it was also paternalist, and took for granted the idea that colonialism was 'natural' and given – even civilizing.

For the first six decades of the twentieth century, the development of school geography depended on socially conservative, 'gentlemanly' public school teachers (Walford, 2001). While this may have been comfortable, the subject lacked intellectual depth: it was heavy on memory but light on the mind. Regional geography in schools lacked rigour. As we saw in Chapter 5, the shock to the system came with the postwar modernization, and geography itself took an applied turn, embracing the 'spatial-quantitative revolution' and contributing to the spatial challenges faced by the UK state at this time (Stamp, 1960). This was a period of nation-building (literally), as the very face of the country changed: with inner-city clearance, suburban growth and New Towns, National Parks, the extension of the road network, agricultural intensification and the problems of affluence.

'New ways' of conceptualizing space were adopted and adapted by a new generation of geography educators and teachers, who found there was a symmetry between rational curriculum planning and the so-called new geography. It also came at a time of expansion of teacher training and a spirit of new professionalism. This was an important period of reform in school geography in terms of both content and methods (curriculum and pedagogy). This spirit of modernization was reflected in how geographers studied 'abroad', with the shift here from 'colonial geography' to the 'geography of development' (Goodenough, 1977). This was in line with British capitalism's attempt to adjust to new circumstances. In the era of decolonization, corporations needed to renegotiate the terms of their relationship with the so-called developing world.

However, the main scholarship and writing in the world of geography education and school teaching during this period was remarkably disengaged from wider educational debates. A good example of this was Bradford and Kent's (1977) best-selling *Human Geography: Theories and Their Application*. It provided comprehensive coverage of the new spatial models, including those associated with modernization theory such as stages of growth and cumulative causation, but in practice it was only the 'application' of these theories that mattered. The social and historical contexts of the theories themselves – where they came from intellectually – was absent. There were notable exceptions, including discussions of political and citizenship education (e.g. Huckle, 1983); how to teach the 'Third World' (e.g. Bale, 1983); tackling bias and stereotyping (e.g. Hicks, 1981a); and 'multicultural issues' (e.g. Gill, 1983). However, mainstream school geography seemed largely content with internal matters. For example, out of nearly 4,000 entries in Foskett and Marsden's (1998) *Bibliography of Geographical Education*, just twenty-one concerned 'multicultural issues'. The main preoccupation of the Geographical Association (GA) and geography educationists during the period of major state reform of education from the 1980s was to ensure geography's continued presence in national policy as a high-status and valued school subject – maintaining 'its place in the sun' (Bailey, 1989). As we have seen, attempts to address race and racism in (and through) geography education remained at the margins of the official, authorized curriculum, which was strongly influenced by the need 'to get to grips with curriculum politics' (Walford, 2001: 205).

The trajectory of geography in British *universities* has been different, as we saw in Chapter 4. Supported by the fact that each year around 7,000 students leave school to study the subject to degree level, geography has been able to build an important base in higher education. The result is that there is a 'gap' between geography as studied and taught in universities and geography as studied and taught in schools. This is not necessarily a problem and is probably to be expected. However, the gap is a political one. As Cox (2014) notes, the hegemonic position in human geography is occupied by critical human geography, a highly eclectic mix made up of a 'soft critique of capitalism' and bits and pieces of "post" thinking. Identity, social construction and discourse dominate. This reflects the turn towards geography as a normative subject in the past two decades. Those who go on to train as geography teachers learn *this* human geography, and one of the challenges they face is to somehow reconcile this with what they find in the national curriculum, examinations specifications and textbooks.

Addressing this reconciliation is not simply a matter of 'auditing' the bits of the school subject they identify they have missed as undergraduates. There are deeper matters to consider including the very purpose of the subject: What is it for, what does the subject do and what educational purposes does it serve? There is an expanding literature about what it means to 'think geographically' (Brooks, 2018; Jackson, 2006; Lambert, 2017; Morgan, 2018; Taylor, 2008). There are different emphases in this work, but what they all share is the idea that thinking geographically means thinking conceptually, since it is this that allows us to gain a deeper and more accurate understanding of the world through better explanations. In the context of UK race and racisms, geography as a discipline has produced new knowledge and insights, as we have seen in Chapters 4 and 6. These can be melded with a broader contextual knowledge of the politics race (Chapter 2) and indeed how education (including geography education in particular) have often struggled to address issues of race and racism (in Chapters 3 and 5, respectively).

## Where Are We Now?

The coalition government elected in 2010 in the UK opted for fiscal conservatism and implemented policies of austerity. Austerity is an ideology which gives primacy to economic matters (insisting that we cannot challenge the natural order of profit and loss). The promise of global consumerism that had kept the whole system going seemed to collapse after the 2008 crash, illustrated with the English Riots of August 2011 and the long road to Brexit. The 2016 Brexit vote was interpreted by many as a case of the older generations imposing the costs (which are now becoming apparent) on the next generations, already burdened with the challenges of dealing with climate change.

All of these developments are mediated through the UK's racialized class system, which ensures that wealth and privilege exist for a few alongside widespread poverty and lack of opportunity. Instead of climbing the ladder of opportunity, many young people are sliding down it. There is a growing radicalism among young people, which has been expressed in the campaigns to decolonize the curriculum and responses to Black Lives Matter (BLM).

One outcome of these movements has been demands for more culturally responsive pedagogies in schools and universities – that is, pedagogies that seek out, acknowledge and respect Black scholarship as well as local, traditional and indigenous knowledges and more diverse ways of knowing. But this appears to put schools and teachers on a collision course with the government, which seeks to maintain tradition within teaching, focus on ensuring 'standards' are maintained and resisting what it regards as the politicization of teaching. The 2013 National Curriculum was seen as an attempt to provide a more 'knowledge-rich' curriculum, now bolstered by a new inspection framework which stresses knowledge and memory. On these terms, geography's place in the curriculum seems assured. However, at a cost, for the curriculum question of what to teach is literally ceded to the government. The 2020 Ofsted review of the 'research evidence' on which school geography is based (Ofsted, 2021) excluded much of the curriculum debates in geography education we have outlined (Chapter 5), aside from the recognition of cultural diversity. Furthermore, in response to BLM, there have been attempts to move against the teaching of Critical Race Theory in schools (emulating aspects of US culture wars where this issue has become an often misrepresented yet extremely divisive political marker), for instance, by a reassertion by the government of the need for 'balance' within teaching of social and political issues.[1]

Teachers operate at the frontline of these cultural shifts, changing political contexts and educational developments, and to find a way through is extremely challenging. Our argument is that by focussing on *the curriculum* – teachers can develop intellectually robust approaches to anti-racist geography through their curriculum making. As we suggested in Chapter 5, the subject community's record on this is patchy, to say the least. There is reason, therefore, to be cautious about Kinder and Pike's (as Chief Executive and President of the GA respectively) response to BLM and the 2021 CRED Report: 'we suggest that examination of racism and neo-colonialism through the lens of the geography curriculum would be better handled from within our subject community' (Kinder and Pike, 2021: 9). We could more confidently embrace this suggestion if the community were truly open and ready to develop an approach that took on *wider* perspectives on the work of geography teachers, such as we have attempted to show in this book.

## Three 'Anti-Racist' Approaches to the Geography Curriculum

Having set out the political economy of the curriculum and examined school geography's contribution to an overt ideology that tends to bolster the status quo, we

---

[1]. https://www.theguardian.com/education/2020/nov/13/education-experts-counter-government-attack-on-critical-race-theory (accessed 30 September 2022).
2. https://www.gov.uk/government/publications/political-impartiality-in-schools/political-impartiality-in-schools (accessed 30 September 2022).

come to this key section. This is a discussion of the options that present themselves to geography teachers in schools keen to develop anti-racist curriculum making strategies. We discuss three alternatives – all of which can reasonably claim to promote 'anti-racist geography'. They are quite different from each other, and here we recourse to Alistair Bonnett's arguments, in *Anti-racism* (Bonnett, 2000), that there is no single anti-racism. Anti-racism can be conservative, liberal or radical. We present three anti-racist alternatives available to departmental teams and the wider geography education community.

- The anti-racist geographical mainstream

We assume there are few geography teachers and geography departments who still believe that there is 'no problem here' or proclaim, 'we're all white thanks'. This was an all too common position in the 1980s and even 1990s, especially in those geographical areas where the proportion of Black, Asian and minority ethnic people was relatively low. Even so, there is no reason to assume that the majority of geography teaching in schools now reflects perspectives on race and racisms – or as we argue in this book, are racially literate.

Geography in many schools has been modernized so as to bring in students' perspectives, frequently adopting an issues-led approach, enquiry learning and insights from learning theory. These attributes reflect commonly held ideas about good practice and matters of pedagogical concern such as, for example, about providing access and equality, and more recently technocratic concerns about raising attainment levels and to demonstrate students 'making progress'. The geographical mainstream goes with the grain of official policy, and it is interesting to note that in terms of candidate numbers at GCSE as a crude measure of popularity and success, geography has done better under Conservative administrations over the past 35 years – in which policy making is generally aligned to shoring up tradition and continuity.

School geography could therefore end up supporting a post-race or colour-blind agenda through an uncritical acceptance of calls for school improvement and educational progress. A long-standing tradition of 'professional neutrality' may lead to a modern curriculum based on an ideology of problem solving, decision making and effective management, whether this is to do with flooding, urban zoning or retail distribution. This positivist approach (e.g. making use of official data and reports) can be made more human (and therefore more palatable to teachers and students) through cultural artefacts and narratives. However, race, if it features at all, will be seen as a spatial 'problem' to be managed through rational decision making, and racism mainly explained in terms of irrational prejudice.

At an institutional level, BLM and criticisms that geography is a white subject have prompted a new wave of reflection in organizations such as the GA and the Royal Geographical Society (with IBG) (RGS-IBG), not least because these perspectives challenge the subject's self-image as progressive, open and diverse. The resurgence of the BLM movement has promoted a range of reactive statements, articles and projects which effectively amount to the attempt to show that 'geography' is doing something. However, the geographical mainstream is relatively silent on questions of knowledge and the curriculum, other than to say that all students should be taught to a 'high standard' and have greater access to 'good' geography. Hence, our contrasting focus on knowledge and curriculum in Chapter 6, for the knowledge question – what counts as good geography – is in our view crucial, and far from settled).

Where curriculum matters are raised in the mainstream, the question will be about sequencing, coherence, the selection of images and the choice of case studies reflecting diversity. Much professional energy and leadership effort is expended on technical issues regarding curriculum coherence (Gardner, 2021), with an understandable focus on *implementation* and *impact*. However, teachers are now also expected to show how they articulate the *intent* of the geography curriculum. In theory, this is promising and will require more and better qualified teachers who are able to make informed, racially literate curriculum decisions. The question remains whether the mainstream is able to accommodate the more demanding conceptual and political questions we have explored in this book.

- Radical anti-racist geography curricula

There has been a vocal call for radical anti-racist and decolonizing geographies that gained momentum in the wake of BLM. It is appealing because it calls for decisive action and operates within a clear and simple framework of good and bad. The self-evident 'good' is decolonization, which advocates rewriting geography in order to expunge its colonial and imperialistic overtones. It has its origins in debates on the critical left, in the anti-racist struggles of the 1970s and 1980s and the growth of World Studies and Development Education. A key difference is that while these earlier approaches were often rooted in an analysis of global capitalism, more recent work has drawn from standpoint epistemologies which focus on the positionality of knowledge (see Chapter 6).

The establishment of a relationship between colonizer and colonized is a binary framework such as found in Paulo Friere's *Pedagogy of the Oppressed*. It casts the teacher as facilitator of emancipation, achieved collaboratively through a process of co-construction of knowledge. Because knowledge is powerful, usually reflecting the interests of the powerful social classes and groups that control the curriculum, it needs to be countered with a 'standpoint' curriculum. Such a curriculum recognizes the role of power in shaping dominant understandings of the world (Au, 2017) and seeks to challenge and *replace* dominant voices and stories with others.

As we have seen in Chapter 6, this 'essentialist' view sees knowledge as linked to the positionality of those who produce it, and logically leads to calls for white voices to be replaced by Black, and for a curriculum written from 'the standpoint of the least advantaged'. This is to challenge the traditional curriculum of exclusion, and it requires *critical pedagogies* which value and recognize the social, economic and political locations of oppressed groups, based on the 'deconstruction' of dominant versions of the curriculum (e.g. Winter, 2006, 2018).

A geography curriculum informed by a radical anti-racist perspective would seek to deconstruct categories such as North and South and developed/developing world. It would be attentive to commonly used terms such as 'slum' which seem to produce negative images (perhaps even issuing advice to teachers not to use certain terms). There would be attention to the positive images and representations of people and place, and avoidance of stereotypical ideas such as those rooted in environmental determinism. More ambitious would be the acknowledgement of power in social and environmental relations and the considered selection of case studies and examples that stress positive change. There would also be a focus on moral issues, especially those that look at how present-day patterns of racial inequality and injustice are linked to processes in the past. There would be a concern to ensure that representations of the nation are inclusive. There may also be a focus on concepts such as racial capitalism, locating the causes of hazards in their 'slow violence' (disproportionately affecting poor people at the margins and 'out of sight').

The obvious appeal of this approach is that it seeks to teach a geography with an overt ideology of anti-racism. It seeks consciously and visibly to counter apolitical and Eurocentric perspectives. It offers a different view of geographic processes and pays attention to views from the global south. However, it risks replacing one 'truth' with another and may even achieve little more than to install an alternative canon of geographical knowledge – which might be as unreflexive, uncontested and inadequately pre-decided and 'given' as the one it replaces.[2] It also risks amplifying the problem of a binary divide between 'black' and 'white' knowledge, and its overtly political stance is likely to bring accusations of bias, for a narrative based on a moral geography risks over-simplification and the elevation of the 'single story'. And there are further issues to address which exist with any widespread adoption of critical pedagogy, the not least of which is students' ability and willingness to give the teacher the answers they seem to want.

Finally, there are questions about the position of scholar-activism underpinning radical anti-racism. It is an open question as to whether teachers can and should adopt the role of social justice warriors. The issue of how ideas at the cutting edge of radical thought are to be 'translated' into school geography lessons is usually left unaddressed.

- A 'powerful knowledge' geography curriculum

The third anti-racist approach (which for the sake of openness is the one we favour) is rooted in the analysis of the curriculum as teachers' work which we set out in this and the previous chapter. It also draws from our discussion of how geography as a discipline has evolved (Chapter 4) and the difficulties that have acted as a drag anchor to geography in schools coming to terms with race and racisms (Chapter 5).

---

[2]We use here the language Young and Muller's (2010) 'three-futures' heuristic in geography education to characterize this 'traditional' curriculum as Future 1. This contrasts with alternative scenarios: Future 2 and Future 3. See Appendix 2 for a summary.

If we accept the earlier argument of this chapter concerning the ideological nature of school geography, then we could summarize its general purpose as providing students with an answer to the question: *to which space do I belong*? This is ideological in the sense that it takes for granted that what we see and explain is somehow 'natural'. It makes little reference to the historical construction of the nation's wealth – of power, exploitation and oppression. Rather, it provides natural and unexamined messages about who belongs where and the unevenness of development.

Geographical explanations can be made to sound very smooth, but they are not. This is because there are real contradictions in the process of accumulation, the foundation of capitalism, and these are never far from the surface. Students experience these contradictions in their own lives, families and communities, and have their own questions. This is what teachers experience all the time, and it is their job to weave all this into a cohesive world picture – a practical curriculum. Teachers have relative autonomy to 'make' the curriculum, though the question of how much is open to question (and also whether there is now more or less autonomy than in previous times). One of the ways in which teachers may feel prevented from addressing the contradictions is the fact that they are kept busy with new demands (dressed up as innovation) and other pressures that prevent them spending time developing the full potential of geography as an educational resource. A further barrier is geography teachers' socialization, which reflects the liberal ideology of professional and political neutrality.

However, as we have tried to show (Chapter 4) geography as an academic discipline, especially since its realignment as a social science, has an important role to play in explaining the production of place, space and environment. The discipline offers a resource that can help geography teachers create a realist 'cohesive world picture', and this includes the way race and racisms work in society. But we acknowledge a significant issue, namely, that geography teachers rarely gain the type of wide-ranging training that can help them develop such a realist account – not from their undergraduate degrees which tend to specialize and rarely cover a rounded philosophy of geography as a whole. Space to do so in their teacher education and training is also limited, as time is increasingly spent on developing technical competence. We find ourselves in easy agreement therefore with the caveats that underpin the Universities Council for the Education of Teachers (UCET) strategic plan and vision to the way teachers are prepared:

> Teacher education should have an academic, intellectual basis alongside a practical focus and should meet the needs of all pupils and students, particularly those facing disadvantage.
> - The teacher education sector should be receptive to challenge and debate and to a diverse range of approaches and structures.
> - The design and provision of teacher education should be informed by high-quality research of regional, national and international significance.
> - The higher education teacher education sector should work collaboratively in a constructively critical way with policymakers and others and be open and receptive to challenge in return.
>
> (UCET, 2020: n.p.)

The kind of anti-racist curriculum we propose, based on Future 3–type curriculum thinking (see Appendix 2), requires a huge intellectual effort. For example, it will require a grasp of colonialism which understands the ways in which it both promoted and used the racist imagination of human hierarchies enabling violence and oppression. It will require an understanding of the evolution of British capitalism and society, the incorporation of a global labour force and struggles over space – and how this has been represented through a changing geography. It will also require culturally sustaining pedagogies which are committed not only to engaging young people with powerful knowledge about the 'ways of the world' but also enabling teachers actively to listen to their lived experience of and encounters with the world. We envisage Future 3 thinking as engaging with selections of powerful knowledge plus how this interacts with other ways of knowing, including indigenous knowledges. Above all, Future 3–type curriculum making is acutely aware of the dangers of a single (simple) story.

## Towards Racially Literate Curriculum Making

In setting out three alternative approaches to 'anti-racist' geography curricula, we hope to generate argument and debate, facilitated by the three-future scenarios framework. The following table (derived from John Huckle's analysis) provides a series of questions that could inform curriculum discussions in schools. On the left are critical questions, and the right-hand column show these questions link to issues of race and racism in school geography.

These questions can be transformed into a set of six principles that underpin a racially literate geography curriculum:

- People and places are dynamic and always changing as a result of the interplay of economic, social, cultural, political and environmental processes; these do not operate neutrally and in the same way for all.
- Geographical facts are nearly always contingent: they are selected, prioritized and can frequently be contested; and there is nearly always another way of looking at them.
- Human agency is rarely unfettered and frequently involves disagreement, tension and struggle: human processes always involve politics (the process by which limited resources are allocated).
- Race is not a biological fact, attribute or phenomenon: race is a social construct and both produces and is a product of economic, environmental, political and social processes that have been racialized.
- Racialization is key to understanding racism: not solely as irrational prejudice held by individuals but also as part of social and economic institutions and structure.
- Theories in geography are not 'given' and are certainly not facts: theorizing always has relevant political, historical, economic, and social context.

**Table 7.1** Critical Questions about the Geography Curriculum

| | Principle | Illustration |
|---|---|---|
| 1 | How many geography lessons cultivate, or even encourage, a voluntary submission to existing social, spatial and environmental relations? | If race and racism are mentioned at all in school geography, they are likely to draw upon the idea that 'inner cities', segregation and/or 'ghettos' are facts of geography, albeit unfair and undesirable. |
| 2 | How often is the subject matter presented as a body of unproblematic facts? | The empirical tradition that still dominates school geography makes use of existing data sets and categories, often used uncritically to map the distribution of social groups (e.g. 'races') without examining the origins of these categories. |
| 3 | Over a course of study in geography, to what extent are pupils given a largely depoliticized and dehumanized view of the world? Does their success in geography depend on their ability to reproduce ideas, skills and attitudes which sustain the status quo? | The complex politics of race and immigration are rarely taught or explored in any depth in geography lessons. While there may be some recognition of personal experiences of migration, this is largely handled through a humanistic approach that stresses common experiences and downplays politics, economic structures and institutions. |
| 4 | To what extent is there a reference to economic, political and social processes which could explain the phenomena being studied? | A key concept required to make sense of race and racism is that of 'racialization'. Although this is widely accepted in the geographic literature, this concept is largely absent in school geography and its texts. |
| 5 | To what extent are problem-solving and decision-making activities in geography usually cast in an apolitical way? That is, within a consensus (managerial) view of society, where conflict is regarded as dysfunctional and little attention is given to radical social alternatives. | If it is mentioned at all, race and racism are regarded as a 'problem' to be managed by social policy. Racism is assumed to be an irrational prejudice, rather than as linked to wider economic and social structures (that can be changed). |
| 6 | To what extent are 'theories' in geography lessons placed in an historical and social context? To what extent are pupils encouraged to see institutions, processes and knowledge as pre-given, neutral and static. | The neglect of 'racialization' means that students are not taught how race and space are constructed. The ways racism operates in diverse societies could also be taught, providing a comparative means to understand how meanings attached to race change over time. |

These are 'key ideas'. They do not prescribe the content of the curriculum, but they are highly suggestive of how content selection may be made and how it should be taught. As Appendix 2 shows, these principles strongly indicate a healthy (Future 3) *approach to knowledge* which teachers may seek to impart to students – recognizing that seeking truthful, better explanations of the world usually requires digging below the surface (which is not easy) and is always open to debate and renewal (which can be unsettling).

Geography teachers today are now in a better position to answer the questions in Table 7.1 than when Huckle first posed them in the 1980s. Geography as an intellectual field has much more awareness of its wider academic significance – its key concepts (e.g. space, place and scale) are seen as crucial to sociologists, cultural theorists, political scientists and historians. But to round off this discussion, let us just stress one overarching and enduring question about school geography: *To what extent does learning geography in school inadvertently encourage young people to naturalize the present?* In other words, through neglecting the unequal distribution of power, diverse perspectives and the agency of ordinary people, to what extent do geographical patterns and processes appear to students as natural, inevitable, logical – and therefore legitimate?

A great advance in school geography would be more overtly to recognize the historicity of geographical patterns – the history behind the geography.

## Conclusion

The one thing we hope that our book achieves is to convince geography teachers that the 'theoretical effort' (not to mention the emotional effort) required to teach about race and racism is worth it. This requires critical self-reflection and the acceptance that there is no quick fix. This, therefore, is an introductory book in every sense. We hope it opens up new areas of debate and discussion and encourages readers to embark on a career-long journey of seeking to know and understand more about school geography's contribution to illuminating the world in which our students live.

Young people study geography for a variety of reasons. One common aspiration is that geography helps young people understand their 'place' in the world. Put this way, it is very important that geography addresses its purposes fairly and productively, so that all young people see their place in its relational settings, ultimately in a global context. This strongly implies the utility of a National Curriculum that sets out in broad terms a shared 'entitlement'. Our advocacy of an approach to curriculum making based on powerful knowledge and the way this *interacts with* experiential and other ways of knowing is in keeping with this vision. This is a principled 'Future 3'–geography curriculum that seeks to build connection and interaction rather than division and separation, especially that based on a deeper understanding of the concept of 'race' and how racism operates to the detriment of all of us.

In a different (US) setting, Heather McGhee expressed this bigger goal in a different way:

> I'm fundamentally a hopeful person, because I know that decisions made the world as it is and that better decisions can change it. Nothing about our situation is inevitable or immutable, but you can't solve a problem with the consciousness

that created it. The antiquated belief that some groups of people are better than others distorts our politics, drains our economy and erodes everything (we) have in common. (McGhee, 2021: p. xxiii)

## Question for Reflection and Discussion

This is a 'synoptic question' requiring an overview.

By way of stimulus, we draw on Priya Satia's (2020) *Time's Monster: History, Conscience and Britain's Empire*. Geography, like history, was and is a significant disciplinary resource in shaping our thinking about empire and the imperial legacy. We should critically examine this notion – not to undermine geography as a discipline but to understand how geography has figured in how people and society at large conceptualize their encounters with the world.

Read what Satia writes about *history* as a discipline, and its role in helping the British embrace empire as principally a force for good.

As you do so, substitute 'geography' for 'history' in the passage: What thoughts come to mind?

> This is a book about how the historical discipline helped make empire – by making it ethically thinkable – and how empire made and remade the historical discipline … that area of rich overlap created by the two meanings of 'history': what happened, and the narrative of what happened. Essentializing representations of other places and people laid the cultural foundation of empire, but historical thinking empowered Britons to *act* on them. The cultural hold of a certain understanding of history and historical agency was not innocent but designedly complicit in the making of empire. (6–7)
>
> History was remade in the crucible of twentieth century anticolonialism, but the discipline has yet to come to terms with its role as time's monster. (10)
>
> Because the historical sensibility that enabled imperialism is still intact, despite the seeing end of empire, we have been unable to sustain a consensus around the moral case against empire. Understanding how historical thinking conspired in imperialism offers a way out of this impasse. By uncovering how ideas of history influenced the actual unfolding of imperial history, we might dispel the perceived ambiguity around the moral case against empire and feel our way towards new modes of historical thinking less likely to bind us to the crimes of empire.
>
> How we remember the British Empire matters. It shapes how we assess the seeming 'failures' of postcolonial countries to 'move on' from their colonial past, how we make sense of Britain's efforts to reinvent its place in the world in the current Brexit crisis, and how we think about imperial activity today. (10–11)

# 8

# Conclusion

Our book can be read in many different ways. For one thing, as with any book, how it is read depends a great deal on what the reader brings to the task. But this book, on this topic, appears to be particularly exposed in this way. Indeed, when we were in the relatively early stages of writing it, several influential individuals in the geography education world publicly advised us, as two white men, not to continue. But continue we did, and with the assistance of a supportive publisher and many others, we have now completed the task. It seems appropriate then to attempt some words in conclusion.

We can begin by reflecting on that public advice. We have been clear about our positionality, both in the introduction and in the coda that follows this conclusion. However, so alert were some individuals to our (and their) inescapable identity as white people that they told us to not even try to write this book. One of our interlocutors explained at length why she had never written about race, her white identity being her disqualification. And in different conversations with a range of academics since, this position has been heard repeatedly to the point it becomes, in some perverse way, a form of white fragility. By way of contrast, in a recent conversation with two young Black men, describing themselves as education activists, one of us asked directly whether a book about racisms in geography education written by two oldish white men (like us) could be taken seriously – by them. Their response was intriguing: it depends, they said, on two things:

- Who you talk with and listen to, and
- The breadth of your scholarship.

There is not even a hint in this response that we had no business trying to write our book. But they were very clear in their challenge: that we had our work cut out. We have lived and worked in a racialized society, studied and tried to engage with it, but we do not have the *experience* of a minoritized person. We therefore cannot claim direct understanding of how our life chances, including in our professional settings, would have been limited or impaired through racialized processes. So, we have roamed widely, especially in our reading, and have listened carefully. Some readers may think we have not listened carefully enough, or to the 'right' people. That is fair enough although we should be clear about the limits we set ourselves, and especially about what we have *not* set out to do in this book. For example, we do not speak *for* black and minority ethnic people, and of course we would have been roundly criticized and ridiculed if we had tried.

Rather, our book addresses issues of race and racisms within our specialist field, geography education, and specifically examines implications for the curriculum. In this sense this book is a culmination of our joint interest in these matters spanning several decades (Morgan and Lambert, 2003, 2005; Lambert and Morgan, 2010) concerning the question of what to teach in school geography. We argue that better explanations of the world can be offered to young people when the school subject is able to embrace a greater racial literacy. We combine three areas of study: race, geography and curriculum, matters that face all teachers of geography even before they begin the intensely practical task of teaching.

However, our young activist interlocutors were telling us that we should be prepared to go beyond any kind of given 'comfort zone' in our scholarship: that is, to step outside of some of the established layers of received wisdom that may exist in the field of geography education. We have taken this challenge very seriously indeed, for it is true that all communities, disciplines and associations can become overly 'settled' on habitual practices, beliefs and processes that blind them to worthwhile and ethical alternatives. Thus, the 2022 All Party Parliamentary Group report on the teaching of Africa in British schools quotes the Canadian Ghanaian humanities educator George Sea Dei:

> We must also see Africa beyond homogeneity by exploring all the emerging contestations, contradictions and ambiguities in people's lives. Africa is a community of difference. The politics of claiming universal sameness served well the interests of those who did not want to see Africa challenge their 'stable knowledge'. Difference challenges that stability and the community of sameness.
> (Royal African Society, 2022: 12)

The Report goes on to argue that these 'stable' generalizations (resulting in stereotypical images and misconceptions) about Africa need to be dislodged and undermined from British mindsets so that a *better* understanding of Africa may be imparted through curriculum subjects such as geography, history, literature and music. So again, just a gentle reminder on what our book is *not* attempting to do: we do not pretend to come up with solutions, or a ready-made anti-racist curriculum to implement or operationalize. Apart from being absurd even to imagine such a thing being possible, it presupposes that the necessary graft, implied by the need to tackle the issues of 'stable knowledge' in geography, has been done. It has not, but we hope that this book makes a contribution to that work.

Thus, we provide a succinct yet layered account of the story of race and racisms in the UK (Chapter 2) and indeed the ways in which issues of race have been taken on within the education system at large (Chapter 3). These accounts form an essential background in supporting our intention to help raise levels of racial literacy in geography education. In Chapter 4 we then open up a discussion of how the discipline of geography itself has been challenged, both internally and through wider movements in the social sciences and beyond, to develop and refine its theoretical and conceptual resources for examining and making sense of the world – with a particular focus on race and racisms. In addition to showing how the discipline has adapted to accommodate and use the socially constructed nature of 'race', the chapter again shows the ways 'geography matters', for example, in the ways place and space are created through racialized processes. Chapter 5 then retraces the story in the context of geography education and teaching in schools. A central theme here has been the apparent insouciance of leaders and influencers to anything other than the adoption of a liberal face to questions of race and racism. It was as if anything else would require upsetting the proverbial apple cart: safer simply to espouse geographical knowledge and its enduring presence in the school curriculum as a good thing and its enduring stability.

So, to Chapters 6 and 7. These chapters begin to grasp the curriculum nettle and ask: 'where next'? We do this by breaking new ground in addressing tough questions about the nature of geographical knowledge and the kind of high-quality ('Future 3') curriculum making that will nurture a deeper, better set of explanations with young people. We draw upon both geography's enduring purpose and place in the school curriculum *and* the contemporary moment that urges radical change – for example, to respect local funds of knowledge and to take steps to decolonize the curriculum.

As Julian Agyeman chose to stress in his foreword, progress towards more balance and fairness in the geography curriculum has been 'partial and incomplete'. Even so, it is startling to recall how far society has travelled:

> When large numbers of black children first went to school in Britain in the 1950s they entered an educational system organized on the assumption of cultural homogeneity, staffed by people with inappropriate training and a curriculum reflecting the racist ideology of Britain's colonial and imperial past. (Carr-Hill and Chadha-Boreham, 1988: 147)

Since then, migration has given rise to 'nothing less than a rapid and quite unprecedented demographic and cultural transformation of British society' (Reynolds, 2020). Our task in this book has been to ask, how has this fact influenced the geography curriculum enacted in British schools today? We conclude, in agreement with Julian, that the development of UK school geography to meet the needs of all students growing up in an uncertain, plural world is at best 'unfinished business'. We hope our book can assist leaders of all kinds (and especially geography teachers) in 'turning the page' as we suggested in Chapter 1.

School geography in Britain has always been concerned with the UK space and its 'position' in the wider world. This has never been 'innocent' or free from values (think Mackinder in *Britain and the British Seas* or Fairgrieve in *Geography and World Power*). Thus, geography was then both about and part of an imperial, exceptionalist account. However, the UK space and its external relations with the world have changed over time, and geographers and geography teachers have (more or less consciously) been involved in representing these changes. In this sense the task has always been to help successive generations answer the question – to which space do I belong? Our book is a contribution to that project, perhaps clarifying for teachers what is at stake if this question is not opened up with young people – or if we stumble and defer for another day the need for school geography to offer fuller, deeper and better explanations of the UK space and its wider position in the world.

This statement, from the British government's official response (CP625, March 2022) to the heavily criticized *Sewell Report*, seems reasonable to us:

> All children should grow up feeling a strong sense of belonging to this country. They need to see themselves as integral parts of the rich, diverse mosaic of traditions, faiths and ethnicities which make up the UK today. Children need to know that the UK is their home and that they will play a part in writing the next chapter of the UK's future. While promoting and celebrating diversity is hugely important, it is meaningless if children do not feel a sense of belonging or inclusion.

What this means for geography teachers is really significant. We hope our book shows why this is so and gives the Sewell statement practical meaning. It is worth stressing a key element to our argument repeated throughout, that addressing racism cannot *just* to be seen as the 'correction' of individual prejudices. Implicit in this clear recognition of the insidious power of structural and institutionalized forms of racism, is the argument that racial literacy includes understanding of how 'race' is understood and how this has shaped UK geography. Comprehending this requires us to acknowledge and understand community solidarity: how both individuals and groups have responded to and resisted the subtle and not so subtle oppression they have experienced. Being sensitive to the plurality of experiences in the student population within wider community, national and ultimately global contexts is therefore a key element of teachers' curriculum thinking. In this context it good to note Zongyi Deng (2022) discuss the part the GeoCapabilities project played in foregrounding educational purposes in the process of making content and pedagogic selections in practical curriculum making: the project asserts that the prior question to what to teach (and why) is 'who are we teaching?'

To finish, let us jump back into the United States for a moment. Racisms in the United States have a different history and show a different trajectory compared with the UK – but occasionally a view from such a different setting can be revealing. One of the most interesting voices on race in the United States has been writer and activist James Baldwin. Born in Harlem in tough, impoverished family circumstances, Baldwin struggled to come to terms with America's 'big lie' present in the first words *'we the people'* of the US constitution. This 'we', he argued, refers only to white people, and from the beginning, people of colour were presumed to be worth less than white people. He never disowned the United States but spent much of his life in France and Turkey, lest his anger at the racial divisions in the United States killed him (as it did many of friends, including Martin Luther King Jnr). Some argued that Baldwin's anger and his involvement in Black political struggle interfered with his product as an artist. Others argued that his anger did not translate sufficiently into direct political action. He was indeed a singular figure. But perhaps the most inspiring legacy we get from Baldwin was his understanding that, despite his visceral experience of racism and racial segregation in the United States, racism will not be resolved by somehow simply 'toppling' white supremacy. His argument is subtle and complex, driven by the need for common humanity to transcend race – not to be blind to difference, but to accept and respect plurality as a normal part of the human condition. As Eddie Glaude (2022) sums up in his portrait of James Baldwin, in a passage focusing on his relations with Black Power in the United States:

> It makes all the sense in the world, then, that black people would look to the fact of their blackness as a key source of solidarity and liberation. White people make black identity politics necessary. But if we are to survive, we cannot get trapped there. (102).

That appears to be a message from a Black writer to people of colour. But we take it as a message to all of us. The geography we teach in school is a vital component of how we grow to understand plurality in a diverse and respectful society. This requires critical open and dynamic engagement not only with geographical knowledge but also how we come to know it.

# Coda: Positionality

## Geography Teaching with Racial Literacy

In writing this book, our intention is to convince geography teachers, the majority of whom are white, that issues of race and racism are of central concern to their work and not some kind of an optional add-on. Our argument is that geographical understanding is partial and incomplete without foregrounding these issues. Our aim has been to write a rigorous, comprehensive and usable book to enhance our collective 'racial literacy' in the field of geography education.

We are not black, but does this mean we cannot 'know' and write about race? While it is true that neither of us has faced oppression and the daily microaggressions resulting from society-wide racism, to assume that we have no business to read, listen and reason beyond our own experiences is wrong, for the following reasons.

First, this would be to accept (unintentionally) that race itself is a given, immutable, biological fact and impossible to transcend. It is dangerous nonsense such as this that enables racists to argue for segregation, exclusion and a lot worse besides. We totally reject such essentialism, the very cornerstone of 'white supremacy' and imperialist projects. Furthermore, we are alert to the dangers that still lurk in modern school geography teaching undertaken under a long, toxic shadow cast by earlier discredited geographical traditions, such as environmental determinism. We want to expose this. Silence about race on account of whiteness is an option: but only as a convenient means to avoid facing some uncomfortable truths.

Secondly, to assume that you need direct experience of phenomena before you can study or think about them undermines the very process of education, which is designed to take people beyond what they already know. Educators understand that their role is to induct people into more abstract thought, how to make safe generalizations, to critique and to appreciate the strength of theoretical perspectives. They do this in order to deepen students' knowledge and understanding of how the world works, and understanding racism is part of that. As we both have an interest in notions of 'powerful knowledge' in the school curriculum, we reject the notion that direct experience is the only, or even the most important, basis for legitimate knowledge acquisition and development. Nevertheless, plural voices are important to seek out and acknowledge in geography, not least in the students we teach.

We also acknowledge *our* white privilege. However, we are conscious that too sharp a focus on difference and identity can encourage separation and division. If only Black, Asian and minority ethnic people are thought to have authentic voices on racism then white people are, in effect, let off the hook: as if it were, literally, not their problem! We utterly reject this. Race and racism are *structural processes* in society. An understanding of society is impossible without grasping powerful concepts such as 'racialization'. It is not satisfactory to leave it to people of colour to argue this.

In geography, perhaps more than most subjects, we 'get' how general principles (such as racialization) are contextualized by local, contextual particularities (thus, UK racism is distinctive in comparison to, say, US racism). So, of course experience matters, and we take this into account through our support of culturally responsive pedagogies and respect for local funds of knowledge. However, in this book our overarching concern is the curriculum question: what shall we teach? And our proposition is that there are no quick fixes. Culturally sustaining school geography lies in the hands of teachers who are committed to working through what we describe as Future 3 curriculum making. Our book contributes to building the racial literacy on which sound curriculum and related pedagogic decisions can be based.

# Appendix 1

# Critical Realism, Powerful Knowledge and Future 3

Critical Realism (CR) assumes the world 'is not immediately apparent' (Bhaskar, 2017: 17). However, reality exists – independently of our human perceptions of the world. Knowledge of the world is always contingent. Subject to development based on informed judgement (not absolute 'proof').

CR sees the world as complex, open, intrinsically dynamic, emergent and full of novelty. Its three pillars are:

- Ontological realism: objects exist independently of our theories about them or our direct experience of them;
- Epistemological relativism: what we believe to be true about the world is socially produced and fallible – and can therefore change;
- Judgemental rationality: the reverse of 'anything goes' – arguments for preferring this or that set of beliefs over other theories or beliefs, have to be made and tested against each other.

A CR understanding of the world is 'layered': it doesn't just depend on one given observation, course of events or experience. There are three principle domains ('layers') of reality:

- Empirical (human sensory *experiences*)
- Actual (*events* that happen in space and time – whether we experience them or not)
- Real (structures, *mechanisms*, tendencies that explain/generate events)

Mechanisms, events and experiences are not always in sequence or even synchronistic.

> For example, in seeking to understand the BLM resurgence in 2020 we can see that demonstrations (*events*) are seen differently – depending on who is describing

them, and from what standpoint they are *experienced*. The *mechanisms* that gave rise to them are more hidden and require exploration. Similarly, as has been pointed out by many commentators, for the US courts to find the policeman involved with George Floyd's death guilty of murder in 2021 was an enormously significant *event*, but it will change nothing on its own (it doesn't get to the *mechanisms* which gave rise to the circumstances of the murder).

So, CR recommends a retroductive approach to understanding. This involves moving from the 'surface phenomena' towards some 'deeper causal' explanation.

This, in turn, suggests an inductive pedagogy.

This is quite different from a deductive approach, whereby theory is presented (sometimes almost as fact) and then applied to reality: think, for example, of teaching Burgess's concentric zone model; Rostow's stages of growth; 'the' demographic transition model; or even push and pull population migration models.

Bhaskar proposed an approach known by its acronym DREIC

- Description (describes the phenomenon as accurately as possible)
- Retroduction (imagine or propose a mechanism(s) or structure(s) that could account for this
- Eliminate (any proposed mechanisms that do not satisfy or are false)
- Identify (mechanisms that may genuinely account for the phenomenon)
- Corrections (return to the phenomenon – does the mechanism(s) offer adequate explanation?)

CR offers a curriculum scenario where human diversity, choice and emancipation are possible. It invites us to consider broadening the scope of human possibility, opportunity and existence. It asks us to balance in our mind, and hold together, both *structures* (social, political, economic and environmental) and *human agency*.

Learning outcomes under a CR approach to the curriculum could be listed as:

Becoming critical thinkers
Developing disciplined thinking
Learning how to argue
Making reasoned judgment
Opening up attitudes to knowledge and diverse ways of knowing
Grasping structure-agency interfaces

## Critical Realism and Powerful Knowledge

CR is a philosophy that is closely related to social realism as espoused by Michael Young in his 2008 book identifying powerful knowledge (PK). Although not really an analytical concept (it doesn't tell us directly what to teach), PK is an important school curriculum principle. It insists that the overarching curriculum principle must be to induct young people into knowledge that is not readily available to them in their everyday lives.

This knowledge is:

- Abstract or theoretical (conceptual)
- Displays high levels of systematicity (part of a system of thought/ideas)
- Reliable (even though evolving and dynamic)
- Sometimes counter-intuitive (not always aligned with 'common sense')
- Usually specialized and discipline based

> Powerful knowledge refers to what the knowledge can do or what intellectual power it gives to those who have access to it. Powerful knowledge provides more reliable explanations and new ways of thinking about the world and acquiring it can provide learners with a language for engaging in political, moral, and other kinds of debates. (Young, 2008: 14)

Young coined the term PK in order to contrast the principle from an earlier, influential idea that saw the school curriculum as based on the knowledge of the powerful. That is, the knowledge of the elite which by design excluded the majority – for whom other less powerful forms of knowledge were deemed satisfactory. To this day this analysis rings true, fuelling argument for decolonizing the curriculum and ridding school knowledge of its partial, excluding white gaze.

The proposition of PK is important not least because it reminds us that educationally, anti-racism is more complicated than simply rewriting the curriculum. Who selects the knowledge to be taught, and on what basis this is done, is still a crucial question. But equally important is the question of how the curriculum is enacted with students: how the particular contents are selected and sequenced by the teacher-as-curriculum maker.

## Future 3 Curriculum Scenarios

Such learning outcomes suggest a Future 3 (F3) curriculum scenario. CR is the philosophy that underpins its close relation, 'social realism' – which argues for PK and F3 curriculum scenarios.

The principles of F3 curriculum thinking are as much about our 'approach' to knowledge as about the knowledge itself. Experience is important. Events are significant. But we must also seek the mechanisms, which requires theory, testing generalizations and engaging in more abstract thought. PK, which is what F3 promotes, explicitly is socially produced (it is not just inert and 'given'). Therefore, in F3 teaching we need to impart the idea that knowledge changes and develops – and geography as a discipline certainly has done that. Knowledge is contingent, dynamic and can be challenged. Indeed, this suggests the very process by which knowledge gains its 'warrant' – it is not set in stone. It must be argued about.

# Appendix 2
# Why Future 3?

Future 3 (F3), used in Chapter 7 of this book, spells out the significance of 'powerful disciplinary knowledge' (PK) in terms of the kind of 'curriculum scenario' in which it would prosper. So, what exactly is 'F3'? Following Michael Young's proposition of powerful knowledge (Young, 2008), he and his collaborator Johan Muller published a paper outlining 'three future educational scenarios' (Muller and Young, 2010). This was designed to show how different theories of knowledge result in contrasting educational scenarios. The three futures heuristic serves as a useful device to compare possible curriculum outcomes.

**Future 1 (F1) curriculum scenarios**: The 'traditional' school model, based on a given and inert selection of *delivered* knowledge-as-fact. This grossly under-socialized view of knowledge risks becoming rigid and unresponsive. It is a conservative curriculum: preserving both existing knowledge and its unequal distribution. F1 tends to promote the knowledge of the powerful and appears alienating to many students.

**Future 2 (F2) curriculum scenarios**: These are often the 'progressive' reaction to F1. F2 is typically generic and considers curriculum content to be arbitrary and flexible. This over-socialized model, encouraged by post-modern thinking in the late twentieth century, risks becoming knowledge averse, ignoring the strength of domain-specific specialized knowledge. However, it is motivated by an inclusive democratic principle, being shaped by the interests, purposes and needs of all students as future citizens.

**Future 3 curriculum scenarios**: These assume that the world is knowable. New knowledge is produced in specialized communities including dynamic, ever-changing academic disciplines. Related school subjects are maintained by teachers. F3 envisions high quality, productive *engagement* (by teachers and students) with PK. F3 is emancipatory not conservative (and in some senses can be imagined as some form of synthesis of F1 and F2). The major pedagogic challenge is how to make the epistemic quality of PK available to all young people, and to enable them to relate this to other ways of knowing.

Both F1 and F3 scenarios describe 'knowledge-based' curricula, but with radically contrasting qualities in this regard. The nature of geographical teaching and learning in F1 and F3 scenarios is likely to be very different requiring different approaches to knowledge. Thus, in F1 knowledge is assumed to be given, prepackaged, stable and 'oven ready', in contrast to F3 in which knowledge is dynamic, contingent and needs to be worked with. In contrast to both is F2. Through its learner-centredness it may become careless with knowledge, a curriculum in which content selections are not thought deeply about. The epistemological universe of F2 curriculum thinking emerged in opposition to the persistence of inequalities associated with F1. Its dominant characteristics are:

1. to emphasize the learner as a co-constructor of knowledge;
2. to shift the emphasis from 'curriculum' to 'pedagogy';
3. to assume that because all knowledge is socially constructed, no knowledge can claim intellectual superiority; and
4. to stress learning, with teaching supporting/facilitating learning (rather than focusing on knowledge and what is to be taught).

It is important to critique this list (or indeed any orthodoxy). For example, although good geography classrooms are full of activity to help students make and clarify meaning, relatively not all knowledge construction needs to take place in situ in the classroom. Furthermore, if knowledge is considered to be quite arbitrary, then the curriculum question (what is worth teaching) is diluted, and the pedagogic cart comes before the curriculum horse. The beguiling truth of this is that teachers (as curriculum makers) are, in effect, let off the hook. Innovative and adventurous pedagogies are in themselves no guarantor of high-quality teaching. Another way to express all this is to suggest that neoliberal F2 curriculum scenarios are in a sense atheoretical when it comes to knowledge: knowledge is nothing more than the stuff or the filling – the vehicle for delivering the value-free 'learning outcomes' which quite possibly have failed to address issues of race and racism in any depth.

Both the strength and potential weakness of F3, the alternative scenario to F1 *and* F2, is that rather like PK itself, it has not yet been fully developed as an analytical concept: there are no settled lists of criteria or tick sheets to judge 'how F3' is in our curriculum. Alaric Maude's five-part typology of powerful knowledge in geography (Maude, 2016) has been helpful in showing the scope of 'knowledge work' in geography and how to avoid knowledge-led curriculum thinking slipping back to F1 teaching. But there are, by definition, no templates and pre-prepared plans to take off the shelf in order to 'deliver' F3. Teachers, and in time the students, need to engage with questions such as 'In what ways is this, or that, powerful knowledge?' And crucially, 'How do we know?'

F3 has social realist theoretical foundations which ultimately find their philosophical roots in Critical Realism (CR). See Appendix 1 for a summary, which is helpful in thinking through the significant differences between the aspirations of F3 curriculum scenarios in contrast to limitations and inadequacies of F1 knowledge-rich curricula.

To achieve F3 requires teachers to be knowledge workers and curriculum makers. One crucial aspect of F3 development particularly relevant to the creation of anti-racist curricula is how to combine the selection and teaching of powerful disciplinary concepts with the experiential knowledge that students already possess. Furthermore, there are questions about how PK relates to other ways of knowing, for example, those that draw from indigenous and community knowledges. A key characteristic of F3, again drawing from the summary of CR in Appendix 1, is that it is concerned with the *approach* to knowledge that it attempts to nurture with students – that knowledge is contentious, and that 'how do we know what we think we know?' needs to be a frequently asked question. This alone encourages teachers to be culturally responsive in their pedagogy.

# References

Agnew, J. (2002). Introduction. In J. Agnew and J. Smith (Eds.), *American space/American place: Geographies of the contemporary United States* (pp. 1–18). Edinburgh: Edinburgh University Press.

Agyeman, J. (1989). A snail's pace. *New Statesman and Society*, *2*(35), 30–1.

Agyeman, J. (2020). Urban planning as a tool of white supremacy: The other lesson from Minneapolis. *The Conversation*. 27 July

Agyeman, J., and Spooner, R. (1997). Ethnicity and the rural environment. In P. Cloke and J. Little (Eds.), *Contested countryside cultures* (pp. 190–210). London. Routledge.

Ahier, J. (1988). *Industry, children and the nation: An analysis of national identity in school textbooks*. Lewes: Falmer Press.

Ahmed, A. (1992). *Postmodernism and Islam: Predicament and promise*. London: Routledge.

Ajegbo, K. (2011). Diversity, citizenship and cohesion. *Teaching Geography*, *36*(2), 46–48.

Akala (2018). *Natives: Race and class in the ruins of Empire*. London: Two Roads Press.

Ali, T. (2020). "Come what may, we're here to stay": Remembering the Asian youth movements. *Tribune Magazine*. https://tribunemag.co.uk/2020/12/come-what-may-were-here-to-stay-remembering-the-asian-youth-movements (accessed 2 October 2022).

All London Teachers against Racism and Fascism (ALTARF). (1984). *Challenging racism*. London: ALTARF.

Allen, T. (1994). *The invention of the white race* (Vol. 1). London: Verso.

Andrews, K. (2018). Preface. In R. Chantiluke, B. Kwoba, and A. Nkopo, (Eds.), *Rhodes must fall: The struggle to decolonize the racist heart of empire*. London: Zed Books.

Andrews, K. (2020). Blackness, empire and migration: How Black studies transforms the curriculum. *Area*, *52*(4), 701–7.

Andrews, K., and Palmer, L. (Eds.). (2016). *Blackness in Britain*. London: Routledge.

Apple, M. (1979). *Ideology and curriculum*. London: Routledge and Kegan Paul.

Arday, J. (2019). *Cool Britannia and multi-ethnic Britain: Uncorking the Champagne supernova*. London: Routledge.

Arday, J. (2020). If we want a more equal Britain, we must teach its true black history. *The Guardian*, 13 June.
https://www.theguardian.com/commentisfree/2020/jun/13/equal-britain-teach-black-history-empire (accessed 2 October 2022)

Ashmore, S. (2006). Far out and way in: London as fashion cosmopolis, 1945-1979. In C. Breward and D. Gilbert (Eds.), *Fashion's world cities* (pp. 201–15). Oxford: Berg.

Au, W. (2017). *A Marxist education: Learning to change the world*. Chicago: Haymarket.

Bailey P. (1989). A place in the sun: The role of the Geographical Association in establishing geography in the National Curriculum of England and Wales. *Journal of Geography in Higher Education*, *13*(2), 149–57.

Bailey, P., and Binns, A. (1987). *A case for geography: A response to the Secretary of State for Education from Members of the Geographical Association.* Sheffield: Geographical Association.

Bain, Z. (2018). Is there such a thing as "white ignorance" in British education? *Ethics and Education, 13*(1), 4–21.

Bale, J. (Ed.). (1983). *The Third World: Issues and approaches.* Sheffield: Geographical Association.

Ball, S. (1994). *Education reform: A critical and post-structural approach.* London: Routledge.

Barnes, T., and Duncan, J. (Eds.). (1992). *Writing worlds.* London: Routledge.

Barnes, T., and Gregory, D. (Eds.). (1997). *Reading human geography: The poetics and politics of inquiry.* London: Arnold.

Battle-Baptiste, W., and Rusert, B. (Eds.). (2018). *W.E.B. Du Bois's data portraits: Visualising Black America.* New York: Princeton Architectural Press.

Beckert, S. (2016). *Empire of cotton: A new global history of capitalism.* London: Allen Lane.

Begum, H. (2022). If the government wants to open up debate in universities, why stifle it in schools? *The Guardian.* https://www.theguardian.com/commentisfree/2022/feb/18/tories-debate-universities-schools-government-impartial-teaching (accessed 2 October 2022).

Belcham, J. (Ed.). (2006). *Liverpool 800: Culture, character and history.* Liverpool: Liverpool University Press.

Benyon, H., and Solomos, J. (Eds.). (1987). *The roots of urban unrest.* Oxford: Oxford University Press.

Bhabha, H. (1994). *The location of culture.* London: Routledge.

Bhambra, G., Gebrial, D., and Nişancioğlu, K. (2018). *Decolonizing the university.* London: Pluto Press.

Bhaskar, R. (2017). *The order of natural necessity. A kind of introduction to critical realism.* London: Gary Hawke.

Bhattacharyya, G. (2018). *Rethinking racial capitalism: Questions of reproduction and survival.* London: Rowman and Littlefield International.

Bhattacharyya, G., Elliott-Cooper, A., Balani, S., Nisancioglu, K., Koram, K, Gebrial, D., El-Enamy, N., and De Noronha, L. (2021). *Empire's endgame: Racism and the British state.* London: Pluto Press.

Bhopal, K. (2018). *White privilege: The myth of a post-racial society.* Bristol: Policy Press.

Bhopal, K., and Preston, J. (Eds.). (2012). *Intersectionality and "race" in education.* London: Routledge.

Biddulph, M., Lambert, D., and Balderstone, D. (2021). *Learning to teach geography in the secondary school* (4th ed.). London: Routledge.

Black Geographers (n.d.). https://www.blackgeographers.com/ (accessed 6 October 2022).

Blaikie, P., and Brookfield, H. (1987). *Land degradation and society.* London: Methuen.

Blaikie, P., Cannon, T., Davis, I., and Wisner, B. (1994). *At risk: Natural hazards, people's vulnerability, and disasters.* London: Routledge.

Bledsoe A. (2021). Methodological reflections on geographies of blackness. *Progress in Human Geography, 45*(5), 1003–21.

Blunt, A., and McEwan, C. (Eds.). (2004). *Postcolonial geographies.* London: Bloomsbury.

Blunt, A., and Rose, G. (Eds.). (1994). *Writing women and space: Colonial and postcolonial geographies.* London: Guilford.

Boardman, D. (1985). Geography and the young school leaver. In D. Boardman (Ed.), *New directions in geographical education* (pp. 65–83). Brighton: Falmer Press.

Bonnett, A. (1993). Contours of crisis: Anti-racism and reflexivity. In P. Jackson and J. Penrose (Eds.), *Constructions of race, place and nation* (pp. 163–80). London: UCL Press.

Bonnett, A. (1996). Constructions of "race", place and discipline: Geographies of "racial" identity and "racism." *Ethnic and Racial Studies, 19*(4), 860–83.

Bonnett, A. (1997). Geography, "race" and whiteness: Invisible traditions and current challenges, *Area, 29*(3), 193–9.

Bonnett. A. (2000). *Anti-racism*. London: Routledge.

Bradford, M., and Kent, A. (1977). *Human geography: Theories and their application*. Oxford: Oxford University Press.

Brah, A. (1996). *Cartographies of diaspora*. London: Routledge.

Brah, A. (2020). Interview. In B. Bhandar and R. Ziadah (Eds.), *Revolutionary feminisms: Conversations on collective action and radical thought* (pp. 33–54). London: Verso.

Brake, M., and Hale, C. (1992). *Public order and private lives: The politics of law and order*. London: Routledge.

Bray, C. (1863). *The British Empire: A sketch of the geography, growth, natural and political features of the United Kingdom, its colonies and dependencies*. London: Forgotten Books.

Bromley, R. (2019). Reading the "Black" in the "Union Jack": Institutionalising Black and Asian British writing. In S. Nasta and M. Stein (Eds.), *The Cambridge history of black and Asian British writing* (pp. 417–31). Cambridge: Cambridge University Press.

Brooks, C. (2018). Understanding conceptual development in school geography. In M. Jones and D. Lambert (Eds.), *Debates in geography education* (pp. 103–14). Abingdon: Routledge.

Brown, C. (1988). The curriculum and national identity. In R. Dale, R. Fergusson, and A. Robinson (Eds.), *Frameworks for teaching: Readings for the intending secondary school teacher* (pp. 222–4). Maidenhead: Open University Press.

Bryan, B., Dadzie, S., and Scafe, S. (1985). T*he heart of the race: Black women's lives in Britain*. London: Virago.

Bullivant, B. (1981). *The pluralist dilemma in education*. Sydney: Allen and Unwin.

Bulpitt, J. (1986). Continuity, autonomy and peripheralisation: The anatomy of the centre's race state statecraft in England. In Z. Layton-Henry and P. B. Rich (Eds.), *Race, government and politics in Britain* (pp. 17–44). London: Macmillan.

Bunce, R., and Field, P. (2017). *Renegade: The life and times of Darcus Howe*. London: Bloomsbury.

Bunce, R., and Linton, S. (2020). *Diane Abbott: The authorized biography.* London: Biteback.

Buras, K. (2008). *Rightist multiculturalism: Core lessons on neoconservative school reform*. New York: Routledge.

Burgess, J. (1985). News from nowhere: The press, the riots and the myth of the inner city. In J. Burgess and J. Gold (Eds.), *Geography, the media and popular culture* (pp. 192–228). Beckenham: Croom Helm.

Burgess, J., and Gold, J. (Eds.). (1985). *Geography, the media and popular culture*. Beckenham: Croom Helm.

Butcher, J. (2020). Should we decolonise geography? *Areo Magazine*. https://areomagazine.com/2020/02/11/should-we-decolonise-geography/ (accessed 2 October 2022).

Butlin, R. (2003). British geographical representations of imperialism and colonial development in the early and mid-twentieth century. In D. Gilbert, D. Matless, and B. Short (Eds.), *Geographies of British modernity* (pp. 229–49). Oxford: Blackwell.

Butlin, R. (2009). *Geographies of empire: European empires and colonies c.1880–1960*. Cambridge: Cambridge University Press.

Butt, G. (2020). *Geography education research in the UK: Retrospect and prospect*. Singapore: Springer.

Camp, J., and L. Pulido (2017). Introduction: The dialectics of Bourbonism and the Blues. In. C. Woods (Eds.), *Development drowned and reborn: The Blues and Bourbon restorations in post-Katrina New Orleans* (xxi–xxiv). Athens: University of Georgia Press. p. 116

Cantle, T. (2008). *Community cohesion: A new framework for race and diversity* (2nd ed.). Basingstoke: Palgrave Macmillan.

Carby, H. (1980). Multi-culture. *Screen Education, 34,* 62–70.

Carby, H. (1982). Schooling in Babylon. In *The empire strikes back: Race and racism in 70s Britain* (Centre for Contemporary Cultural Studies) (pp. 183–211). London: Hutchinson.

Carr-Hill, R., and Chadha-Boreham, H. (1988). Education. In A. Bhat., R. Carr-Hill., S. Ohri (Eds.), *Britain's black population: A new perspective* (pp. 147–176). Aldershot: Radical Statistics Race Group.

Carrington, B. (2008). Where's the white in the Union Jack? In M. Perryman (Ed.), *Imagined nation: England after Britain* (pp. 109–133). London: Lawrence and Wishart.

Carrington, B. (2010). *Race, sport and politics: The sporting black diaspora*. London: Sage.

Cashmore, E. (2012). *Beyond black: Celebrity and race in Obama's America*. London: Bloomsbury Academic.

Castree, N. (2014). *Making sense of nature*. London: Routledge.

Castree, N., Hulme, M., and Proctor, J. (Eds.), (2018). *Companion to environmental studies*. London: Routledge.

Centre for Contemporary Cultural Studies. (1981). *Unpopular Education: Schooling and social democracy in England since 1944*. London: Hutchinson.

Chambers, E. (2016). *Roots and Culture: Cultural politics in the making of Black Britain*. London: I.B. Tauris.

Chisholm, M. (1971). *Resources for Britain's future*. London: Penguin.

Clarke, J. (1984). 'There's no place like…': Cultures of difference. In D. Massey, J. Allen, and J. Anderson (Eds.), *Geography matters!* (pp. 54–67). Maidenhead: Open University Press.

Clark, G., and Dear, M. (1984). *State apparatus: Structures of language and legitimacy*. London: Allen and Unwin.

Cloke, P., Crang, M., and Goodwin, M. (2014). *Introducing human geography* (3rd ed.). London: Routledge.

Coard, B. (1971). *How the West Indian child is made educationally subnormal in the British school system*. London: New Beacon Books.

Cohen, P. (1998). On teaching arts and 'race' in the classroom. In D. Buckingham (Ed.), *Teaching popular culture: Beyond radical pedagogy* (pp. 153–76). London: UCL Press.

Cole, M. (2009). *Critical race theory and education: A Marxist response*. Basingstoke: Palgrave Macmillan.

Cole, M. (2017). *Critical race theory and education: A Marxist response* (2nd ed.) Basingstoke: Macmillan.

Collins, M. (2004). *The likes of us: A biography of the white working class*. London: Granta.

Commission on Race and Ethnic Disparities (CRED). (2021). *The report*. London: HMSO. https://assets.publishing.service.gov.uk/government/uploads/system/uploads/attachment_data/file/974507/20210331_-_CRED_Report_-_FINAL_-_Web_Accessible.pdf (accessed 2 October 2022).

Commission on the Future of Multi-ethnic Britain. (2000). *The future of multi-ethnic Britain (The Parekh Report)*. London: Profile.

Corbridge, S. (1986). *Capitalist world development: A critique of radical development geography*. Basingstoke: Macmillan.

Couch, C. (2003). *City of change and challenge: Urban planning and regeneration in Liverpool*. Aldershot: Ashgate.

Cox, K. (2014). *Making human geography*. New York: Guilford Press.

CP625. (2022). *Inclusive Britain: Government response to the Commission on Race and Ethnic Disparities*. https://www.gov.uk/government/publications/inclusive-britain-action-plan-government-response-to-the-commission-on-race-and-ethnic-disparities/inclusive-britain-government-response-to-the-commission-on-race-and-ethnic-disparities (accessed 2 October 2022).

Cresswell, T. (1996). *In place/out of place*. Minneapolis: University of Minnesota press.

Crush, J. (1994). Post-colonialism, de-colonization and geography. In A. Godlewska and N. Smith (Eds.), *Geography and empire* (pp. 333–50). Oxford: Blackwell.

Crush, J. (1995). *Power of development*. London: Routledge.

Curtis, P. (2004). MPs warn of growing racial divide in schools. *The Guardian*, 14 May. https://www.theguardian.com/education/2004/may/14/schools.uk2 (accessed 24 September 2022).

Curtis, P. (2008). Education: Black Caribbean children held back by institutional racism in schools, says study. *The Guardian*, 5 September. https://www.theguardian.com/education/2008/sep/05/raceineducation.raceinschools (accessed 24 September 2022)

Curry, M. (1996). *The work in the world: Geographical practice and the written word*. Minneapolis: University of Minnesota Press.

Dale, R., Robinson, A., and Fergusson, R. (Eds.), (1988). *Frameworks for teaching: Readings for the intending secondary teacher*. London: Hodder and Stoughton.

Davis, A., Dent, G., Meiners, E., and Richie, B. (2022). *Abolition. Feminism. Now*. Chicago: Haymarket.

Davison, S., Grayson, D., and Forkert, K. (2020). Editorial: Challenging the structures of racism. *Soundings: A journal of politics and culture,* (75), 4–12.

Dear, M. (1988). The postmodern challenge: Reconstructing human geography. *Transactions of the Institute of British Geographers*, NS 18(4), 460–80.

Delaney, D. (2002). The space that race makes. *Professional Geographer, 54*, 6–14.

Deng, Z. (2022). Powerful knowledge, educational potential and knowledge-rich curriculum: Pushing the boundaries. *Journal of Curriculum Studies*. doi: https://doi.org/10.1080/00220272.2022.2089538.

Department of Education. (2022). Political impartiality in schools: Guidance. https://www.gov.uk/government/publications/political-impartiality-in-schools/political-impartiality-in-schools (accessed 2 October 2022).

Department of Education and Science (DES). (1972). *New thinking in geography*. London: HMSO.

Department of Education and Science (DES). (1977). *Education in Schools*. London: HMSO.

Department of Education and Science (DES). (1985). *Education for all: Report of the committee of enquiry into the Education of Children from Ethnic Minority Groups* (The Swann Report; Cmnd. 4953). London: HMSO.

Department of Education and Science (DES). (1990). *The national curriculum*. London: HMSO.

Department for Education and Skills (2007. *Curriculum review: Diversity and citizenship* (The Ajegbo Report). PPSLS/D35/0107/14. London: DfES.

Dhondy, F., Beese, B., and Hassan, L. (1982). *The black explosion in British schools*. London: Race Today.

DiAngelo, R. (2018). *White fragility: Why it's so hard for white people to talk about racism*. Boston, MA: Beacon Press.

Dinkele, G. (1993). Geography and multicultural education. In A. Fyfe and P. Figueroa (Eds.), (1993). *Education for cultural diversity: The challenge of a new era* (pp. 168–76). London: Routledge.

Donald, J. (1992). *Sentimental education*. London: Verso.

Dorling, D., and Tomlinson, S. (2018). *Rule Britannia: Brexit and the end of Empire*. London: Biteback.

Driver, F. (2001). *Geography militant: Cultures of exploration and empire*. Oxford: Blackwell.

Driver, F., and Gilbert, D. (Eds.), (2003). *Imperial cities*. Manchester: Manchester University Press.

Dufour, B. (Ed.). (1988). *The new social curriculum*. London: Routledge.

Dumenil, G., and Levy, D. (2011). *The crisis of neoliberalism*. Cambridge, MA: Harvard University Press.

Duncan, J., and Gregory, D. (Eds.). (1999). *Writes of passage: Reading travel writing*. London: Routledge.

Duncan, J., and Ley, D. (Eds.). (1993). *Place/culture/representation*. London: Routledge.

Duneier, M. (2016). *Ghetto: The invention of a place, the history of an idea*. New York: Farrar, Strauss, and Giroux.

Dyer, R. (1988). White. *Screen, 29*(4), 44–64.

Dyer, R. (1997). *White*. Routledge: London.

Eatwell, R., and Goodwin, M. (2018). *National populism: The revolt against liberal democracy*. London: Penguin.

Ebert, T. (2009). *The task of cultural critique*. Urbana: University of Illinois Press.

Eddo-Lodge, R. (2018). *Why I'm no longer talking to white people about race*. London: Bloomsbury.

Edwards, G. (1996). Alternative speculations on geographical futures: Towards a postmodern perspective. *Geography, 81*(3): 217–24.

Eliot-Hurst, M. (1985). Geography has neither existence nor future. In R. Johnston (Ed.), *The future of geography* (pp. 59–91). London: Methuen.

Embery, P. (2021). *Despised: Why the modern left hates the working-class*. Cambridge: Polity.

Esson, J., and Last, A. (2019). Learning and teaching about race and racism in geography. In H. Walkington, S. Hill, and S. Dyer (Eds.), *Handbook of teaching and learning in geography* (pp. 227–40). London: Edgar Elgin.

Fairbank, J. (2020). *English pastoral: an inheritance*. London: Penguin.

Feagin, J. (2013). *The white racial frame* (2nd ed.). New York: Routledge.

Felli, R. (2021). *The great adaptation: climate, capitalism and catastrophe*. London: Verso.

Fien, J. (1983). Humanistic geography. In J. Huckle (Ed.), *Geographical education: Reflection and action* (pp. 43–55). Oxford: Oxford University Press.

Forest, B. (2002). A new geography of identity? Race, ethnicity and American citizenship. In J. Agnew and J. Smith (Eds.), *American space/American place: Geographies of the contemporary United States* (pp. 231–63). Edinburgh: Edinburgh University Press.

Forsyth, T. (2003). *Critical political ecology*. London: Routledge.

Foskett, N., and Marsden, W. (Eds.). (1998). *A bibliography of geographical education, 1970–1997*. Sheffield: Geographical Association.

Foucault, M. (1977). *Discipline and punish: The birth of the prison*. New York: Pantheon Books.

Frankenberg, R. (1993). *White women, race matters: The social construction of whiteness*. London: Routledge.

Freund, D. (2007). *Colored property: State policy and white racial politics in suburban America*. Chicago: University of Chicago Press.

Fryer, P. (1984/2018). *Staying power*. London: Pluto Press.

Fyfe, A., and Figueroa, P. (Eds.). (1993). *Education for cultural diversity: The challenge of a new era*. London: Routledge.

Fyson, A., and Ward, C. (1973). *Streetwork: The exploding school*. London: Routledge Kegan and Paul.

Galeano, E. (1973). *The open veins of Latin America: Five centuries of the pillage of a continent*. New York: Monthly Review Press.

Gardner, D. (2021). *Planning your coherent 11–16 geography curriculum: A design toolkit*. Sheffield: Geographical Association.

Gattrell, P. (2019). *The unsettling of Europe: the Great Migration 1945 to the present*. London: Allen Lane.

Geographical Association (1975). Teaching about the Third World: A report of a symposium. *Geography*, 60(1), 52–8.

Gibbons, S. (2018). *City of segregation: One hundred years of struggle for housing in Los Angeles*. London: Verso.

Gibson, M. (1981). Realism. In M. Harvey and B. Holly (Eds.), *Themes in geographic thought* (pp. 148–62). London: Croom Helm.

Gill, D. (1982). *Geography for the young school leaver: A critique* (Centre for Multicultural Education. Working Paper No. 2). London: Institute of Education.

Gill, D. (1983). *Geographical education in a multicultural society* (Research report commissioned by the Schools Council). London: Council for Racial Equality.

Gill, D. (1999). Geography. In M. Cole and D. Hill (Eds.), *Promoting equality in secondary schools* (pp. 157–73). London: Cassell.

Gillborn, D. (1995). *Racism and anti-racism in real schools*. Buckingham: Open University Press.

Gillborn, D. (2005). Education policy as an act of white supremacy. *Journal of Education Policy*, 20(4), 485–505.

Gillborn, D. (2008). *Racism and education: Coincidence or conspiracy?* London: Routledge.

Gillborn, D., and Youdell, D. (2000). *Rationing education: Policy, practice and equity*. Buckingham: Open University Press.

Gilmore, R. W. (2007). *Golden gulag: Prisons, surplus, crisis, and opposition in globalizing California*. Los Angeles: University of California Press.

Gilroy, P. (2004). *After empire*. London: Routledge.

Gilroy, P. (2005). Melancholia or conviviality: The politics of belonging in Britain. *Soundings: A Journal of Politics and Culture*, (29). 35–43.

Gilroy, P. (2007). *Black Britain: A photographic history*. London: SAQI Books.

Glaude, E. S., Jr. (2022). *Begin again: James Baldwin's America and its urgent lessons for today* (Vintage ed.). London: Penguin Random House.

Goodenough, S. (1977). *Values, relevance and ideology in Third World geography*. Milton Keynes: Open University Press.

Goodhart, D. (2004). Too diverse? *Prospect Magazine*. 20 February. https://www.prospectmagazine.co.uk/magazine/too-diverse-david-goodhart-multiculturalism-britain-immigration-globalisation (accessed 2 October 2022).

Goodhart, D. (2014). *The British dream: Successes and failures of post-war immigration*. London: Atlantic Books.

Goodyer, I. (2009). *Crisis music: The cultural politics of rock against racism*. Manchester: Manchester University Press.

Graves, N. (1975). *Geography in education*. London: Heinneman.

Graves, N. (1979). *Curriculum planning in geography*. London: Heinneman.

Graves, N. (1996). Curriculum development in geography: An ongoing process. In A. Kent., D. Lambert., M. Naish, and F. Slater (Eds.), *Geography in education: Viewpoints in teaching and learning*. Cambridge: Cambridge University Press.

Greenberg, M. (2008). *Branding New York: How a city in crisis was sold to the world*. London: Routledge.

Greenspan, A., Wooldridge, A. (2019). *Capitalism in America*. London: Allen Lane.
Gregory, D. (1994). *Geographical imaginations*. Oxford: Blackwell.
Gregory, D. (2004). *The colonial present*. Oxford: Blackwell.
Gregory, D., and Walford, R. (Eds.). (1989). *Horizons in human geography*. Basingstoke: Macmillan.
Gregory, K. (2000). *The changing nature of physical geography*. London: Arnold.
Grimwade, K., Reid, A., and Thompson, L. (2000). *Geography and the new agenda*. Sheffield: Geographical Association.
Guinier, L. (2006). From racial liberalism to racial literacy: *Brown v, Board of Education* and the interest-divergence dilemma. *Journal of American History, 91*(1), 92–118.
Gwynne, R., and Kay, C. (Eds.). (1999). *Latin America transformed*. London: Edward Arnold.
Habermas, J. (1971). *Knowledge and human interests*. Boston: Beacon Press.
Habib, S. (2018). Fundamental British values: Moving towards anti-racist and multicultural education? In K. Johnson R. Joseph-Salisbury (Eds.), *The fire now: Anti-racist scholarship in times of explicit racial violence* (pp. 209–22). London: Zed Books.
Haggett, P. (1996). Geography into the next century: Personal reflections. In E. Rawling and R. Daugherty (Eds.), *Geography into the twenty-first century* (pp. 11–18). Chichester: Wiley.
Haggerty, S., Webster, A., and White, N. (Eds.). (2008). *The empire in one city? Liverpool's inconvenient imperial past*. Manchester: Manchester University Press.
Haider, A. (2018). *Mistaken identity: Race and class in the age of Trump*. London: Verso.
Hall, D. (1976). *Geography and the geography teacher*. London: Allen and Unwin.
Hall, J. (1978). *London: Metropolis and region* (Rev. ed.). Oxford: Oxford University Press.
Hall, J. (1990). *Metropolis now: London and its region*. Cambridge: Cambridge University Press.
Hall, S. (1967). *The young Englanders*. London: National Committee of Commonwealth Immigrants.
Hall, S. (1989). Imaginary identification and politics (transcript of a talk given at the Institute for Contemporary Arts). London: Institute for Contemporary Arts.
Hall, S., Crictcher, C., Jefferon, T., Clarke, J., and Roberts, B. (1978). Policing the crisis: Mugging, the state, and law and order. London: Macmillan.
Hamilton, A. (2020). The white unseen: On white supremacy and dangerous entanglements in geography. *Dialogues in Human Geography, 10*(3), 299–303.
Hammond, L. (2021). London, race and territories: Young people's stories of a divided city. *London Review of Education, 19*(1), 1–14. doi: https://doi.org/10.14324/LRE.19.1.14.
Hannah, M. (2005). Representation/reality. In N. Castree, A. Rogers, and D. Sherwood (Eds.), *Questioning geography: Fundamental debates* (pp. 151–66). Oxford: Blackwell.
Hartman, C., and Squires, G. (Eds.). (2006). *There is no such thing as a natural disaster: Race, class and Hurricane Katrina*. New York: Routledge.
Harvey, D. (1969). *Explanation in geography*. London: Edward Arnold.
Harvey, D. (1974a). Population, resources and the ideology of science. *Economic Geography, 50*, 256–77.
Harvey, D. (1974b). What kind of geography for what kind of public policy? *Transactions of the Institute of British Geographers, 63*, 18–24.
Harvey, D. (1984). On this history and present condition of geography: An historical-geographical materialist manifesto. *Professional Geographer, 36*(1), 1–11.
Harvey, D. (1989). *The condition of postmodernity*. Oxford: Blackwell.
Harvey, D. (2005). *A brief history of neoliberalism*. Edinburgh: Edinburgh University Press.
Harvey, D. (2014). *Seventeen contradictions (and the crises of capitalism)*. London: Profile Books.

Harvey, D. (2015). Response to Alex Dubilet. *Syndicate* (1 April). syndicatetheology.com
Harvey, D. (2016). *The ways of the world*. London: Profile Books.
Hayes, N. (2020). *The book of trespass: Crossing the lines that divide us*. London: Bloomsbury Circus.
Head, L. (2000). *Cultural landscapes and environmental change*. London: Hodder.
Hebdige, D. (1983). *Cut 'n' mix*. London: Comedia.
Herbert, D., and Smith, D (Eds.). (1979). *Social problems and the city*. Oxford: Oxford University Press.
Her Majesty's Stationery Office (HMSO). (1967). *Children and their primary schools: The Plowden Report.* London: HMSO.
Hewitt, K. (Ed.). (1983). *Interpretations of calamity from the viewpoint of human ecology*. Boston: Allen and Unwin.
Hewitt, R. (2005). *White backlash and the politics of multiculturalism*. Cambridge: Cambridge University Press.
Hickman, M., and Walter, B. (1995). Deconstructing whiteness: Irish women in Britain. *Feminist Review*, 50, 5–19.
Hicks, D. (1981). The contribution of geography to multicultural misunderstanding. *Teaching Geography*, 7(2), 64–7.
Hicks, D. (1981a). Bias in geography textbooks (Working Paper No. 1). London: Centre for Multicultural Education.
Hill, D., and Cole, M. (Eds.). (1999). *Promoting equality in secondary schools*. London: Cassell.
Himley, M., Havice, E., and Valdivia, G. (Eds.). (2022). *The Routledge handbook of critical resource geography*. London: Routledge.
Hirsch, A. (2018). *Brit(ish): On race, identity and belonging*. London: Vintage.
Hirsch, E. D. Jr. (1987). *Cultural literacy: what every American needs to know*. Boston: Houghton Mifflin.
Hoggart, R. (1957). *The uses of Literacy*. London: Chatto and Windus.
Hoggart, R. (1958). *Speaking to each other*. In N. Mackenzie (Ed.), Conviction (121–38). London: MacGibbon and Kee.
Holloway, L., and Hubbard, P. (2001). *People and place: The extraordinary geographies of everyday life*. London: Prentice Hall.
Home Office. (1965). *White paper on immigration from the commonwealth* (Cmnd 2739). London: HMSO. https://discovery.nationalarchives.gov.uk/details/r/C1385012 (accessed 28 September 2022).
Home Office. (1978). *The West Indian community: Observations on the report of the Select Committee on Race relations and Immigration* (Cmnd 7186). London: HMSO.
Huckle, J. (ed.) (1983). *Geographical education: Reflection and action*. Oxford: Oxford University Press.
Huckle, J. (1985). Geography and schooling. In R. Johnston (Ed.), *The future of geography* (pp. 291–306). London: Methuen.
Huckle, J. (1986). Confronting the ecological crisis. *Contemporary issues in Geography and Education,* 2(2), 2–13.
Hulme. M. (2008). *Why we disagree about climate change*. Cambridge: Cambridge University Press.
Hulme, M. (2020). *Climate change*. London: Routledge.
Husen. T. (1979). *The school in question: A comparative study of the school and its future in Western society*. London: Taylor and Francis.
'Interview with Holberg Laureate Paul Gilroy'. (2019). *Holberb Prized*. https://holbergprize.org/en/news/holberg-prize/interview-holberg-laureate-paul-gilroy (accessed 2 October 2022).
Institute of Race Relations. (1983). *The roots of racism*. London: Institute of Race Relations.

Jackson, N. (2016). The ties that bind: Questions of empire and belonging in black British educational activism. In K. Andrews and L. Palmer (Eds.), *Blackness in Britain* (pp. 117–129). Abingdon: Routledge.

Jackson, P. (Ed.) (1987). *Race and racism: Essays in social geography*. London: Croom Helm.

Jackson, P. (1988). Beneath the headlines: Racism and reaction in contemporary Britain. *Geography*, *73*(3), 202–7.

Jackson, P. (1989). *Maps of meaning: An introduction to cultural geography*. London: Unwin and Hyman.

Jackson. P. (1996). 'Only connect': Approaches to human geography. In E. Rawling and R. Daugherty (Eds.), *Geography into the twenty-first century* (pp. 77–94). Chichester: Wiley.

Jackson, P. (2006). Thinking geographically. *Geography*, *91*(3), 199–204.

Jackson, P. (2008). Afterword: New geographies of race and racism. In C. Dwyer and C. Bressey (Eds.), *New geographies of race and racism* (297–304). Aldershot: Ashgate.

Jackson, P., and Jacobs, J. (1996). Postcolonialism and the politics of race. *Environment and Planning D: Society and Space 14*, 1–3.

Jackson, P., and Penrose, J. (Eds.). (1993). *Constructions of race, place and nation*. London: UCL Press.

Jackson, P., and Smith, S. (1984). *Exploring social geography*. London: Allen and Unwin.

James, C. L. R. (1969). Black studies and the contemporary student. Detroit, Friends of Facing Reality Publications.

Jazeel, T. (2019). *Postcolonialism*. London: Routledge.

Jeffcoate, T. (1984). *Positive image*. London: Writers and Readers.

Jeffries, S. (2022). *Everything, all the time, everywhere: How we became postmodern*. London: Verso.

Jenkins, D., and Leroy, J. (Eds.). (2021). *Histories of racial capitalism*. New York: Columbia University Press.

John, G. (2008). Racism in education: Have we learned nothing? *The Guardian.* https://www.theguardian.com/commentisfree/2008/sep/05/raceineducation.raceinschools (accessed 24.09.2022).

Johnston, R. (1983). *Philosophy and human geography*. London: Edward Arnold.

Johnston, R. (Ed.). (1985). *The future of geography*. London: Methuen.

Johnston, R. (1986). *On human geography*. Oxford: Blackwell.

Johnston, R. (1989). *Environmental problems: Nature, economy and the state*. London: Belhaven Press.

Jones, A. (2006). *Dictionary of globalization*. Cambridge: Polity.

Jones, K. (1983). *Beyond progressive education*. Basingstoke: Macmillan.

Jones, K. (1992). Re-creation. *Ten.8, 2*(3), 96–105.

Jones, K. (2016). *Education in Britain: 1944 to the present* (2nd ed.). Cambridge: Polity.

Jones, M. (Ed.). (2017). *The handbook of secondary geography*. Sheffield: Geographical Association.

Joseph-Salisbury, R. (2020). *Race and racism in English secondary schools*. London: Runnymede Trust.

Kaufman, E. (2018). *Whiteshift: Populism, immigration and the future of white majorities*. London: Allen Lane.

Kearns, G. (2020). Topple the racists 1: Decolonizing the space and institutional memory of the university. *Geography*, *10*(3), 116–25.

Kearns, G. (2021). Topple the racists 2: Decolonizing the space and institutional memory of geography. *Geography*, *106*(1), 4–15.

Khan, O., and Shaheen, F. (Eds.). (2017). *Minority report: Race and class in post-Brexit Britain*. London: Runnymede Trust.

Kincheloe, J., and Steinberg, S. (1997). *Changing multiculturalism*. Buckingham: Open University Press.

Kincheloe, J., Steinberg, S., Rodríguez, N., and Chennault, R. (Eds.). (1998). *White reign: Deploying whiteness in America*. New York: St. Martin's Press.

Kinder, A., and Pike, S. (2021). Policy matters. *Geographical Association Magazine, 48*, 9

King, L. J., Vickery, A. E., and Caffrey, G. (2018). A pathway to racial literacy: Using the LETS ACT framework to teach controversial issues. *Social Education, 82*(6), 316–22.

Kingsnorth, P. (2008). *Real England: The battle against the bland*. London: Granta.

Kinsman, P. (1995). Landscape, race and national identity: The photography of Ingrid Pollard. *Area, 27*(4), 300–10.

Kirp, D. (1979). *Doing good by doing little: Race and schooling in Britain*. London: University of California Press.

Kundnani, A. (2007). *The end of tolerance: Racism in 21st century Britain*. London: Pluto Press.

Lambert, D. (2017). Thinking geographically. In M. Jones (Ed.), *The handbook of secondary geography*. Sheffield: Geographical Association.

Lambert, D. (2018). The road to Future 3: The case of geography. In D. Guile, D. Lambert, and M. Reiss (Eds.), *Sociology, curriculum studies and professional knowledge: New perspectives on the work of Michael Young*. Abingdon: Routledge.

Lambert, D., and Morgan, J. (2010). *Teaching geography* 11–18. Buckingham: Open University Press.

Lambert, D., and León, K. (2023). The value of geography to an individual's education. In M. Biddulph, S. Catling, L. Hammond, and J. H. McKendrick, (Eds.), *Children, education and geography: Rethinking intersections*. London: Taylor & Francis.

Lander, V. (2014). Initial Teacher Education: The practice of whiteness. In R. Race and V. Lander (Eds.), *Advancing race and ethnicity in education* (pp. 93–110). Basingstoke: Palgrave Macmillan.

Lane, T. (1987). *Liverpool: gateway of empire. London*: Lawrence and Wishart.

Lane, T. (1996). *Liverpool: City of the sea. London*: Lawrence and Wishart.

Lave, R. (2017). Getting back to our roots: Integrating critical physical and social science in the early work of Michael Watts. In S. Chari, S. Freidberg, J. Ribot, W. Wolford, and V. Gidwani (Eds.), *Other geographies: The work of Michael Watts* (43–54). Oxford: Wiley-Blackwell.

Lave, R., Biermann, C., and Lane, S. (Eds.). (2018). *The Palgrave Macmillan handbook of critical physical geography*. Basingstoke: Palgrave Macmillan.

Lawrence, E. (1982). Just plain common sense: The 'roots' of racism. In *The empire strikes back: Race and racism in 70s Britain* (Centre for Contemporary Cultural Studies) (pp. 47–94). London: Hutchinson.

Lawson, V. (2007). *Making development geography*. London: Routledge.

Lawton, R., and Pooley, C. (1992). *Britain 1740–1950: An historical geography*. London: Edward Arnold.

Leach, B. (1973). The social geographer and black people: Can geography contribute to race relations? *Race, 15*(2), 230–41.

Lee, R. (1983). Teaching geography: The dialectic of structure and agency. In D. Boardman (Ed.), *New directions in geographical education* (pp. 199–216). Brighton: Falmer Press.

Lee, R. (1985). The future of the region: Regional geography as education for transformation. In R. King (Ed.), *Geographical futures* (pp. 77–91). Sheffield: Geographical Association.

Legrain, P. (2020). *Them and us: How immigrants and locals can thrive together*. London: Oneworld.

Lewis, M., and Wigen, K. (1997). *The myth of continents: A critique of metageography*. Berkeley: University of California Press.

Lipsitz, G. (2007). The racialization of space and the spatialization of race: Theorizing the hidden architecture of language. *Landscape Journal*, *26*(1), 10–23.

Livingstone, D. (1992). *The geographical tradition*. Oxford: Blackwell.

Lyell, C. (1830/1997). *Principles of geology*. London: Penguin.

Mac an Ghaill, M. (1994). *The making of men*. Maidenhead: Open University Press.

Mac an Ghaill, M. (1999). *Contemporary racisms and ethnicities: Social and cultural transformations*. Basingstoke: Open University Press.

MacKenzie, J. (1984). *Popular culture and imperialism*. Manchester: Manchester University Press.

Mackenzie, J. M. (1984). *Propaganda and empire: The manipulation of British public opinion, 1880–1960*. Manchester: Manchester University Press.

McEvoy, D. (1983). Updating Urban Geography: Asian immigrants in British cities: The study of ethnic segregation. *Teaching Geography, 8* (3), 99–102. http://www.jstor.org/stable/23750 520 (accessed 2 October 2022).

McGhee, D. (2005). *Intolerant Britain? Hate, citizenship and difference*. Buckingham: Open University Press.

McGhee, H. (2021). *The sum of us: What racism costs everyone and how we can prosper together*. London: Profile Books.

McGuigan, J. (1996). *Culture and the public sphere*. London: Routledge.

McGuigan (2010). *Cool capitalism*. London: Pluto Press.

McIntosh, P. (1989). White privilege: Unpacking the invisible knapsack. *Peace and Freedom Magazine,* July/August, 10–12.

McKenzie, L. (2019). The British class system is in great shape. *Progressive Review, 26* (3), 230–7.

McKittrick, K. (2006). *Demonic ground: Black women and the cartographies of struggle*. Minneapolis: University of Minnesota Press.

McKittrick, K., and Peake, L. (2005). What difference does difference make to geography? In N. Castree, A. Rogers, and D. Sherman (Eds.), *Questioning geography: Fundamental debates* (pp. 39–54). Oxford: Blackwell.

Mahony, M., and Randalls, S. (Eds.). (2020). *Weather, climate, and the geographical imagination: Placing atmospheric knowledges*. Pittsburgh: University of Pittsburgh Press.

Mangan, J. (1986). The grit of our forefathers: Invented traditions, propaganda and imperialism. In J. M. McKenzie (Ed.), *Imperialism and popular culture* (pp. 113–39). Manchester: Manchester University Press.

Marsden, W. (1976). *Evaluating the geography curriculum*. London: Oliver and Boyd.

Marsden, W. (1978). *The changing geography of the UK*. London: Oliver and Boyd.

Marsden, W. (1995). *Geography 11–16: Rekindling good practice*. London: David Fulton.

Marsden, W. (2001). *The school textbook: History, geography and social studies*. London: Woburn Press.

Massey, D. (1984). *Spatial divisions of labour*. Basingstoke: Macmillan.

Maude, A. (2016). What might powerful knowledge in geography look like? *Geography*, 101(1), 70–76. https://doi.org/10.1080/00167487.2016.12093987.

Meghji, A. (2019). *Black middle class Britannia: Identities, repertoires, cultural consumption*. Manchester: Manchester University Press.

Marriner, S. (1982). *The economic and social development of Merseyside*. London: Croom Helm.

Merriam, T. (1973). Geography is bunk. *Times Educational Supplement* (6 October).

Mignolo, W. (2005). *The idea of Latin America*. Malden, MA: Blackwell.

Mignolo, W. D. (2000). *Local histories/global designs: Coloniality, subaltern knowledges, and border thinking*. Princeton: Princeton University Press.

Miles, R., and Phizacklea, A. (1984). *White man's country: Racism in British politics*. London: Pluto Press.
Miller, D., Jackson, P., Thrift, N., Holbrook, B., and Rowlands, N. (1998). *Shopping, place and identity*. London: Routledge.
Milner, D. (1975). *Children and race*. London: Penguin.
Minoli, S. (2000). Migration and mutability: The twice-born fiction of Salman Rushie. In A. Davies and A. Sinfield (Eds.), *British culture of the postwar: An introduction to literature and society 1945-99* (pp. 43–62). London: Routledge.
Mirza, M. (2010). Rethinking racism. *Prospect Magazine* (October) https://www.prospectmagazine.co.uk/magazine/munira-mirza-multiculturalism-racism (accessed 2 October 2022).
Morgan, J. (2012). *Teaching secondary geography as if the planet matters*. London: Routledge Falmer.
Morgan, J. (2018). Are we thinking geographically? In M. Jones and D. Lambert (Eds.), *Debates in geography education* (pp. 287–97). Abingdon: Routledge.
Morgan, J., and Lambert, D. (2001). Geography, 'race', and education. *Geography, 86*(3), 235–46.
Morgan, J., and Lambert, D. (2003). *Place, race and teaching geography*. Sheffield: Geographical Association.
Morgan, J., and Lambert, D. (2005). *Geography: Teaching school subjects 11–19*. London: Routledge.
Morgan, J., and Lambert, D. (2018). For Knowledge – but whose knowledge? Confronting social realism's curriculum problem. In B. Barratt, U. Hoadley, and J. Morgan (Eds.), *Knowledge, curriculum and equity: Social realist perspectives*. Abingdon: Routledge.
Mullard, C. (1973). *Black Britain*. London: Allen and Unwin.
Mullard, C. (1984). *Anti-racial education: The 3 'O's*. Washington, DC: National Association for Multicultural Education.
Mullard, C. (1985). *Race, power and resistance*. London: Routledge Kegan and Paul.
Murray, W. (1999). Natural resources, the global economy and sustainability. In R. Gwynne and C. Kay (Eds.), *Latin America transformed: Globalization and modernity* (pp. 128–52). London: Arnold.
Myers, G. (2011). *African cities*. London: Zed Books.
Nassy Brown, J. (2005). *Dropping anchor, setting sail: Geographies of race in black Liverpool*. Oxford: Oxford University Press.
Nayak, A. (2003). *Place, race, and globalization*. London: Berg.
Nayak, A., and Jeffrey, A. (2011). *Geographical thought*. London: Routledge.
Neal, S., and Agyeman, J. (Eds.). (2006). *The new countryside? Ethnicity, nation and exclusion in contemporary rural Britain*. Bristol: Policy Press.
Nixon, R. (2011). *Slow violence: Environmentalism and the poor*. Cambridge: Harvard University Press.
Noronha, L. de. (2022). Everyday racism and the violence of borders. *Decolonising Geography*, 12 March. https://decolonisegeography.com/ (accessed 2 October 2022).
Noxolo, P. (2018). Laughter and the politics of place-making In K. Johnson and R. Joseph-Salisbury (Eds.), *The fire now: Anti-racist scholarship in times of explicit racial violence* (pp. 250–60). London: Zed Books.
Noxolo, P. (2022). Geographies of race and ethnicity 1: Black geographies. *Progress in Human Geography*, 46(5), 1232–40.
O'Daley, P., and Murrey, A. (2022). Defiant scholarship: Dismantling coloniality in contemporary African geographies. *Singapore Journal of Tropical Geography, 43* (2), 159–76.

Offe, C. (1984). *Contradictions of the welfare state.* Cambridge, MA: MIT Press.

Ofsted. (2021). *Research review series: Geography.* June 2021. https://www.gov.uk/government/publications/research-review-series-geography (accessed 2 October 2022).

O'Keefe, P., Westgate, K., and Wisner, B. (1976). Taking the naturalness out of natural disasters. *Nature, 260* (566–7), 137.

Omi, M., and Winant, H. (1986). *Racial formation in the United States: From the 1960s to the 1980s.* London: Routledge Kegan and Paul.

Oswin, N. (2020). An other geography. *Dialogues in Human Geography, 10*(1), 9–18.

Parekh, B. et al. (2000). *The future of multi-ethnic Britain.* London: Runnymede Trust.

Parsons, C. (1987). *The curriculum change game: A longitudinal study of the schools council "Geography for the Young School Leaver".* Lewes: Falmer Press.

Paul, K. (1997). *Whitewashing Britain: Race and citizenship in the post-war era.* Ithaca, NY: Cornell University Press.

Peach, C. (1996). Does Britain have ghettos? *Transactions of the Institute of British Geographers, 21*(1), 216–35.

Peake, L., and Kobayashi, A. (2002). Anti-racist policies and practices for geography at the millennium. *Professional Geographer, 54,* 50–61.

Peet, R. (1991). *Global capitalism.* London: Routledge.

Pepper, D. (1986). Why teach physical geography? *Contemporary issues in Geography and Education, 2*(2), 62–71.

Perry, P. J. (1975). *A geography of 19th century Britain.* London: Batsford.

Phillips, R. (1997). *Mapping men and empire: A geography of adventure.* London: Routledge

Phillips, T. (2005). 'After 7/7: Sleepwalking to segregation'. Speech to the Manchester Council for Community Relations, 22 September.

Phillips, M., and Phillips, T. (1998). *Windrush: The irresistible rise of multi-racial Britain.* London: HarperCollins.

Pitcher, B. (2016). *Consuming race.* London: Routledge.

Plomin, J. (2001). Schools failing ethnic minority students. *The Guardian.* 17 October. https://www.theguardian.com/education/2001/oct/17/ofsted.schools (accessed 24 September 2022).

Ploszajska, T. (2000). Historiographies of geography and empire. In B. Graham and C. Nash (Eds.), *Modern historical geographies* (pp. 121–45). London: Prentice Hall.

Pluckrose, H., and Lindsay, J. (2020). *Cynical theories: How universities made everything about race, gender and identity.* London: Swift.

Pocock, D. (1981). *Humanistic geography and literature.* London: Croom Helm.

Pollack, M. (1972). A suggested Black Studies syllabus. *Teachers Against Racism, 7,* 10–11.

Porter, B. (2004). *The absent-minded imperialists: What the British really thought about Empire.* Oxford: Oxford University Press.

Porter, P., and Sheppard, E. (1998). *Worlds of difference: Society, nature, development.* New York: Guilford Press.

Power, M. (2000). *Rethinking development geographies.* London: Routledge.

Proctor, J. (2003). *Dwelling places: Post-war Black British writing.* Manchester: Manchester University Press.

Puttick, S., and Murrey, A. (2020). Confronting the deafening silence on race in geography education in England: Learning from anti-racist, decolonial and Black geographies, *Geography, 105*(3), 126–34.

Quijano, A. (2000). Coloniality of power and Eurocentrism in Latin America. *International Sociology, 15*(2), 215–32.

Rabbett, P. (1993). Introduction. In A. Fyfe and P. Figueroa (Eds.), *Education for cultural diversity: The challenge of a new era* (pp. 9–16). London: Routledge.

Radcliffe, S. (2022). *Decolonizing geography: An introduction.* Oxford: Wiley.

Radhakrishan, R. (2003). *Theory in an uneven world*. Malden, MA: Blackwell.
Raskin, J. (1971). *The mythology of imperialism*. New York: Monthly Review Press.
Rattansi, A. (2007). *Racism: A very short introduction*. Oxford: Oxford University Press.
Rawling, E. (1997). Geography and vocationalism – opportunity or threat? *Geography*, *82*(2), 173–8.
Rawling, E. (2001). *Changing the subject: The impact of national policy on school Geography, 1980–2000*. Sheffield: Geographical Association.
Reynolds, D. (2020). *Island stories: An unconventional history of Britain*. London: Penguin.
Richardson, B. (2005). *Tell it like it is: How our schools fail Black children*. London: Bookmarks.
Rigg, J. (2007). *An everyday geography of the global south*. London: Routledge.
Robbins, P. (2004). *Political ecology: A critical introduction*. Chicester: Wiley.
Roberts, M. (2003). *Enquiry through geography*. Sheffield: Geographical Association.
Roberts, M. (2013). *Geography through enquiry*, 2nd edition. Sheffield: Geographical Association.
Roberts, R. (1971). *The classic slum*. Manchester: Manchester University Press.
Robinson, C. (1983). *Black Marxism: The making of the Black radical tradition*. London: Zed Books.
Robinson, V. (1987). Race, space and place (the geographical study of UK ethnic relations 1957–1987). *Journal of Ethnic and Migration Studies*, *14*(1–2), 186–97.
Robinson, V. (1989). Economic restructuring, the urban crisis and Britain's black population. In D. Herbert and D. M. Smith (Eds.), *Social problems and the City: Geographical perspectives* (pp. 247–70). London: Routledge.
Roediger, R. (1991). *The wages of whiteness: Race and the making of the American working class*. London: Verso.
Rose, G. (2020). Editorial introduction by Professor Gillian Rose: Diversity and Inclusion. *Routes*, *1*(2), 138–41.
Royal African Society. (2022). *APPG Education Enquiry Report*. London Royal African Society.
Rushdie, S. (1982). The new empire within Britain. *New Society* (9 December).
Rutherford, A. (2020). *How to argue with a racist*. London: Weidenfeld & Nicolson.
Saad, L. F. (2020). *Me and white Supremacy: How to recognize your privilege, combat racism and change the world*. London: Quercus.
Said, E. (1978). *Orientalism*. London: Routledge and Kegan Paul.
Said, E. (1993). *Culture and Imperialism*. London: Chatto and Windus.
Sanghera, S. (2021). *Empireland: How imperialism has shaped modern Britain*. London: Penguin Viking.
Sardar, Z. (1998). *Postmodernism and the other: The new imperialism of Western culture*. London: Zed Books.
Sarup, M. (1996). *Identity, culture and the postmodern world*. Athens, GA: University of Georgia Press.
Satia, P. (2020). *Time's monster: History, conscience and Britain's empire*. London: Allen Lane. p. 257
Sayer. A. (1985). Realism. In R. Johnston (Ed.), *The future of geography* (pp. 159–73). London: Methuen.
Sayer, A. (2000). *Realism and social science*. London: Sage.
Scafe, S. (1989). *Teaching black literature*. London: Virago.
Schwarz, B. (2011). *The white man's world: Memories of empire* (Vol. 1). Oxford: Oxford University Press.
Schwartz, R. (2019). *Ghetto: The history of a word*. Cambridge: Harvard University Press.
Sen, A. (1999). *Development as freedom*. Oxford: Oxford University Press.

Sethi, A. (2021). *I belong here: A journey along the backbone of Britain*. London: Bloomsbury.

Sewell, T. (2008). Racism is not the problem. *The Guardian*. https://www.theguardian.com/commentisfree/2008/sep/05/raceinschools.raceineducation (accessed 2 October 2022).

Shabazz, R. (2015). *Spatializing Blackness: Architectures of confinement and masculinity in Chicago*. Champagne-Urbana: University of Illinois Press.

Sharp, J. (2005). *Geographies of postcolonialism*. London: Sage.

Shilliam, R. (2018). *Race and the undeserving poor: From abolition to Brexit*. London: Agenda Publishing.

Short, J. R. (1998). *New worlds, new geographies*. New York: Syracuse University Press.

Short, J. R., and Kirby, A. (Eds.). (1984). *The human geography of contemporary Britain*. Basingstoke: Macmillan.

Shurmer-Smith, P., and Hannan, K. (1994). *Worlds of desire, realms of power*. London: Edward Arnold.

Sibley, D. (1995). *Geographies of exclusion*. London: Routledge.

Sims, S. (2000). *An introduction to postmodern thought*. London: Fontana.

Sivanandan, A. (1983). Challenging racism: Strategies for the 80s. *Race and Class*, 25, 1–11.

Sivanandan, A. (1990). *Communities of resistance: Writings on black struggles for socialism*. London: Verso.

Skelton, T., and Valentine, G. (Eds.). (1997). *Cool places: Geographies of youth cultures*. London: Routledge.

Slater, F. (1982). *Learning through Geography*. London: Heinemann.

Small, G. (1994). *Racialised barriers: The black experience in the United States and England in the 1980s*. London: Routledge.

Smith, N. (1993). Homeless/global: Scaling places. In J. Bird, B, Curtis, and T. Putnam (Eds.), *Mapping the futures: Local cultures, global change* (pp. 87–119). London: Routledge.

Smith, S. J. (1994). Urban geography in a changing world. In D. Gregory, R. Martin, and G. Smith (Eds.), *Human geography* (pp. 232–51). London: Palgrave.

Smith, L., Cubbit, G., Wilson, R. and Fouseki, K. (Eds) (2011). *Representing enslavement and abolition in museums: ambiguous engagement*. New York: Routledge.

Smithers, R. (2002). Racism rife says school expert. *The Guardian* 17 March. https://www.theguardian.com/uk/2002/mar/12/politics.race (accessed 24 September 2022).

Soja, E. (1989). *Postmodern geographies*. London: Verso.

Solomos, J. (1988). *Black youth, racism and the state: The politics of ideology and policy*. Cambridge: Cambridge University Press.

Solzhenitsyn, A. (1985). *The gulag archipelago* (abridged edition) London: HarperCollins.

Stedman Jones, G (1982). *Languages of class*: Studies of English working-class history 1832–1982. Cambridge: Cambridge University Press.

Stone, M. (1981). *The education of the black child: The myth of multiracial education*. London: Fontana.

Stamp, D. (1960). *Applied geography*. Harmondsworth: Penguin.

Standish, A. (2017). Geography. In A. Standish, and A. Sehgal Cuthbert (Eds.), *What should schools teach? Disciplines, subjects and the pursuit of truth* (pp. 137–53). London: UCL-IOE Press.

Storm, M. (1975). Third world studies and the environment. In G. Martin and K. Wheeler (Eds.), *Insights into environmental education* (pp. 106–14). London: Oliver and Boyd.

Story, B. (2019). *Prison lands*: Mapping carceral power across neoliberal America. Minneapolis: University of Minnesota Press.

Stott, P., and Sullivan, S. (Eds.). (2003). *Political ecology*. London: Edward Arnold.

Streeck, W. (2016). *How will capitalism end?* London: Verso.

Taylor, P. (1985). *Political geography: World-economy, nation-state, and locality*. London: Longman.

Taylor, P. (1989). The error of developmentalism. In D. Gregory and R. Walford (Eds.), *Horizons in human geography* (pp. 303–19). Basingstoke: Macmillan.

Taylor, L. (2008). Key concepts and medium-term planning. *Teaching Geography, 33*(2), 50–4.

Thompson, E. P. (1963). *The making of the English working-class*. London: Victor Gollancz.

Timothy, N. (2020). *Remaking one nation: The future of conservatism*. Cambridge: Polity.

Tomlinson, S. (1983). *Ethnic minorities in British schools: A review of the literature 1960–82*. London: Heinemann Educational Books.

Tomlinson, S. (1989). The origins of the ethnocentric curriculum. In G. Verma (Ed.), *Education for all: A landmark in pluralism* (pp. 26–41). Lewes: Falmer Press.

Tomlinson, S. (2020). *Rule Britannia? Education for honesty*. https://www.transformingsociety.co.uk/2020/06/30/rule-britannia-education-for-honesty/ (accessed 2 October 2022).

Toyne, P., and Newby, P. (1971). *Techniques in human geography*. London: Nelson-Thornes.

Troyna, B., and Carrington, B. (1990). *Education, racism and reform*. London: Routledge.

Turner. P. (1976). *Spotlight on the UK*. London: Nelson.

UNESCO. (1974). *African geography for schools: A handbook for teachers*. London: Longman.

UCET. (2020). *Strategic Plan* 2020–2025. https://www.ucet.ac.uk/downloads/12134-UCET-Strategic-Plan-2020-2025.pdf (accessed 2 October 2022).

Unwin, T. (1992). *The place of geography*. Harlow: Longman.

Valentine, G. (2001). *Social geographies: Space and society*. London: Routledge.

Verma, G. (Ed.). (1989). *Education for all: A landmark in pluralism*. Lewes: Falmer Press..

Walford, R. (1985). *Geographical education for a multi-cultural society: Report of the Working Party set up by the Geographical Association*. Sheffield: Geographical Association.

Walford, R. (2001). *Geography in British schools, 1850–2000*. London: Woburn Press.

Walford, R., and Haggett, P. (1995). Geography and geographical education: Some speculations for the twenty-first century. *Geography, 80*(3), 3–14.

Walter, B. (2001). *Outsiders inside: Whiteness, place and Irish women*. London: Routledge.

Walton, S. (2019). Why the critical race theory concept of "White supremacy" should not be dismissed by neo-Marxists: Lessons from contemporary Black radicalism. *Power and Education, 12*(1), 78–94.

Ware, V. (2022). *Return of a native: Learning from the land*. London: Repeater Books

Warmington, P. (2014). *Black British intellectuals and education: Multiculturalism's hidden history*. London: Routledge.

Warmington, P. (2020). Critical race theory in Britain: Impact and opposition. *Identities, 27*(11), 20–37.

Waters, R. (2020). *Thinking Black: Britain 1964–85*. Los Angeles: University of California Press.

Watts, M. (1983). *Silent violence*. Berkeley: University of California Press.

Watts, M. (1993). The geography of post-colonial Africa: Space, place and development in sub-Saharan Africa. *Singapore Journal of Tropical Geography, 14*(2), 173–90.

Webster, W. (1998). *Imagining home: Gender, 'race' and national identity, 1945–64*. London: UCL Press.

Whitty, G., and Young, M. (Eds.). (1976). *Explorations in the politics of school knowledge*. Nafferton: Nafferton Press.

Williams, J. (1979). Perspectives on the multi-cultural curriculum. *Social Science Teacher, 8*(4), 126–33.

Williams, J. (2017). The 'decolonise the curriculum' movement re-racialises knowledge. *Open Democracy*. https://www.opendemocracy.net/en/decolonise-curriculum-movement-re-racialises-knowledge/ (accessed 2 October 2022).

Williams, S. (1989). Foreword. In G. Verma (Ed.), *Education for all: A landmark in pluralism* (pp. vii–ix). London: Falmer Press.

Wilson, A. (1978). *Finding a voice: Asian women in Britain*. London: Virago.

Wilson, D. (2007). *Cities and race: America's new black ghetto*. London: Routledge.

Wilson, R. (2000). *America's Johannesburg: Industrialization and racial transformation in Birmingham*. Athens: University of Georgia Press.

Wilson, R. W. (2022). *Abolition geography: essays towards liberation*. London: Verso.

Winant, H. (1994). Racial formation and hegemony: Global and local developments. In A. Rattansi and S. Westwood (Eds.), *Racism, modernity and identity: On the western front*. Cambridge: Polity Press.

Winter, C. (2022). The geography GCSE curriculum in England: a white curriculum of deceit, *Whiteness and Education*, DOI: 10.1080/23793406.2022.2132179.

Winter, C. (2006). Doing justice to geography in the secondary school: Deconstruction, invention and the National Curriculum. *British Journal of Educational Studies*, *54*(2), 212–29.

Winter, C. (2018). Disrupting colonial discourses in the geography curriculum during the introduction of British Values policy in schools. *Journal of Curriculum Studies*, *50*(4), 456–75.

Woods, C. (1998). *Development arrested: Race, power, and the Blues in the Mississippi Delta*. London: Verso.

Woods. C. (2017). *Development drowned and reborn: The Blues and Bourbon restoration in post-Katrina New Orleans*. Athens: University of Georgia Press.

Wooldridge, S., and East, G. (1955). *The spirit and purpose of geography*.

Wray, M. (2006). *Not quite white: White trash and the boundaries of whiteness*. Durham, NC: Duke University Press.

Young, L. (1996). *Fear of the dark: 'Race', gender and sexuality in the cinema*. London: Routledge.

Young, L., and Pollard, I. (1995). Environmental images and imaginary landscapes. *Soundings: A Journal of Politics and Culture*, *1*, 99–110.

Young, M. (Ed.). (1971). *Knowledge and control: New directions for the sociology of education*. London: Methuen.

Young, M. (2008). *Bringing knowledge back in: From social constructivism to social realism in the sociology of education*. Abingdon: Routledge.

Young, M., and Lambert, D. (2014a). *Knowledge and the future school*. London: Bloomsbury.

Young, M., and Lambert, D. (2014b). What should we teach? *SecEd*. https://www.sec-ed.co.uk/blog/what-should-we-teach/ (accessed 2 October 2022).

Young, M. and Muller, J. (2010). Three educational scenarios for the future: lessons from the sociology of knowledge. *European Journal of Education*, *45*(1), 11–27.

Younge, G. (2018). Foreword. In P. Fryer (Ed.), *Staying power: The history of black people in Britain* (pp. xi–xii). London: Pluto Press.

Yusoff, K. (2019). *One billion black Anthropocenes (or none at all)*. London: Verso.

Zukin, S. (2010). *Naked city: The death and life of authentic urban places*. Oxford: Oxford University Press.

# Index

Ahier, J. 97
anti-racist education 6, 39, 41–2, 162, 163
Asian Britain 23–4
assimilation 6, 20, 36

Black Britain/British 21, 22, 38, 115
Blackness 21, 23, 120
Black Geographers 119
Black Lives Matter (BLM) 5, 11, 29, 30, 42, 118, 160, 161
Black Studies 38–9, 124–5, 126
Brexit 29, 115, 160
British Nationality Act
  1948 18
  1981 24
Bryan, B., Dadzie, S., and Scafe, S., *The heart of the race: Black women's lives in Britain*, 6, 35
Burgess, J. 59

capitalism 152, 153–4
Coard, B., *How the West Indian child is made educationally subnormal in the British school system* 37
Cohen, P. 44, 113
coloniality 78–9, 83
Commission for Racial Equality (CRE) 26, 106, 116
Commission on Race and Ethnic Disparities (CRED) x–xi, 155, 157, 161
class 50–1
Critical physical geography 85–90
Critical Race Theory (CRT) 45–8
Critical resource geography 88–9
Crush, J., *The power of development* 80
cultural racism 157
curriculum 8, 37, 124, 151–2, 161–6

Decolonizing Geographers 119, 142–4
Department of Education and Science (DES) 39–40, 96
dependency theory 76
Development 75–8
diaspora 42, 44

Eddo-Lodge, R. (*Why I'm longer talking to white people about race*) 13, 29
Education Reform Act (ERA) 153
exclusion 26

Feagin, J., *The white racial frame* 67
Fryer, P., 11, 12, 13, 17

Geographical Association (GA) 97, 159, 164
Geography/geographies
  abolition 74
  behavioural and humanistic 57, 106, 111, 129–30
  cultural 18, 57, 58
  decolonizing 7, 81–5
  development 75–8
  postcolonial 7, 79–81
  post-development 7, 76, 78
  postmodern 69, 133, 134
  rural 61
  social and economic 7, 57
  urban 57
  welfare 7, 106
Geography for the Young School Leaver (GYSL) 8, 105, 106, 108
Ghetto 66, 114
Gill, D. 8, 105–9, 112–13, 131
Gillborn, D., 45–6
globalization 82
Goodhart, D. 28–9
Graves, N. 100, 127, 129, 130
Gregory, D., 134
Gwynne, R. and Kay, C. (*Latin America Transformed*) 82

Hall, S. 34, 42
Hicks, D. 101–3
Huckle, J. 152, 158, 166
hybridity 44

identity 42
immigration 17–21, 23–4, 27–8
imperialism 53
inclusion 26
inner city 59

institutional racism 26, 47
integration 6, 20, 27, 36

Jackson, P. 57, 59–60, 64, 65, 109
Johnston, R. J. 111, 131
Joseph-Salisbury, R. (*Race and racism in English secondary schools*) 9

knowledge
   critical perspective on 131
   fields of 128
   forms of 128
   liberal view of 127, 128
   phenomenological approach to 129–30
   postmodern view of 156
   powerful knowledge 123, 135, 138–9, 164

Mackenzie-Porter debate 99
Marsden, W. 100, 101, 130, 134
modernization theory 75
multicultural education 6, 39–40, 110–11
multiculturalism 25, 41

national curriculum 9, 41, 110, 112, 155, 161
neoliberalism 48, 82, 156
new ethnicities 42–3
New Right 41
Noxolo, P. 63–4, 120
1944 Education Act 34
1962 Commonwealth Immigration Act 20, 24

Omi, M., and Winant, H., *Racial formation in the United States* 67
Orientalism 60, 79, 136, 137

Parekh Report 25–6
political ecology 86–8
Porter, B., *The absent-minded imperialists* 98–9
positionality 136
postcolonialism 79, 81
post-development 76

postmodernism 76, 132–3, 134, 135
post-race 48–9, 155, 157
post-racial society 49

race 3, 4, 51, 56, 57, 61
racial capitalism 51, 65, 65, 68, 146, 148
racial literacy 9–11, 151, 166–7
racialization, of space 57, 68–9
racism 1, 2, 6, 41, 43
realism
   critical 139–40
   naive 127, 128
   scientific 127
Robinson, C. 68
Robinson, V. (*Economic restructuring, the urban crisis and Britain's black population*) 58

Said, E. 60, 79, 98, 137
Segregation 66
Rutherford, A., *How to argue with a racist* 1
Sewell Report, *The commission on race and ethnic disparities* 49
standpoint theory 136, 137
Swann Report, *Education for all* 41, 96, 155

textbooks
   academic 62
   school 96–9, 100, 101–4, 131
Tomlinson, S. 96–7, 100, 154, 155

Walford, R. 106–8, 134, 135, 158
Walter, B., 44
white ignorance 120
whiteness 42, 43–4, 68
   of geography 53–4, 63–4, 120
Wilson, R. (*America's Johannesburg*) 70–1
Woods, C. (*Development drowned and reborn*) 71–2

Yusoff, K., *A billion Black anthropocenes (or none at all)* 89–90

# Race, Racism and the Geography Curriculum

**ALSO AVAILABLE FROM BLOOMSBURY**

*Knowledge and the Future School,* Michael Young and David Lambert, with Carolyn Roberts and Martin Roberts

*Mastering Primary Geography,* Anthony Barlow and Sarah Whitehouse

*Sustainability Education,* Stephen Scoffham and Steve Rawlinson

*Developing Culturally and Historically Sensitive Teacher Education,* edited by Yolanda *Gayol Ramírez*, Patricia Rosas Chávez and Peter Smagorinsky

*Education for Social Change,* Douglas Bourn

*Doing Diversity Differently in a Culturally Complex World,* Megan Watkins and Greg Noble

*Special Educational Needs and Disabilities in Schools,* Janice Wearmouth

*Navigating Teacher Education in Complex and Uncertain Times,* Carmen I. Mercado

*Reflective Teaching in Secondary Schools,* Andrew Pollard and Caroline Daly, with Katharine Burn, Aileen Kennedy, Margaret Mulholland, Jo Fraser-Pearce, Mary Richardson, Dominic Wyse and John Yandell